From the lush, windy cloud forest of Monteverde in Central America comes the story of pioneering conservationist Wolf Guindon. Jailed in the United States in 1949 as a conscientious objector, Wolf and his bride Lucky were among a small group of Quakers who left Alabama a year later in search of a new life and found it on a wet mountaintop in Costa Rica. For the next twenty years, Wolf labored to transform the land to make it habitable and productive, even as he was falling in love with the flourishing jungle around him. In 1972, he found a new purpose when he helped establish the Monteverde Cloud Forest Reserve. Since then he has worked relentlessly to secure the protection of the surrounding wilderness so that the flora and fauna of this vast, incredibly beautiful and biologically diverse region will be intact for generations to come.

In 1990, following her first experience of walking with Wolf for several days through the rainforest, Canadian social activist Kay Chornook gave Wolf a tape recorder. She encouraged him to record his many remarkable tales of cutting trails through the dense vegetation, following tapir tracks across the ridges, discovering the wonders of the wild abundance, and sharing innumerable cups of coffee with homesteaders, biologists and fellow adventurers. *Walking with Wolf* is a personal memoir, but it is also the history of a place and a movement as well as a celebration of lives lived amongst the trees of both Canada and Costa Rica.

With prose often as pristine as cloud forest mist, Kay Chornook's lyrical homage to one of Earth's original deep ecologists is intimate and inspiring. Her labor of love well serves both her mentor and our imperiled planet.
Paul McKay, journalist and author

This splendid slice of Costa Rican social history, beautifully presented by Kay Chornook, tells it as it really was. It is a heartrending story of one man's love of adventure and wild places set alongside his love for his growing family and his ties with the Quaker community in which he lives. Through his innate kindness and ability to change the perspective of those around him, Wolf has enriched many peoples' lives. Now, through reading this great book, others can share his unconventional way of looking at life.
Patricia and Michael Fogden, international wildlife photographers

Walking with Wolf

Wandering Words Press first published in 2008
Printed on recycled paper

Edited by Jane Pavanel
Designed by Laurie Hollis-Walker
Photographs by Kay Chornook unless otherwise credited
Maps by Yúber Rodríguez

Illustration Judy's Entrance (2005) by Lucky Guindon.
For prints of Lucky Guindon's pen and ink drawings contact
www.alquimiaartes.com or (506) 645-5847.

Chornook, Kay, 1958-
    Walking with Wolf : Reflections on a life spent protecting the
    Costa Rican wilderness / Kay Chornook and Wolf Guindon.

    Includes bibliographical references and index.
    1. Guindon, Wolf, 1930-. 2. Reserva del Bosque Nuboso de
Monteverde (Costa Rica). 3. Cloud forest conservation--Costa Rica. 4.
Rain forest conservation--Costa Rica. 5. Monteverde (Costa Rica)--
History. 6. Conservationists--Costa Rica--Biography. 7. Quakers--Costa
Rica--Biography. 8. Monteverde (Costa Rica)--Biography. I. Guindon,
Wolf,1930- II. Title.

    SD411.52.G85C46 2008   333.75'16092   C2008-900274-1
    ISBN 978-0-9809085-0-3

                    Wandering Words Press
        154 Macauley St. E., Hamilton, Ontario, Canada L8L 3X6
                        905-523-4354
        kchornook@hotmail.com or kchornook@rogers.com

Walking with Wolf

Reflections on a life spent
protecting the Costa Rican wilderness

Kay Chornook and Wolf Guindon

Peace
K Chornook

Wandering Words Press
Hamilton, Ontario

Contents

Foreword

In 1982, at 4:30 a.m., the Peñas Blancas valley seemed a long slog from Monteverde. The trade winds howled and threw something between mist and rain full in the face. It took coffee and *cajeta,* a gooey, caramelized wad of sugar, to make trekking a load of camping gear uphill feel feasible. But there was the lure of seeing the sunrise from the Continental Divide, a lesser chance of rain in the early hours on the Atlantic side, and perhaps even the prospect of lingering sunshine. There's nothing as grand as walking in sunlight in Peñas Blancas with swallow-tailed kites soaring above the ridges of trackless cloud forest.

The road through the Monteverde Cloud Forest Reserve was a mess. In those days there were still cows in upper Peñas Blancas and enough hoofed traffic to turn the track into a corrugated quagmire of slimy clay creases interspersed with ooze. It was always a relief to get beyond the clearings and into the forest on the downhill side. Gravity became an ally, but soon the trail went rocky. Our cheap rubber boots wore holes in our socks and then our skin. The nagging question of the day was where to cross the Peñas Blancas River, a choice determined by how much water was surging over its path of slick boulders, the weight and contents of the packs on our backs, and the available fording techniques. Water waist high was usually capable of tipping anyone over, and the riverbed shifted often enough to make crossing an unpredictable event. Rain or drizzle began mid-morning, and by the time a shelter came in sight in the afternoon, we were sodden.

No matter, the house owned by Eladio Cruz almost always had room for visitors. It was a rustic haven. Rice and beans were warming on the wood fire and before long a pitcher of fragrant sour-orange *refresco* appeared. Specimens of tree hoppers and beetles were sorted on the rough wooden table. After the sun set, candles flickered and spattered as moths and caddis flies dived through the flames. We heard a holler coming from the direction of some dark, lonely ridge. We heard it again and knew it could only be one person. Half an hour later we saw the beam of a dim flashlight emerge from the forest. Wolf Guindon, wet, grinning, eyes twinkling, and hefting a well-worn machete, ascended the steps to the house calling for coffee. He then gave us a recounting of his trek, and typically, it was multiples of the hike we had just made, a route that looped away from a tapir track and followed a ridge towards a distant town and then descended through the impossible tangle before somehow finding its end at Eladio's. The rain came and went in torrential episodes and the attendant noise on the tin roof drowned out all conversation. By eight in the evening the day felt complete. Damp, dirty and aching, we slept the blessed sleep of biologists wandering in a place of biological marvels.

In the hour before dawn we listened for the deep blowing tone of the bare-necked umbrellabird. Wolf was gone at first light. I watched him striding off, a rangy man all sinew and heart, a mighty heart, heading back into the still, dark forest.

I never met before or since those days a more scopius and merry hiker than Wolf Guindon. He walked with a purpose. He loved and still loves the cloud forests of Monteverde. For more than three decades he was the chief protector and indefatigable advocate for the wilderness of Monteverde and Peñas Blancas. Only he knew what was transpiring in the farthest reaches – who was hunting where, what the tapirs were eating, where a landslide had closed a trail. Wolf has played an inspirational role in protecting one of the most significant cloud forest areas remaining in Central America. He is fused with this landscape. His life and the fate of these luxuriant forests are forever intertwined.

I am deeply grateful to Kay Chornook for writing this wonderful record of a good man in a great place at a critical time in its history. Wolf and his many allies detailed in this book can be proud of what they have protected. Without them there would be nothing left but cows and weedy pasture. Much was learned in the campaign to save these forests. What I learned was that money and knowledge are necessary but not sufficient to reach the goal of conservation. In the end, nothing gets conserved without passionate, committed individuals like Wolf. His spirit and his love for the forest was the ultimate resource. It's an enduring pleasure and honor to have walked a ways with Wolf.

Adrian Forsyth, PhD
Vice President for Programs, Blue Moon Fund

Dedication

This book is dedicated to Vi Chornook, who shared freely with others her passion for being in the woods. Vi supported Wolf in his dream of establishing a long-distance hiking trail and encouraged Kay to love nature, laugh often, and write this book. She would have written her own book had she lived long enough.

Judy's Entrance   Lucky Guindon 2005

ONE

If you go out in the woods today...

"I'm out here looking over the treetops, across the old clearings to the ridge and the Continental Divide, thinking about those early years. That's always been my problem – I like to do my dreaming on the trail. When you get to this stage in life and start slowing down physically, you have more time to dream. You have the opportunity to look back as well as forward.

"The funny thing about the dream is how it changes. We can see those changes in the forest. We used to bring in chainsaws, take down the trees, cut out pastures, and be happy with our work. These days it's satisfying to come here and see that same land mostly covered with secondary forest. We put it all in the bank we call the Monteverde Cloud Forest Reserve. Now I can just sit back and see what the next generation will do with it."

Wolf pressed the stop button on the little black recorder. He dropped it into his knapsack, eased his stiff body off the stump he had been perched on, and forced his tired old knees to move forward. As soft mist sifted down on him from the fleeting clouds, he hesitated, wondering if he should head back home. An instant later, a keen ray of sun briefly penetrated the leafy canopy, provoking steam out of the damp ground. The metallic tones of a black-faced solitaire's song pierced the momentary stillness. Wolf turned his face skyward and howled in response. He listened as his cry was swept away by a sudden breeze. Spotting a fallen tree limb he grabbed his machete, delaying his decision. He started once more down the muddy trail, chopping as he went, searching for signs of animal or human activity.

All around him was the emerald jungle, the mistress he had been carrying on with for decades while his wife took care of their family and home in Monteverde. Rounding the next bend in the trail another story crept into his mind. He reached into his pack, retrieved the tape recorder and began again, "Well, Kay, I was thinking..."

I met Wolf in 1990 on that lush green mountaintop known as Monteverde, situated in the Tilarán Mountain range of northwestern Costa Rica. We began our friendship in February during an exhilarating six-day hike through the vibrant, tangled mass of wilderness called the Peñas Blancas valley, following trails Wolf and others had cut and maintained for more than forty years. It was my first trek through such a soggy world. We walked seventeen kilometers, beginning in the Monteverde Cloud Forest Reserve, continuing through the land known as the Children's Eternal Rain Forest, and eventually arriving on the eastern edge of the protected land in a place called Poco Sol, where the valley spills out into the country's San Carlos region.

It was Costa Rica's conservation efforts that drew me to the tiny Central American country. I was born and raised in a middleclass city in southern Ontario, but I am a bush babe at heart and have managed to spend my adult life residing in some of Canada's most beautiful wild spaces. Although I come from a homogenous suburban setting, each community I have been part of has taught me more about the mosaic of values and philosophies that make up our social existence. I have always had great respect for those dedicated people who work towards a healthy and harmonious planet, and have lent my support to many environmental and peace causes. It was a dream to visit a community with a reputation for having a collective social conscience.

Monteverde's beauty easily seduced me. I soaked my senses in the moist rainforest, pondered the world as the mists of the cloud forest enveloped me, and grew familiar with the society that exists there. I discovered that Wolf and his wife Lucky had lived in Monteverde since arriving in 1951 as part of a small group of American Quakers. They had moved to Costa Rica in search of a peaceful life, disillusioned by the military machine that was revving up in their native country. As these pioneers cleared land for their farms, they chose to leave intact 554 hectares of forest to ensure the conservation of their watershed. In the 1960s biologists started visiting Monteverde, and with them came a growing interest in the incredible biodiversity of the region. In the 1970s the Monteverde Cloud Forest Reserve laid a blanket of protection over the wooded mountainside. Today the Reserve forms part of a complex of protected areas that encompasses over 60,000 hectares.

As I walked the trails of Monteverde during that first visit, I realized I was benefiting from the foresight of those young settlers. I was soon to learn that the path they had followed as they went from putting aside that small tract of forest to conserving such a large piece of wilderness was as demanding and convoluted as the one we took on this journey from Monteverde through the Peñas Blancas valley to Poco Sol. It was only my second week in the country when I innocently embarked on that hike with Wolf, who had not only helped create the Reserve, but had spent the rest of his life nurturing it. At the time I had no idea that my life was about to be forever transformed by the magic of these woods and the company of Wolf Guindon.

Since those early days of Monteverde more than a million people have wandered the central paths of the Reserve known as the Triangle, but relatively few have ventured deeper into the jungle. That was where we were headed. Our little group consisted of Maryjka Mychajlowycz, the Canadian woman who had introduced me to Monteverde, Art Pedersen, a professional trail guide and park consultant from Texas, and me. We were told to start the hike without Wolf, who I had met a few days earlier while volunteering at the Monteverde Conservation League. Throughout his life Wolf had walked faster than most, so he could leave a day later and easily catch up with us.

As soon as we left the Reserve's reception area we were immersed in a dripping mass of chlorophyll. We followed El Camino, the old horse track that homesteaders had used to access the Peñas Blancas valley decades ago. Now a muddy, furrowed roadway, it brought us through the woods to the path that follows the Continental Divide. We emerged from the shelter of the trees and were greeted by views of the vast green quilt of forest that spreads miles eastward across the valley towards the Caribbean lowlands and westward to the Gulf of Nicoya on the Pacific Ocean. We were lucky to have those vistas - when the clouds are low it can be impossible to see more than three feet in front of you.

The trails here are maintained by workers who are continuously swinging their machetes to cut back the endlessly creeping vines and billowing bushes, for if a trail is left unattended, in a matter of weeks it will be difficult to find. Many days are warm and bright at this high elevation of 1,600 meters, and on those days it is almost possible to hear the plants growing upward to find the sun above the dense canopy. It is more usual to find the forest capped in clouds, often with a strong wind blowing the mists through the trees, or a breezeless downpour soaking the spongy earth. All that rain and consistently moderate temperatures create a growing climate that never sleeps.

As we walked, the roadway narrowed to a zigzagging path that plunged down to the Peñas Blancas River, the trail almost constantly bordered by pink impatiens. An African plant brought on European boats, it was obviously comfortable in its new surroundings. In places these plants were shoulder high, tumbling over each other in an attempt to fill up every bit of unclaimed threshold between path and forest, seeking the sun's kiss on their sodden leaves. Deep mauve ageratum also fancied this climate, and delicate begonias fought to be noticed amongst the greenery. Beyond these familiar garden species I saw a biodiversity of plant life that brings biologists literally to their knees as they search for the secrets stored in this open-air laboratory. From the tiniest orchid to the largest umbrella leaf, from the balancing bromeliads to the trailing vines and climbing lianas, there are thousands of plant species living in delicate harmony within this green micro-planet.

Walking through this glory I was overwhelmed, almost frightened, by the potency of the vegetative growth. Yet there was a calm that lingered in the shadow of the arboreal giants, their twisted trunks patiently reaching through the layers of foliage and cloud towards the promise of blue sky. These trees were surely the Latin American cousins of Tolkien's Ents, standing erect for centuries despite the many forces that would see them fall.

As we descended in elevation we started to feel the heat and humidity closing in on us. Although there were signs all around us of the heavy moisture that sustains life on the mountain, our first day out was hot and sunny and the cool of the rainforest was welcoming. Surrounded by a chorus of insect voices, we followed the path for about five hours, walking nine kilometers before arriving at one of the area's main *refugios*. These original homesteading cabins are known by the names of their most famous or most recent inhabitant, and this one, called El Alemán, or the German's, was named after Klaus Stein, who sold it to the Reserve in the late 1980s. Scattered throughout the forest, the cabins provide a dry and relatively comfortable night's rest for the Reserve's forest guards and work crews. They are also a dry oasis for saturated hikers, quite often students on tropical biology courses.

The going had been tough on the trail and I was drooping with fatigue. The path had wound its way down and up and down again, over rambling roots and treefalls, giving our knees and lungs a good workout. We were at a lower elevation – it drops to 900 meters near the river – and the air was warm and humid and water was constantly dripping down our skin. We were never sure whether this was water dropping from the canopy or mist or drizzle or sweat, or maybe even monkeys peeing on us, which they are known to do if you get underneath them.

The sound surrounding us was pure atmospheric jungle: peeps and warbles, coos and cackles, drips and whispers, rustles and hums. It was hard to take our eyes off the huge array of leaf shapes, moss-covered branches, vibrant yet diminutive flowers, and the breathtaking views that appeared without warning. Glimpses of brightly colored birds and shiny bugs begged our attention. But we had to constantly watch the path ahead of us, anticipating slippery rocks or twisting vines anxious to grab our ankles and pull us down into their green recesses. We had heard that if we were lucky we might spot the footprints of a puma or Baird's tapir, the seldom seen original denizens of the forest. And, of course, we had to look out for snakes.

This was the land of legendary serpents: poisonous fer-de-lance, colorful coral snakes, eyelash vipers and aggressive black snakes. The chance of seeing a venomous snake was low and the probability of being bitten by one remote, but we were told to keep an eye out for them, even though the fear people sometimes carry concerning snakes is much more likely to ruin their day than any snake itself.

We arrived at the German's to the smell of wood smoke and the sound of male voices. Entering the cabin, we introduced ourselves to the work crew. My understanding of our conversation was limited as I spoke next to no Spanish and they spoke only a few words of English. Many of these young men became friends of mine over the years, but at the time they were for the most part typically shy *Ticos* – the commonly used nickname for Costa Ricans – and as timid with me as I was with them. The man slicing pieces of meat and throwing them into a hot pan was Eladio Cruz. He seemed to be the one in charge, and his kind eyes and humble manner made us feel welcome.

With a smile, he offered me a piece of *mortadela*. Starved as I was, I still remember how that scrap of processed meat tasted as good as prime rib. Eladio had fed hundreds of students studying in the rainforest and knew how hungry hikers could be, especially upon arriving to the smell of cooking food. I have no doubt that we looked as famished and tired as we felt, and I will be forever grateful to Eladio for that simple gift of nourishment.

Darkness falls between 6 and 6:30 p.m. year-round that close to the equator, and down in a valley such as the one we were in the shadows deepen much earlier. Exhaustion pushed us into bed as the night critters were getting warmed up. We settled down in the bunkroom to the sound of the howler monkeys roaring, the dink frogs' staccato song and the river gurgling over the rocks. A hard wooden slab barely softened by a thin foam pad made up my bed, but despite the lack of comfort, I only heard those lullabies for minutes.

It seemed I had barely fallen asleep when I awoke to a discordant howl. My eyes popped open and I tried to focus in the dim dawn light.

"What in the world was that?" asked Maryjka from the bunk above me.

We could hear the workers moving around in the kitchen, the low din of their voices passing through the thin wooden walls, someone chopping firewood.

Then, another "CO-CO-RI-CO," followed by laughter erupting from the next room. I didn't know whether to leap from my bed or hide under it.

"Hey, what's everyone doing, sleeping in there?" shouted a friendly voice. "You folks should be dressed and halfway to San José by now."

"I'd guess that's Wolf," offered Art as he crawled out of his bedroll. "That must be our wakeup call."

"What time is it?" I asked, starting to stretch out my aching body.

"Five-thirty, by my watch," Art replied, already heading out the door.

"Oh, my God! Where'd he come from?" Maryjka groaned. We weren't quite awake, but we realized we wouldn't be falling back to sleep so we got up from our beds and began putting our clothes on. The smell of fresh coffee and wood smoke drifted through the cracks in the wall, igniting hunger pangs.

6

Moments later, Wolf clomped up the steps and the door flew open. "Well, girls, good morning! I thought you'd have been up for hours. Those beds must've been too comfortable."

In the early morning light, Wolf was aglow with beads of sweat rolling down his face. His thick graying hair was matted to his scalp as he wiped the moisture from his brow with one large, rough hand. The smile that twinkled in his eyes echoed in his words. "Thought I'd make sure we got a good start today."

"How far have you walked in the dark?" Maryjka asked as she shook her socks out. "It's barely light out there."

"I left home about three-thirty. I could've got here faster but I thought I'd do a bit of trail clearing. No use doing all that walkin' without getting some work done," Wolf replied. He sat down on the wooden bench and pulled off his rubber boots, exposing his dirty, sock-less feet, calloused and shriveled from hours spent inside damp darkness.

Wolf must have been as powerful as a mountain lion when he was young because now, at sixty, he was all long, sinewy muscle and not much else. He had somewhat of a farmer's tan, his neck and forearms a ruddy brown in contrast to the pale torso and hairy white legs that were revealed when he unabashedly changed his sweaty T-shirt and pants for a slightly dryer and cleaner set he had in his pack. A tangle of hair crept down his face as wooly sideburns, and bushy eyebrows protected his expressive eyes from the sweat and rain that had slowed to a trickle across his forehead. With prominent cheekbones that were even more exaggerated when he laughed, his face was a constant commentary on his emotions, which changed as rapidly as his narrative. Tears welled readily in his eyes, disclosing painful memories or betraying a flash of anger, but just as quickly he would break into a wide grin that both humored and explained everything. As I discovered during that hike, Wolf's large heart and soft soul were evident in every feature of his face and in every story that he shared.

After breakfast, the four of us hiked eight kilometers to the *refugio* at Poco Sol, where a small lake provides a watering hole for cattle and the white egrets that accompany them. For us there was *mucho sol* as we observed and were fascinated by the abundant bird population and prolific plant life. I was more out of shape than I had imagined, and Wolf always returned to me when I lagged behind. He relieved my bag of whatever he could, and sometimes carried the whole pack so I could

7

make the long uphill sections in a decent time. I couldn't understand why I was so slow. I had been raised hiking – following the Bruce Trail across the rugged escarpment of southern Ontario – and could usually keep up with a group. Now here I was, only thirty-one years old, and being seriously out-walked by someone twice my age! It would be months before I understood what had slowed me down that day.

Wolf fell in love with this steamy jungle on his first trek through it in 1952. Since then he has walked countless miles, often alone, in the tropical wilderness, looking for signs of squatters or hunters or tree poachers, clearing boundary lines and following animal tracks towards distant ridges. Armed with his trusty machete, he has never wasted a chance to keep the greenery at bay, to chop out a deadfall blocking the path or knock back the impatiens so any walkers coming behind wouldn't get too wet.

Wolf wields his machete like the guest conductor of a woodland symphonic orchestra, his outstretched arm and the sharp metal appendage maintaining a steady tempo as he adds his own syncopation. The tone and rhythm of his chopping changes as he cuts wooden stems close to the ground — *thwack!* then punctuates his song with a slice through a high hollow vine — *ping!* Rattling insects, quivering leaves and whistling birds fill in the melody. Every once in a while Wolf stands still and listens, his satisfied smile suggesting that surely there is nothing sweeter than the acoustic harmony of a forest full of life.

When I began walking with Wolf I stayed to the back of him because I didn't trust that machete coming up behind me, and I couldn't outpace him anyway. I soon learned to keep at least an arm-and-machete length away because as he walks and swings, he often turns around, his machete in mid-air. As we spent more time hiking together over the years I moved to being in front of him, still keeping a safe distance, so I could set the speed and listen to his commentary more clearly.

Along with all his walking and chopping, Wolf is constantly talking. In his unique mixture of Alabamian English and local Spanish, stories pour out of him like manna from heaven. Wolf talks in the same way he walks, often in circles, switching directions frequently. If you can interpret his mumbles and follow his storyline you will be endlessly entertained by his tales of visiting with the old hunters, forging raging rivers and tracking the elusive tapir. He has experienced the Costa Rican wilderness like few others have, running nonstop for hours along the trails, often in the dark by the light of the moon or with a small flashlight to guide him, drenched in sweat, a pack full of provisions on his back. He has accompanied renowned biologists, spent hours searching for missing hikers, and gone many kilometers into the forest only to race back to Monteverde in time for yet another meeting that dealt with the preservation of the land. Wolf is well known not only by Costa Rican politicians, international environmentalists and professional scientists, but also by all the inhabitants of the area, including those who live in the most remote of the homesteads.

By the end of that hike, Art, Maryjka and I decided to encourage Wolf to record his stories. We thought a portable device would be ideal since Wolf seldom sat still for long, and we realized that it was when he was in the jungle that his passion for this jewel flowed out of him. I knew I was capable of transcribing the tapes if he made them. Although Wolf initially balked at the idea, it didn't take him long to say he would give it a try. By then I was working for a biologist, Nalini Nadkarni, and I borrowed a recorder from her assistant and gave it to Wolf, saying, "If you tell the stories, I'll translate the Wolfspeak to the written form."

This book is the result of all that walking and talking. Seventeen years have passed since our first hike together. During that time Wolf's monologues and our subsequent conversations led us down many winding trails. The following are Wolf's stories, often told by him to the tape recorder, other times sifted like gold from his stream of consciousness as we walked together. I deciphered and organized the meanderings from the tapes and worked with Wolf to clarify his dialogue. The challenge was to retain as much of his dialect as possible while attempting to make his musings understandable. As my life unfolded during this process my own experiences made their way onto the pages, describing how our friendship grew and our perseverance kept us moving forward. Over the years I gathered more tales from the Guindon family and other friends who wanted to share their experiences of walking with Wolf. Together we present the journey of a unique man who moved from Alabama to Costa Rica and never stopped learning, loving and laughing as he hiked the back trails of this mountainous tropical paradise.

TWO

From whence we come

"I'm going to dedicate this day to my father and mother who thought up my coming into the world. They're the ones who receive the credit for getting me here. My kids picked up the idea when they were little ones at school that before they were born they were just a shadow behind God's eye. That would be where I was until day one.

"So a good word to my parents for allowing me to get to where I am now, to taking this hike to the river's edge. I pulled in here about a quarter to midnight. I've got the lights beaming and I'll take a break. I've got coffee already in my cup and after an hour or two will carry on and try to get to where I'm going by about the time the rooster crows." *Wolf in Peñas Blancas*

Since our paths converged in 1990, I have only become richer for knowing this modest man who manages to find humor in just about every situation. One of the first impressions I had of Wolf was that he was a person of great self-deprecation, despite the fact that he was an educated and well-traveled gentleman, a community leader and a nationally and internationally recognized conservationist. Wolf comes from humble beginnings. He was raised as a Quaker with a philosophy of life that opened his mind to learning and his heart to other people and their ideas.

The Religious Society of Friends, or Quakers, arose in England in the mid-seventeenth century, a period of great religious and political ferment. As English translations of the Bible became more accessible to the public, large numbers of people began seeking other ways to worship outside the traditional churches. George Fox founded the Society of Friends of Truth and for the first time brought people together in silence to realize the presence of God. Many "Friends," as they called themselves, were persecuted for their dissention and it was not unusual for them to be brought to court and imprisoned. On one occasion, while testifying before a courtroom, Fox stated that the justices and those around him should tremble at the name of God. The derogatory term "Quaker" was then applied to Fox and the Friends, but later was adopted by the group themselves.

For its followers, Quakerism is a way of life. It is a non-dogmatic movement based on certain attitudes such as open-mindedness and forgiveness that are expressed through personal and collective practices. Quaker fundamentals include being receptive to new insights, tolerant of differing opinions and ready to work for reconciliation wherever there is conflict. Nonviolence in thought, word and deed is central to Quakerism, and for this it is regarded as one of the traditional "peace churches." Quakers tend to live with moderation but are not puritanical. Their meetings may include spoken messages, prayers, songs or quotes offered from the heart by any member who feels moved to share, or they may consist only of silent worship. For Quakers, no church or organization, not even the words of the Bible, has ultimate authority. The Friends do not claim that their path is the only true path, and they welcome inquisitive visitors without pressuring anyone to join them.

Wolf credits his family and Quaker education for providing him with a strong foundation. He has weathered many storms and moves like the willow tree, possessing deep roots and flexible branches that survive the winds of change with grace. His sense of humor has not only added many laugh lines to the other wrinkles that life has etched across his kind face, but has surely eased him through difficult times and endeared him even to those who have disagreed with him.

Wilford Francis Guindon's life began in the United States in the tough years of the depression. He was born in Barnesville, a small town in the eastern part of Ohio, on the morning of August 17, 1930, to Albert Guindon and Bertha (Hall) Guindon. For the first five years of his life the family stayed in Barnesville to be near his mother's relatives. His father's people, originally from Vermont, had taken up residence in Fairhope, Alabama.

Both sides of Wilford's family were Quakers, and he and his siblings were educated in Quaker schools. Wilford was the fourth of five children: his brothers, William and Clifford, an older sister Mary Eva and a

12

younger sister Sara. The children were sent to the one-room school-house known as the Friends Quaker School. In Wilford's sixth year, the family moved to Fairhope so that his father could care for his ailing parents. The strain of uprooting a young family was made even worse when it became clear they would have to leave Wilford's mother behind.

"One of the first things I had to face in my youth was being told by my father that our mother would have to go to the Ohio State Mental Institution. She had to be where she could have care and treatment because she wasn't able to manage the household. As children, we wondered what she was being punished for, being sent away like that. I didn't understand the situation. Over the years I've remembered this – not having my mother at home – as a sad part of growing up. I've reflected on it many times, both in my youth and as an adult.

"Daddy's explanation in later years was that my mother was frail. He said she was in poor health and felt dominated by her older sister, who was both strong and confident. My mother was hospitalized beginning in 1935. Later she was released and lived with her parents near Barnesville. She had been to Fairhope years before, but she felt strongly that she could never live there. So she never did return to Alabama. She stayed in Ohio and we'd go visit her when we could. It wasn't until my high school years, when I went back to Ohio for boarding school, that I got better acquainted with my mother."

In Fairhope, Wilford continued his education first at the Quaker School and then at the Organic School of Education. This was a private institution founded by Marietta Johnson, who believed that education should be organic and that learning is a life-long process. Lessons in academics were given, but the important part of the schooling was learning skills through crafts such as woodworking, leatherworking and ceramics. The students participated in folk dancing and put on exhibitions for the parents and community. Organic was a hands-on school that provided the right activities to keep young, restless boys like Wilford busy and interested in learning.

"We had small classes and were graded as much on our conduct as we were academically. The emphasis was on teaching us to be 'ladies and gentlemen,' as our teacher would say. There was only one test a year at

Organic, which was quite different from what I experienced later at boarding school with its emphasis on scholastics. A big part of the curriculum was family events. It was during those times that I missed having my mother to see my performances.

"I suppose it was there that I started to gather a lot of my philosophy, picked up by osmosis from the Quaker way of not telling you what to do and not do. Instead it is more about guiding and showing and understanding the value of being honest, honoring your body and health, and practicing nonviolence in all aspects of life. I realized that it was rewarding to live in an upstanding manner. We were furnished with the value of having positive relations with one another. We learned to approach life by doing what we knew to be right as opposed to just following the crowd."

When Wilford returned to Ohio in 1945 it was to attend the Friends Boarding School on the outskirts of Barnesville. The school was unofficially known as Olney, a nickname derived from the title of a poem, "Olney Green," written by a former teacher and minister, Louis Taber, and agreed upon by the student body back in 1876. Stately red brick buildings housing classrooms and dormitories stood amidst grand old hardwoods. On the sprawling campus students had access to sports fields, a dairy herd, an orchard, a small lake and an old-growth forest.

Youth from all over North America and beyond still come to Olney (now called Olney Friends School) to receive an education supported by Quaker values. The green, rolling hillsides of the area are unlike the flatlands of western Ohio. Woodlots mark farm boundaries and narrow roads curve around elegant century-old houses, although smaller, simple homes predominate in the region. This is Amish as well as Quaker country, where horse-drawn buggies meander along the roads, slowing the pace of modern automobiles.

Wilford's maternal relatives, the Halls, still lived in the area, as did his brother, Clifford, and two sisters, who had returned to Ohio. He had cousins at Olney who helped him adjust to living in a dormitory and to studying in an environment that followed a formal grading system.

"We had to take annual state tests to be rated for college. Throughout the year it was a challenge to come out with at least a C-minus average or it would mean extra work or a failing grade. I managed to keep one foot above the dividing line. If I'd worked harder I probably could have done better, but a big part of my learning was social – meeting gals and guys, living with roommates, learning how to share and get along, how to tease and how to be teased, and maybe when not to tease. I formed my basic outlook on politics and people. I figured out what life was all about, what was important and what wasn't.

"I had four years of being exposed to some of the best teachers you could ever ask for. They were aboveboard morally and they were completely dedicated. They taught us to try to solve our frustrations rather than take them out on a teacher or roommate or whoever.

"Boarding school was where I picked up my nickname. At assemblies the boys were seated on one side of the hall and the girls on the other. Being a Quaker from the South, I didn't like the idea of segregation of any kind, so at one function I sat on the side of the room with the females. Some fellows started to call me Wolford. In those days, soldiers flirting with young women would vie for their attention with wolf whistles, and they became known as 'wolves.' Due to my opposition to the rules that kept the males and females separated, I became Wolf. Obviously, it stuck."

Boarding school was an enlightening and formative time for Wolf. He made several great discoveries that would stay with him for the rest of his life. The first of these resulted from his involvement in sports, which was a school requirement. He joined team sports and particularly enjoyed basketball, but nothing compared to the sense of freedom he felt as he hiked through the surrounding countryside.

"At Olney, playing basketball, soccer and baseball, I learned teamwork. We emphasized good sportsmanship. We knew that playing our best was what counted. Through the school's point system we worked towards earning athletic letters, especially the big 'O,' the big letter, which only about five or six people earned each year. Besides team sports, there was a hiking program. They gave us a point for each mile we covered. So I learned how to hike, and because of hiking and the other sports I did, I managed, in all four years, to earn my big letter.

"The hiking is something to talk about. We followed planned routes that covered much of the area around the community. We did a lot of hiking in the morning before breakfast, although we couldn't head out until after 5 a.m. and had to be in at 8 a.m. sharp. If we arrived late for breakfast we'd lose points, but we usually tried to do eight or nine miles before eating.

"Following the trails and roads in the least traveled and less populated areas was a real good way for me to be introduced to the outdoors. There were camping trips to small woodlots and along rivers near Barnesville. Though I didn't know it then, those hikes contributed to my enjoyment of getting out in the countryside and walking, and through this, building a physical relationship to a place. I didn't realize that this was going to be one of the major assets I'd have when I came to Monteverde. Since the early years in Costa Rica I've wandered all over by foot and by horseback. I've enjoyed getting out and meeting the people.

"In my four years at boarding school, the hiking I did was enough to go to Alabama and back to Ohio. A round trip would be about 2,430 miles. That was quite an accomplishment."

Olney had an active social scene, but as a boy from the South, Wolf didn't expect to find anyone at the school who would be more appealing than the southern belles at home. To his good fortune, in his senior year he met Emma Lucille Standing, a Quaker girl from Earlham, Iowa, who would turn his head and later become his wife.

"There was another asset of going to a small private boarding school. This kind of school was called a 'match factory,' and it was true. It was quite a factory. Put teenagers together for four years and usually they'll sort things out and find a mate in that length of time. I had three years before I really got tuned in and met the girl who is now my wife. Lucky was one of those tall corn-fed gals from Iowa. She's a great person and I never regret going all the way up north to accomplish that.

"Eston Rockwell, my great friend who was the senior class president, had a vehicle, a Model T. In our senior year he drove it out to school from Iowa just to prove he could. He was to put it in storage before classes started, but before he did that we wanted to drive it around one last time. We saw a couple of girls walking along the highway and we picked them up. As luck would have it there wasn't room for everybody so one of them had to sit on my lap. We got to school and dumped the girls out because all that was in our minds was getting one last ride in that Model T. It was all about the car, no question about it.

"Later I found out that the girl on my lap, Lucille Standing, was the younger sister of Florence, the wife of my cousin Carrol Guindon. I had noticed that marriage had really settled him down and I thought that maybe that might be a good thing. Although I was set on not going steady with any girl in my senior year, I decided to send Lucky a note to see if we could get together at some social do. My good friend Herb Smith from Iowa told me what a special person Lucky was, and then I found out firsthand that she was super nice. The other girl in the Model T was Mary Chamness, who would later become Eston's wife, so perhaps that last ride really wasn't just about the car.

"Lucky recently reminded me that at the first social event of that year someone set off a firecracker and loudly proclaimed, 'This is to get us off to a big bang.' The seniors were responsible for the first social and I was probably the only one who had a firecracker because in Alabama we could get them year-round. She wondered who the heck that person was and someone said it was Guindon. She said, 'Oh, Guindon! I have a sister married to a Guindon.' Of course she put things together. Even though our families were related, I don't think we knew each other before that year.

"Lucky was in her sophomore year when we met. In her senior year, I proposed. I didn't give her the ring until she graduated."

Olney's academic life also had a profound impact on Wolf. His interest in biology, as well as chemistry and physics, started there. He had excellent teachers who not only made these difficult subjects understandable, they taught the importance of them in daily life. This basic knowledge provided Wolf with valuable information he would draw on when he later worked with scientists in the diverse Costa Rican forests.

"I've grown to realize how important Olney was in giving me a proper education. When I look back and think of what I learned from different peers and who really influenced my life, I see that a lot of that happened at boarding school. I learned a whole lot about how to get along with people, and I decided which direction I wanted to go in. I thought it was more important to be a good role model in the little leagues than a star in a higher occupation. There's value in not smoking and drinking as well as in the rigid rules my grandmother had us follow, rules about not doing those things plus a whole lot more.

"I've learned to appreciate more and more my father's influence on my life, not having had much contact with my mother. He was often away working and his sister was the one who gave me motherly love. It was my dad and my Aunt Mary who showed me the basics of discipline and kept me going in the right direction. They were super examples, and so were my brothers and sisters. I don't think I really knew what being a birthright Quaker meant until I became an adult and understood where my opinions and values had come from.

"During boarding school I was able to get more involved with my mother's side of the family. My grandparents lived on a ridge just fifteen minutes across the valley from Olney. I got there by walking cross-country through a couple of pastures and over a small stream. I dropped over on Saturdays in my free time. All I had to do was write in the sign-out book, 'I'm going to Gramp's.'

"My mother was living in her parents' home at the time. It was new being near her. Mama mostly stayed in her room upstairs, but sometimes she would come down to visit and dip in the sugar bowl, satisfying her sweet tooth. In my third year at Olney my grandmother's health required a full-time helper, but Mother wouldn't allow another person in the house. That's when she was committed to an institution in Cambridge, Ohio, where she was diagnosed with the depression that had plagued her for most of her life. She was also diagnosed with diabetes.

"I visited her several times and she was always cheerful and glad to see me. She remembered dates, such as our birthdays and her wedding day. Although Mama was never violent, at one point she burnt our birth certificates. Her mind was probably irrational and she didn't understand the importance of the documents. Her confusion may have stemmed from the Quaker principle of standing up to governmental policy. She'd had electric shock treatments and I wondered if that was why she didn't converse more. While she was living with her parents, Mother wrote letters to my father in Fairhope. Her concern was for him to return to their old home place in Ohio.

"I remember Mother as having a real loving spirit. I've always felt that modern understanding and treatment could have healed my mother's mental hurts. She did receive treatment for diabetes and that extended her life. She died in 1969 of complications from diabetes while still in the institution. My brother Cliff and his wife Dottie were at her bedside, so at least she didn't die alone."

During Wolf's first year at boarding school several events occurred internationally that had a profound impact on the world: Hitler committed suicide, Mussolini was executed, the United Nations was formed, the United States dropped atomic bombs on Hiroshima and Nagasaki, and V-E Day brought the end of World War II. In the United States, President Franklin D. Roosevelt died of a cerebral hemorrhage and Harry S. Truman moved into the Oval Office.

Truman, with his social welfare reforms and civil rights legislation, faced heavy opposition even from his own Democratic party. A faction of the party in the South strongly disagreed with his attempts to desegregate their schools. The military complex within the United States was growing and increasingly exerting influence on political decision-making. Despite his somewhat softer domestic policies, it was President Truman who authorized the use of the atomic bombs on Japan. The distrust of all things Soviet pushed Truman to instigate the Cold War, which would continue for fifty years. In 1950 he led the American military into the Korean War. Truman did manage to find a compromise between his conflicting agendas when he abolished segregation in the armed forces in 1948.

There was general unrest in the United States through the late 1940s, when America's fear of communism influenced many policy decisions. On the civil rights front, a movement was growing. Labor unions were struggling on behalf of workers' rights and strikes were rampant. The postwar economy brought growth, but at the same time there were shortages of essential products, creating restlessness in the population. The Selective Training and Service Act of 1940, which regulated the conscription of young men into military service, was also going through changes.

In 1948, Wolf's last year of high school, two events occurred that aggravated regional conflicts and troubled pacifists worldwide. The newly formed United Nations sanctioned the partitioning of Palestine to create a Jewish state called Israel, and Mahatma Gandhi was assassinated in the newly independent India. At Olney, the Quaker students were constantly discussing world events, and in particular were watching the unfolding of their country's draft policy with more than a passing interest.

After graduating, Wolf returned to Fairhope. Lucky stayed behind to finish her last two years though they had agreed that when her studies were completed they would build a future together. In the meantime, Wolf would help with his father's dairy. When his father learned that Wolf and Lucky were planning to marry, he purchased twenty acres to add to the family's holdings, anticipating that they would all live and work together.

By the end of 1948, the American government reinstated the draft. Along with his friends from the Fairhope Monthly Meeting of Friends, Marvin Rockwell and his nephews, Howard Jr. and Leonard Rockwell, Wolf had to decide how he would respond to this peacetime draft. As Quakers, they were, by conviction, conscientious objectors.

"Everybody was aware of what was going on internationally. During World War II my brother Cliff was drafted and sent to the Civilian Public Service (CPS) camps. Money was donated at Quaker meetings to sponsor people in these camps. Conscientious objectors were classified for alternative service, on conservation projects or as staff in mental hospitals. Some young men volunteered as human guinea pigs in government-sponsored experiments. After working as a forester in a CPS camp, Cliff volunteered as a guinea pig. He spent two years on Staten Island involved in experiments with blood-thinners – what's known as Warfarin – and being subjected to frostbite through the use of dry ice.

"While at Olney I was already thinking about what I'd do if the war continued as I'd be of draft age after graduating. It was a great relief when the war ended and I didn't have to register. Then came the big surprise, when the draft only took a hiatus in 1947-1948 and it was announced that the Selective Service would be remodeled a bit and then reinstated. The Universal Military Training Act of 1948 was passed and so first thing after high school in the summer of 1948, I was faced with how to respond to this program that would conscript men between the ages of eighteen and twenty-six into the military.

"At this time Americans could and should have been involved in relief work in impoverished countries worldwide. I suppose those of us belonging to peace churches were raised with the belief that if you registered in this period, when there wasn't an actual war, there would be another program for conscientious objectors. But there was nothing planned, though it was understood that you would do some sort of civilian service. We found out that if we didn't register we'd be subject to the due process of law and get a prison sentence. The maximum was a $5,000 fine and/or five years in prison.

"The four of us in the Friends meeting at Fairhope, the three Rockwells and myself, decided not to register for the peacetime draft. We each wrote a letter to the draft board explaining our reasons and waited for 'due process.' We were arrested in December of 1948 and on October 26, 1949, we were sentenced to a year and a day. We were sent to the Federal Correctional Institution in Tallahassee, Florida.

"On arriving we were subject to a rotation time for applying for parole. The parole board met every four months and we had the luck, you might say, to go before the board in our first month. So we managed to spend only four months in prison.

"Those four months were really an education in themselves. I learned about what other inmates had been sentenced for, mostly bootlegging and writing counterfeit checks, and came to understand a bit about how they thought. But in prison everyone is handled the same, you're just a number. We were called up by our number six times a day for inspection. I managed to get a good job working in the prison dairy and didn't have to be at standing call most of the day. I still know my number by heart – 7310 – and that's all the system called me while I was incarcerated."

The four boys were released on February 27, 1950. Wolf returned to Fairhope, expecting to continue working with his father on the family farm. But during that four-month incarceration period his father had had what appeared to be a minor accident, and the Guindon family soon suffered a profound loss.

"I was especially close to my father since we did many things together. In Fairhope, my father had sixty acres that supported crops such as spring potatoes and roasting ear corn. He built up a dairy herd, and since he wasn't always there to take care of things, from a young age I took on responsibilities in the dairy. My father also did custom tractor work for neighbors, as tractors weren't very plentiful then. Back in 1929 he had the first tractor in Belmont County, Ohio. It was a CASE steel-wheeled, spade-lug tractor, the first competition to horses. When we moved he had it shipped to Fairhope. He was able to do a lot of custom work on the flat fields of southern Alabama, preparing land for planting, as well as harvesting and silo-filling.

"Daddy was never one to dictate or preach to us. I somehow understood that when we were repairing a tractor, doing farm work or traveling together, we weren't to ask a lot of questions. But when subjects were introduced that were very much of interest to my father, he'd be quite concerned that we see what he did and learn from the seeing. So it's a habit that's become part of my nature, not to ask questions but rather to try and find out all the little details by listening and observing.

"My father prepared the ground for neighbors and it was a unique thing that he frequently hired Negro tractor drivers. As a family we had the experience of having young Negroes work for us at harvest time, and they always ate at the table with us. We felt that it was a privilege to have them there, whereas mostly it was very frowned on by our neighbors. If we'd belonged to another faith or practice, we would have felt the indignation of our neighbors and likely the effects of the Ku Klux Klan. But it was accepted that Friends would do this, work with Negroes and sit at the same table.

"The only exception to this openness at our dinner table that I remember was when a Quaker member of the harvesting crew from North Carolina said he wouldn't feel comfortable sitting at the table with Negroes. So Aunt Mary said that it wouldn't be a problem, she'd fix him a place at a table in the utility room.

"Fairhope was an open type of community, filled with settlers who were into different and often more enlightened thinking such as the Organic School of Education and the Henry George Single Tax Colony. This is a tax structure where the organization collects tax on land value as the sole source of revenue and production efforts are exempt. Because this encourages the efficient use of land it's a system that's supported by many alternative thinkers. The Quakers arrived in Fairhope around 1918 to establish their own meeting in this area, possibly because of the Single Tax Colony, but probably more due to the openness of the community.

"Even with that enlightened atmosphere, a Negro settlement still existed. They had an area to live in and that was it. 'Don't let the sun be setting on you in the town of Fairhope' if you were a Negro. In Fairhope itself society was more tolerant because of the background of the settlers, but racism always existed. The Negroes were still restricted to the two rows of seats at the back of the bus. They had a school in the settlement that had an annual concert, and they would invite us over. White people generally didn't go into that area but members of our Friends meeting would attend their graduation ceremonies. It was quite significant that we were able to make a stand against the racism we often faced and frequently had to live with.

"I was in prison in Tallahassee when my father had his accident. He was a tall man and was working with two other men on a pry lever, using a pole to lift up and pivot a large cement watering tank. It slipped off the fulcrum and the lever came down on his head. It didn't knock him out and afterwards, when he was having headaches, he didn't think they were due to the accident. But then he had more and more pain, mainly in his neck. He tried various treatments, but still the doctors and chiropractor working with him couldn't figure out what was wrong. They sent him to a specialist in Mobile who discovered there was a blood clot, and a brain surgeon from Birmingham performed an operation. This was successful in removing the clot, but at his age, which was fifty-six and sure doesn't seem very old to me now, his brain kept shrinking instead of healing. Within a few days he died.

"I'd just returned from Ohio where I'd gone to give Lucky the ring. My siblings and I had been told there was an emergency, but we were later told that the operation had been successful and we thought that Daddy was okay. He died just a couple of months after I got out of prison, in the spring of 1950.

"It was very hard for me to go back to doing the chores and jobs that we had shared before Daddy's death. When the group of us decided to go to Costa Rica it was very difficult for me to leave Fairhope, but one of the consolations I had was that I didn't have to leave my father."

Like Wolf, Hubert and Mildred Mendenhall were members of the Fairhope Monthly Meeting of Friends. With Quaker sensitivity, they looked on with distress at the increased use of taxpayers' money for military purposes and at the overwhelming state of poverty and hunger in the world. They worked with other Quaker farmers from across the country to find ways to use unprecedented food surpluses in the U.S. to meet international needs. In May, 1950, they joined an agricultural tour of Central America. They were already considering leaving the United States, having found themselves so often at odds with their own government. When they arrived in Costa Rica they were immediately impressed with the friendliness of the people and the general air of contentment in the country. The army had recently been abolished and the government was looking to develop its farmland. By the time they were settled in the airplane for their flight home they knew that this tiny country was "where their destiny lay." The Mendenhalls brought their enthusiasm back to the Fairhope Meeting.

"When the Rockwells and I were released from prison we had to work under a parole program until the end of our sentence period. That became a problem when we decided to go to Costa Rica as none of us on parole were allowed to leave the area without permission. We certainly weren't allowed to leave the U.S. We had to wait for the parole period to be over, but fortunately it didn't hold us up that much.

"Twenty-five or so people from the Fairhope Friends Meeting decided to move to Costa Rica following the Mendenhall's report. We began by sending three people to Costa Rica to make more contacts. The rest of the group had time to learn a little Spanish and to make preparations for leaving the country.

"The most important thing for me from that period was making a stand against what we knew to be wrong, which was that for the first time the United States government would be instituting compulsory conscription during peacetime. We opposed it by not registering and by not directly supporting the institution of war. Our opposition was expressed not only by not registering for the military, but also by taking the next step and coming to Costa Rica."

THREE

Looking for peace

"Talking about the decision to come here and how we evolved into what we are now, if evolving is the right word…anyway, about how we accomplished what we did in our own way. The hardest decision for some of the younger ones was to not register for the peacetime draft. The support we got from the Fairhope Meeting was very important then as well as when we were considering coming to Costa Rica as a group. Of course, one of the big things in favor of Costa Rica was the new constitution that abolished the army. That was the bonus as well as the reason to come down here.

"For Lucky and me, making the actual trip down and getting started was only made possible by having the financial support of Hubert and Mildred, which they offered after my father's death. My inheritance was enough to help us get started, to have a horse and some cattle, but coming here was more than we could ever have financed on our own."
Wolf taking a break on the River Trail

Costa Rica is a small, developing country in Central America. Nestled between Nicaragua and Panama, it is the bridge between powerful North America and feisty South America. It has had its share of invasions, social unrest and polarized political struggle, but the civil war of the 1940s resulted in progressive social reforms, including the abolition of the country's army in 1948. Since that time Costa Rica has attracted people from around the world who are drawn by the ideal of a nonmilitary society existing amidst lush rainforests and the soft sands of tropical beaches.

The *Ticos* themselves are as warm and welcoming as a cup of freshly brewed coffee. Along with sugar cane and a variety of fruits and veg-

etables, coffee is one of the many crops grown on the undulating hillsides that characterize much of the landscape. Although Costa Rica has
been a shining star in ecological policy and political stability, in recent
years, as is so often the case, some negative aspects of its progress and
development have tarnished both its reputation and its clean environment.

I knew very little about Costa Rica when, in January of 1990, I
decided to end my miserable marriage. A few months prior to my decision I had met Maryjka Mychajlowycz when we were blockading the
construction of a logging road in Temagami, Ontario. She had recently
returned from volunteering in Monteverde. She spoke frequently of the
beauty of the area and of the interesting community of Quakers who
were deeply involved in conservation and peace issues.

When I finally made up my mind to leave my husband, the idea of
getting out of our small northern community and convalescing in
Monteverde appealed to me. Maryjka was returning to continue her volunteer work there and I decided to head south with her. As I read up on
Costa Rica I was fascinated that this little country had no standing army,
though it was surrounded by countries that were so often stricken with
military chaos and the social unrest that goes with it. The relative green-
ness of the government gave me hope, and the lure of Latin rhythms
was the final seduction. As I searched for peace in my own troubled soul,
I thought this was possibly the place to find it.

The decision by Wolf and Lucky and the other Fairhope Friends to
move to Costa Rica was similarly about seeking a place to be at peace.
The 1940s was a time when the United States was developing as a military power. It was impossible to live in America and do business as a citizen without paying taxes towards the growing military machine. The
Quakers knew they had to seriously consider moving to another country. U.S. District Judge John McDuffie, presiding over the trial of the
four young men from Fairhope who had resisted the draft, found himself in a tough position. Neither wanting to make them martyrs by hand-
ing down too severe a sentence nor wanting to let them off completely,
he made his position clear with words that were taken to heart by all who
heard them: "…this is a government of laws and not of men, and so
long as you live here, you should abide by the laws of the land…those

who oppose the laws of this country and this form of government, even when it goes to war, should get out of this country and stay out."

In their search for a new beginning the group's requirements included a country with a physical environment and political climate they could endure living in that also had affordable land they could make productive. They considered Canada as a possibility but the idea of moving to a colder climate didn't appeal to them. When Hubert and Mildred Mendenhall returned from their trip to Central America with the strong impression that Costa Rica was the country that could realistically support their dream, the decision was made and the plan put into action.

"I didn't know anything about Costa Rica. In our civics class at Olney we studied events that were happening in Latin America, but I never heard tell of the country until I read an article in Reader's Digest quoting Pepe Figueres, who'd been the main character involved in leading the revolution in 1948. It was Figueres who invited people from developed countries to come and invest in Costa Rica. He requested help in making productive farmland out of the largely forested countryside, which was more than fifty percent of the total land area. That got me interested in trying to develop forested land, which I also discovered would be much cheaper to buy."

In November of 1950 the Quakers started moving their families to Costa Rica. A small contingent went overland, their vehicles loaded down with personal belongings. It was an eventful journey that lasted three months to the day. The others went by air, sending their household goods by ship. Wolf and Lucky were part of the group that flew to their future home.

"That was a period of time with a lot of stress. My father had died, and at the tender age of twenty I was responsible for harvesting the crops and overseeing the needs of our dairy farm. Then we were getting ready for the big wedding and right after that preparing to come to Costa Rica. Lucky and I were married on October 14, 1950. It was only a few months from the time we first decided to come until we were actually married and heading south. That time was quite a busy one and would have been unique in anyone's life.

"On November 21 we flew out of New Orleans in a large four-engine plane with Pan American Airlines. When we landed in Guatemala City we changed over to a smaller plane that could land at La Sabana Airport, which was outside of San José, the capital of Costa Rica. We were greatly pleased that Eston and Mary had also decided to come to Costa Rica. Having the companionship of these two good friends who we had known since boarding school made it much easier for us to come to such a new environment.

"All the families settled in houses around the San José area. In the first week a group of us visited an area in the southern part of the country near what is now known as San Vito. It turned out to be completely unsuitable. After that, land search teams headed out to visit parcels of land that might hold promise for our future community.

"It was very telling to see land when it was dry and looked feasible to settle in and then to see it again at the end of an extraordinarily rainy period when it would have been impossible to bring things in even by plane. I'm talking about the necessities of everyday life and everything we'd brought from the States. We'd also need access to a market for our crops. It was immediately obvious that we couldn't consider certain areas as possibilities. We started making contacts with Costa Ricans and Americans who'd settled here and could tell us more about the year-round weather conditions and show us different places to purchase. Exploring Costa Rica was much more difficult then than it would be now because of the lack of roads in those early years.

"Eston had enough Spanish to interpret for us when we went out looking at farms. I was gradually learning Spanish by picking up on Eston's conversations. I drifted into feeling confident enough to speak. I learned the language a word at a time, mimicking sounds like a parrot.

"During that period we seemed to have a lot of time on our hands and so we got to travel around San José a bit. For entertainment we went to see movies, visited museums or the zoo, or sat in city parks and watched the parade of males and females eyeing each other. We didn't really have anything constructive to do except wait for the day when we'd find the place where we could go and live on the land and set about creating a home and community."

The search for the perfect location for their community intensified. Small groups sent out on scouting trips seriously considered land near the Panamanian border, in the Valle General in southwestern Costa Rica, and in the San Carlos region in the north. In each case the land was either too rough for productive farming, too hot, too wet or too expensive. In the meantime, as the Guindon's meager savings dwindled away, Wolf needed to make some money. Leaving his young wife in Heredia, he found paying work in Turrialba at a research facility.

"I found out about a temporary job that was available at the Inter-American Institute for Agricultural Studies, what is now CATIE. Of course, the big drawback was that I'd have to be away from the group for the whole week and sometimes two weeks in a row. Worst of all it meant being away from my new wife, who was just realizing what her morning sickness was. But the money I made was significant enough to make it worth the effort. I was given room and board and about $60 for six weeks of work.

"The most interesting aspect of the research was the work being done with cattle. They had brought in a type of cattle to study, a crossbreed with a bloodline that showed the characteristics of the original cattle that had come from Spain. There was a small area near the Nicaraguan border where they had remained somewhat pure. This breed was of interest to the Institute because they gave more milk. Tests showed that in Costa Rica's hot, dry lowlands, they were better for dairy than the Jerseys that were being imported from the U.S. and crossed with Brahma cattle. My job was working in the dairy, something I really enjoyed doing.

"Equipment was put in to create a climatic-control room for the cattle. The room had refrigeration and heating units that could duplicate the humidity, temperature and modulations of a particular climate. That was when I learned from the experiments that Brahma cattle change their character when brought to cold climates. They're more nervous and violent. In that room you could see that they changed drastically. Many years later, when our hired man went to work on a farm at a high elevation with cool weather, the owners brought up fifteen head of Brahma as beef cattle. They couldn't handle those animals. Some of the cattle would run you over given the chance. They were nervous and wouldn't graze enough and they got thin. It was interesting to see the cattle react in the field just as the control-room research had predicted they would.

"I was allowed to use the library, and I met many professors. I got better acquainted with Dr. Leslie R. Holdridge, who'd come to see us in San José. He'd read in the paper about a group of Quakers settling in the country and had wanted to introduce himself. He was a forester from the United States affiliated with tropical biology in Costa Rica. His grandmother was a Quaker, which was another thing that interested him about our group.

"Dr. Holdridge would go on to establish La Selva Research Station in 1954 on what was his cocoa farm in eastern Costa Rica. In 1962, ten years after we met him, he was one of the founders of the Tropical Science Center, what we all call the TSC, an organization that was created to support and facilitate biological research and study in the tropics. Ten years after that, the TSC became the administrator of the Monteverde Cloud Forest Reserve. Dr. Holdridge had also developed a life zone classification system that's still widely used internationally. From the start he was a great help to our group, describing the types of forests in different parts of the country as well as telling us where the climate was most suitable for farming.

"It was a very hard time for Lucky because she was diagnosed with amoebic dysentery. She had pain that medication didn't take away. It was probably an early indication of ovarian trouble. As a teenager she'd had similar pain during the winter and had thought it was related to the cold. Whatever it was, it eventually developed into a cyst that we didn't discover until her fifth pregnancy. At the time, though, she was pregnant with our first child. While I was working in Turrialba friends in the community had to take care of her. It was very difficult for us to be apart. I felt both neglectful and jealous!"

It was a tough start to their marriage. At eighteen, Lucky had had no idea what she was getting into. Her account of the time describes events from a young woman's point of view.

"In my last year at Olney Wolf wrote and asked if I'd like to go to Costa Rica. Well, I didn't know anything about Costa Rica. Like everyone else I thought it was Puerto Rico. I wasn't particularly the adventurous sort, but if that was where he was going, that was where I was going. The whole thing wasn't my idea, but I followed along. Yet I've never, ever been sorry. I didn't know the other people, the Mendenhalls and

Rockwells, except for Eston and Mary, who I called Loo. They had decided to go, so we went down together. We had lots of fun doing all kinds of things but it was a difficult way to begin a marriage.

"I wouldn't want to go through that first year of married life again. First we went to a new country with new food, then I got pregnant right away, which I hadn't intended. I couldn't figure out why I felt sick all the time. I thought it must be the food. We were supposed to be using the rhythm method of birth control, but my rhythm was off.

"We were all living together in the same house when we arrived in Costa Rica. Loo, Eston, Wolf and I fixed our kitchen apart. There were all these people telling me what I should and shouldn't do as far as being pregnant was concerned, so there were pressures on all sides. There were a lot of extra emotional things, a new marriage being emotional enough. I would never want to live through that first year again."

At the end of six months, with none of the areas they had visited fully meeting their needs, the group was reaching a crisis. They seriously discussed dividing the group in two to pursue different directions. In the end this solution was rejected because the more financially able members of the group remained committed to helping the younger members. Of equal importance was the group's belief that staying together for worship and schooling was essential to their future as a community.

As the group struggled with the difficult decision of choosing between locations that were less than perfect, they were visited by the man who would introduce them to the land that was to become their home. Ingo Kalinowsky and a partner had taken up options to buy out the squatters living in a remote area on the Pacific slope of the Tilarán Mountain range. The land was owned by the Guacimal Land Company. Three of the Quakers accompanied Kalinowsky on horseback to the tiny mountain community of Cerro Plano. Virgin cloud forest covered the highest slopes and skirting the woods was reasonably level, partially cleared terrain with scattered homesteads. Seeing all of this, the men realized that this was the best land they'd visited.

They returned with such enthusiasm for the area that the group agreed to pursue the land solely on the men's recommendation. Negotiations followed and a price of U.S. $50,000 was reached for approximately 1,400 hectares. They had to purchase the title from the

Guacimal Land Company and buy out the squatters, who had cleared small parcels of land. Many of the squatters stayed in the area, moving their possessions to nearby land where they began new clearings. The local *Ticos* always played an important role in the development of the community. Beyond selling them land, the *Ticos* welcomed the newcomers and shared their knowledge and experience with them.

The Quakers found that the pastures and forests were kept lush by abundant rainfall and frequent mists, and the cultivation of crops year-round would be possible as there was plenty of sunshine and moderate temperatures. This led the group to name their new community Monteverde, or green mountain. At the time there was nothing more than an oxcart trail leading up the mountain, which meant that the group's first task was to build a better road to transport provisions to their new home.

"The first time I went up the mountain was with Cecil Rockwell and Hubert Mendenhall. We wanted to get an idea of how we were going to take over the management of the property and get our families moved up. We had to remove large rocks from the trail and go through gates that were meant for oxcarts, not for a jeep. We frequently had to dig down the middle of the road as a ridge had risen up between the ruts made by oxcart wheels and this was a major problem for the lower axle on the jeep. When we reached the land we were able to ride around on horseback to see the many clearings that had already been made by the Costa Ricans.

"On my second visit I was shown more of the area by Eston, who had been there for a couple of weeks. Everything was one big adventure. We went around talking to the area people, those who we'd bought out and those who'd be our new neighbors. We considered which properties we might like to own one day and I bought a cow from one of the Costa Rican families that was leaving. Everything we saw was new for us. We were constantly thinking and talking about the future. I had a really good time."

On May 29, 1951, the first families started up the mountain on the newly widened road. The mostly light-haired, light-skinned foreigners with jeeps and trailers overflowing with possessions drew the interest of the locals, who surely had never seen anything like this parade before. In the two trips Wolf made, the road needed fixing and overloaded vehicles broke down. The Quakers' first exposure to the mountain had been at the end of the dry season, but by now the rainy season was upon them. Hard rains would first turn the roadway to mud and eventually wash it away. In many places, natural springs would sprout up and create bottomless bog holes. These conditions necessitated chains to be put on all four wheels to have any sort of traction.

In July, as the rest of the group cleared land, erected tent platforms for temporary homes, hauled water from streams and helped each other navigate the mud-slick road, Wolf and Lucky went to Ohio to await the birth of their first child. Lucky's sister and brother-in-law, Helen and Lawrence Sprigal, provided a house for the couple to live in. Wolf worked on his brother-in-law's dairy farm, making precious cash to help on their return to Costa Rica. Alberto Guindon was born on August 17, his papa's birthday. In December of 1951 the young family, with hopes and dreams in hand, returned to begin their life in Monteverde.

FOUR

Stepping stones

"I once heard a speaker share this thought: if you look for bridges and they aren't to be found, then look for stepping stones. As I was crossing the last stream, I was thinking that this is what worked when we were building our relationships with Costa Ricans. We didn't have much opportunity to make big changes or to dominate in any one area, be it education or roads or whatever, but we did try to have high standards at our schools and to promote a better education for people in this area. This was also true when it came to sharing our medical knowledge or trying to improve a road by fixing up the worse spots. Small steps working towards improving the bigger picture." *Wolf crossing the Quebrada Cuecha*

Monteverde has been a hospice for me on more than one occasion. On my first visit I arrived with a heart wounded on the marital battlefield. I had planned to heal in Costa Rica for two months, but life was so good I lingered there for another six. I did some work for biologist Nalini Nadkarni, who was analyzing the composition of the forest canopy. I spent several weeks crawling through the woods following her assistant, Rodrigo Solano, as we prepared study plots and collected data. This part-time job gave me the opportunity to ascend one of the massive trees in the Cloud Forest Reserve. When I poked my head above the sea of leafy green, with white-faced monkeys cursing me from nearby branches, I felt like I'd climbed into a dream. I volunteered in the office of the Monteverde Conservation League and helped develop a program for volunteers at the Monteverde Institute. I lived with a university group in the rustic *casona* at the Reserve, serving as a liaison between the Institute and the Reserve staff as well as a surrogate mother to the visiting students.

While living at the Reserve I helped coordinate the morning nature walks and became familiar with the guides and the trails. My friendship with Wolf evolved as I followed him through the Peñas Blancas valley and started transcribing his stories. I lived on the cool mountain but escaped to the heat of the lowlands as often as possible. I discovered not only the beauty of the Costa Rican rainforest and the pleasures of beach life, but the humility, sincerity and humor of the country's people, developing friendships I treasure to this day. My spirit began to soar and my soul regained the ground it had lost in wedded unhappiness.

At the same time I was losing weight, my breathing had become laborious and my physical energy was ebbing away. At first I ignored what was happening to my body, but in September, after I fainted into the hibiscus flowers outside a local restaurant, I booked my ticket home. My heart was once again intact, but my body was breaking down. When I returned to Canada it was the people in Costa Rica I missed the most, and it is the people who have drawn me back year after year.

After three months of doctors' examinations and tests, on Christmas Eve of 1990 I was diagnosed with Hodgkin's disease, a lymphatic cancer. Immediately I began, one step at a time, my long journey back to health and wholeness.

Step by step, civilization came to the Tilarán Mountains. The Fairhope Quakers weren't the first inhabitants of this area they now call home. Artifacts indicate that indigenous people once lived there, though little is known about them. Modern history begins in this area in the early 1900s with the establishment of a gold mine at Guacimal, in the lowlands southwest of Monteverde. In their free time miners would hike into the forest-covered hills to hunt. Gradually, families spread throughout the land, making clearings to grow crops and raise livestock. By the time the Quakers arrived about 175 subsistence farmers lived in the region.

Monteverde's closest neighbor to the west is Cerro Plano, which at the time of the community's founding had several dwellings, a two-grade school and a church. Pastures in the area had been cleared and claimed through the system of squatters' rights. On the other side of Cerro Plano was Santa Elena, which was a small pueblo where the local authorities were stationed. The main part of the village originally sat on the road arriving from Las Juntas, a mining town where the area's early residents went for supplies. Eventually, a Catholic church was built on donated land closer to Cerro Plano and Santa Elena's center was relocated and grew up around the new church.

The inhabitants of Cerro Plano and Santa Elena received the Quakers with typical Costa Rican warmth. Of course, the *Ticos* were curious about these foreigners, but life continued peacefully. Happy to return to such a welcoming environment, Wolf and Lucky, with their new baby in tow, staked out the boundaries to what is still, fifty-five years later, the Guindon family farm.

"Right from day one, with those first visits to Monteverde, I was attracted to the woods and the back trails and tromping just to see what I would find at the end of the path. Attempting to develop a farm from forest, producing a variety of crops on land where nothing for human consumption had been produced before, was part of my theme. Here was this wild woods that only supported monkeys and the trees they lived in, and my goal was to be able to tell the monkeys to move over and make room for me and my family, though, of course, we were happy to stay on the ground.

"By the time we returned from the U.S. with Berto, the land the group had purchased was pretty well divided up. Most of the families had already moved onto their land so we had the chance to see who our neighbors might be. There were still three parcels that were large enough for our family to settle on and develop. It turned out that one of those properties was what we were looking for, a beautiful piece almost entirely covered with primary forest. That was a good beginning. The trail I made to our place was wide enough for a jeep, which allowed us to move our possessions in with an oxcart. That hand-dug right-of-way was one of the number one necessities that we started with.

"Our piece of land had two small clearings. It was important to have a place where we could have a garden and plant crops. *Ayote*, a kind of squash, was already growing in one of the clearings and we ate lots of it. We got to thinking about where we'd put our house since there wasn't one on the property.

"We made a clearing for our first temporary tent house. Earlier, some of the families had agreed to go together to buy large heavy canvas tents. Each family also bought a wood-burning stove from Sears and Roebuck. We sawed lumber and built platforms with partial walls that we could put the canvas tents on so we'd have clear headroom from wall to wall.

"We had to dig a well and that was quite a process, but it finally got done. I believe there are guardian spirits looking out for you and what happened at our place was that some water seeped out and showed us signs of a natural spring. I dug down thirty feet and there was pretty good water in the rainy season but it dried up in the dry season. So I dug down to fifty feet and found a vein of water that lasted. The good fortune was that I was digging in what they call a *cascajo,* a sandstone outcrop, which meant pick and shovel work, but it didn't have to be cased up. Once the well was dug we took the same bucket we'd used to take out dirt and used it as our water bucket. The well was a big job, but it furnished us with water during the first few years that we lived here.

"We put our tent right in the woods. We often saw monkeys in our trees and we had coatis, what are locally called *pizotes,* eat from our corn patch. We got pigs right away and would feed our squash to them. The squash also fed the coatis and the kinkajous. We had a lot of nightlife with the animals. We were homesteading on this little chunk of land and it was an enjoyment just to see anything, whether it was a forest squirrel or having a cat bring in a weasel. It was one thing or another, quite a zoo.

"So there we were, perched at the end of the road, almost hanging over the cliff edge. That's where I started clearing land for our pastures. Those years must have been pretty lonesome for Luck because she was surrounded by all this forest and it was a good ways off to go visiting. One of the big things Lucky had to adjust to was how independent she needed to be.

"In 1952 both Lucky and I, along with several others in the community, got hepatitis, although none of us seriously. At this time Lucky was pregnant with our second child, but sadly we lost the baby due to jaundice on May 25, 1952. We named her Rebecca Jane after our mothers. The funeral was held the next day and our baby was the first person to be buried in the Monteverde cemetery. I remember that Marvin, Clara and Arthur Rockwell gave us a calla lily to mark the gravesite. Unfortunately, that area became overgrown and I'm not sure we could find the burial plot now.

"In May of 1953, after we'd been living in the tent for over a year, it began to leak. We decided that if we were to survive the wet and windy season, we needed to try and treat the canvas. To waterproof the tent you were to treat it with a mixture of turpentine and paraffin, which you could buy in big chunks. So one morning, as Berto played outside, we decided to go ahead and do it.

"The mixture had to be hot enough so you could spread it. Well, the paraffin wasn't melting and we grew impatient. The rain was starting so we decided to speed up the melting process by taking the lid off the woodstove and putting the kettle directly over the fire. Some of the mixture went over the side and ignited. When we put water on it, rather than putting out the flame, the flame spread and our tent caught fire.

"We had our things on shelves made from the wooden crates our belongings had been shipped in, with fabric tacked on the front. The fire burnt our clothes and tablecloths and many of our other possessions. There was only Luck and me there to put out the fire. At the time Lucky was over six months pregnant with our son Tomás. She got trapped in the kitchen corner and had to run through the flames to get out. When she did that she burnt her arm rather badly.

"We threw what we could outside. We ended up losing a lot of things that we'd thrown out, things we thought weren't burning but that came back into flame while we were still fighting the fire. Some of our things only got burnt on the folds, so we could still use them. Luck later sewed together pieces of towels to make larger, usable ones.

"In general, we just weren't thinking or we would have done that one differently. We were very thankful that Berto was playing outside at the time. The only benefit from the fire was that we got to eat the tasty well-smoked bacon that was hanging over the stove. We were given a place to stay by neighbors until we managed to get tarps over the charred frame so we could move back into our home again. Later we put a metal roof on the structure.

"It became clear that we needed to relocate our house to another spot mainly to access a better water source. We moved to a site closer to our neighbor John Campbell's spring. For many years we continued to haul water with milk cans carried on our shoulder. Several years later we put in a water line of plastic pipe. This line brought water from John's spring and it was only satisfactory as long as he had extra water there.

"It would be 1962 before we built our permanent home on a site more centrally located on our property and soon after we hooked up to the public water system. As more houses were built in the area, the increased demand for water created a need to bring a waterline from a better source further up the mountain. For a good many years this was satisfactory and several families hooked up to it. But accessing water has always been a major problem. We had always expected and hoped that we would have our own spring on our property.

"The community inherited a small hydroelectric generator that provided limited electricity. Eventually, Hubert brought in a bigger generator that supplied his house, the meeting house, his neighbors' houses and the cheese plant. It only provided electricity at night and in the daytime was used exclusively to run the sawmill. The rest of us got electricity in 1957 when Reuben Rockwell established a hydroelectric plant in Lindora, several miles from Monteverde, and installed lines to bring power to the community. There were times when we didn't have electricity because of a landslide or other water problems, but for the most part it was a dependable current. This meant we could have a refrigerator, which made a big difference. We really appreciated that. The Lindora plant serviced the community as far as Santa Elena until the demand got too great with more people owning refrigerators and water heaters. The community switched to public power in 1990."

The Friends always recognized the importance of a reliable water source. Although the area receives large amounts of precipitation, harnessing it is another matter. Through the rainy season, from May to November, there is rainfall almost daily that ranges from a drizzle to a deluge. As the tropical winter gets into gear the mornings are often clear and calm with varying amounts of rain falling in the afternoons. As the season progresses there can be weeks when water is everywhere, the roads a foot deep in mud, an umbrella just about useless. Sturdy rubber boots are the fashion accessory of choice.

Signs that the season is changing arrive in mid-November or early December, when trade winds from the northeast pick up and the rainfall decreases. Monteverde becomes a wind tunnel, with the air gusting so forcefully that people on foot can be blown along the roads appearing to barely touch the ground. As the dry season progresses, the winds continue to bring cloud and mist to the upper parts of Monteverde. The clouds dissipate as they move westward, bringing less and less moisture to the Pacific slope. Only at its highest elevation, in the cloud forest, is there a year-round supply of hydration.

When the wind and mists combine, it is as if ice pellets are hitting the zinc roofs of Monteverde's houses, but outside the sky will be blue and the sunshine warm. The winds begin to ebb in March until one day there is a noticeable stillness across the countryside. As with the coloring of the autumn leaves in North America, this is the signal that winter is around the corner and the rains will come again.

Despite all the rainfall, the region still experiences water shortages. The rainwater runs down the steep hillsides, deforestation aiding its descent. While the remaining forest consumes its share of the water, the trees are essential for preventing erosion, catching mist and evening the flow of water to the streams. Water contamination often occurs around farms and industries. From the beginning, the Monteverdians agreed on a plan for dividing the land that would meet the community's development needs while protecting their watershed for the future.

"The division of the land was determined by everyone's needs, but at the same time was influenced by the money some families had to pay for larger properties or land already in production. The first parcels were in the central part of the community where the main road ended. Those of us with less money to invest or with the desire to work forested land, or community members who had no immediate need for a road, chose properties further from the hub. The land that wasn't taken immediately was divided into two parts. One part was to be sold later as other people came or to any of us who wanted to add to our property. This land needed to be road accessible.

"The other part wasn't suitable for developing due to the lay of the land and the way the ridges ran. This was a forested area that was inaccessible by road. We set aside this part as a community reserve that we called the Monteverde Watershed. The idea was to protect the forest that held the natural springs. We knew right off the bat that looking after our watershed was going to be very important as we needed pure water for our community needs and a good water supply to generate electricity and run the sawmill. Although water shortages weren't an issue at that time, we still recognized that developing land above the community would endanger our water source.

"Some of us were just being practical, but from the beginning Mildred Mendenhall said we should be saving the forest. She always had a concern that we didn't cut down 'the last tree.' Even as we were cut-

ting down trees for lumber for our homes she was emphatic that we did-
n't keep on clearing without considering the value of the forest. So we
held onto that one piece, which amounted to 554 hectares. We all had a
share in it according to the size of the holding that we each had originally purchased.

"For twenty-five years the community worked together to protect
this land, maintaining its boundary lines and, on three occasions, working with authorities to remove squatters who had started clearings. This
land is now known as Bosqueterno S.A., which means the eternal forest.
In 1975 we leased it for ninety years to the Tropical Science Center as
part of the Monteverde Cloud Forest Reserve."

Even before arriving on the mountaintop the group recognized that
the needs of the new community had to be met with intelligence and
commitment, and of course with old-fashioned toil and sweat. As the
group was unpacking, men were already heading out to cut down trees
and haul logs, and soon lumber was being milled at the sawmill that was
built on one of the streams. A woodworking shop was set up and a sugar
mill was erected that required a lot of firewood to boil down the cane
juice. Many of the buildings that were constructed are still standing
today and businesses were developed that continue to prosper. Wooden
homes, often resembling New England farmhouses, gave an identity to
the community that is unique in Costa Rica.

"In the early years we worked together a lot as a community. As
Lucky and I produced children we became more involved in the school.
The Monteverde Friends School was held in a one-room house until
1957, when we finally built a permanent building. We had a Quaker committee that managed the school and implemented our ideals. Our philosophy is that education is not only intellectual but also physical and spiritual. These three things are at the basis of what we try to teach.

"Our children had the advantage of learning from a very special
teacher, Mary Mendenhall, Hubert's sister. Mary made a great contribution to our community. She was the head of the school for most of our
children's education, from elementary through high school. She created
such a capacity and discipline for learning in her students that those who
went on to university or some kind of technical training had no difficulty relating to the learning process at a higher level. Our school empha-

sized the importance of becoming good strong community members, no matter where you live.

"The children benefited from the involvement of all the parents and the community in general. For us it was important to have recreational and social events that contributed to the balance in the community. One of the things we participated in was family night when, once a month, a different family would organize entertainment for the community. Luck and I introduced square dancing, a social event which brought in the Costa Ricans and let people of all ages share an evening together. In the same way other members taught special classes. We took advantage of the individual skills of each person.

"Many young people came to the Friends School from San Luis, the community that sits in the valley below Monteverde. The children would walk up the long hill and back down every day. José Luis Vargas Leitón, Eugenio and Carlos Vargas, and several others have become very prominent people in the community. For those and others from San Luis who've found success both here and outside of this area, it helped being bilingual, having learned English at our school. Nowadays, although the basic subjects are the same, more and more classes at the Friends School are taught in Spanish. There are three private bilingual schools in the Monteverde area: the Friends School, the Cloud Forest School and the Seventh-Day Adventist School. All are committed to the principle of teaching a way of learning which is organic, that is learning that continues to grow throughout your life. Something that is relatively new but very important is teaching environmental education, which includes learning about the protection of natural areas. This is one of the twists of schooling particular to this area.

"We had a lot to learn in those first years and we really depended on the knowledge of the local people. Our Costa Rican neighbors were gracious in teaching us things that we were basically ignorant about. For example, they taught us to plant crops in protected areas that were less exposed to the wind. In Monteverde we could plant pasture at any time of the year but knowing what to plant in which season was very important with all the other crops. I hoped in turn to share with our new neighbors some of the things we thought might be useful such as the benefit of having good schools and the value of not drinking or smoking.

"We established a credit union because we were concerned for our neighbors. We found out that the Costa Ricans were paying the high interest rate of five percent per month on borrowed money. They practically never borrowed except for medical emergencies, such as when a woman needed special care in her pregnancy or any family member needed an operation. If a man was having problems paying back his loan, he could lose whatever he had that was giving him an income and making it possible to feed his family. The family's cows, pigs and horses would go first, followed by their land. People would often be faced with a greater emergency because they'd gotten a loan.

"Eston Rockwell's father, Abner, who'd been a member of a credit union in the U.S., had the idea of establishing a credit union here. He suggested getting people to put in money so that money could be lent out when needed.

"Eston, David Rockwell, Howard Rockwell Jr., Fermín Arguedas and I got it going in 1953. It was the first organization in the Santa Elena area that I was involved in. We called it the Coopesima, and it was known as *La Cima*. It was very successful for several years but later failed because people didn't conscientiously pay back their loans. There was no one on the committee making sure that the borrowers repaid the money.

"We were sponsored by the Co-op Department of the National Bank in San José. *La Cima* lasted until the banks began to make loans and promote savings. The National Bank itself came into Santa Elena in the early 1980s."

Fermín Arguedas is a Costa Rican whose grandfather was one of the first people to settle in the Cerro Plano area. He and his brothers were farmers and had one of the original dairies in the area. Fermín has worked throughout his life for the betterment of the community. He was twelve years old when the Quakers arrived in Monteverde. According to Fermín, their arrival brought positive changes to the region.

"For us, it was a great thing when the Quakers came because they brought new ideas. But it was more than that. The Quakers were non-drinkers. Many of the people whose land they bought had been heavy drinkers and we'd suffered greatly from their use of alcohol. Several of these people were poor without great ideas about what to do with their lives and were happy to have some money for their land. When they left, a new tranquility descended on the community. It was like a new dawning and it was wonderful. Those of us who stayed became great friends with the Quakers. With them, peace came to our mountain."

In Monteverde the expertise and personal dreams of each community member were thrown into the communal pot. Town meetings followed the process of consensus, which encouraged everyone to play a role in decision-making. Consensus attempts to meet the underlying concerns of each stakeholder through talk, good faith, understanding and the willingness to compromise, all Quaker ideals. Discussions would continue until everyone agreed they could live with the final proposal.

Early on the group realized the need for each family to have an income. They considered what businesses would benefit the whole area and could include their Costa Rican neighbors. Mindful of their remote location and the poor quality of the road to Monteverde, they needed a product with a high enough value for its weight that the expense of transport would be offset. They also needed a product that was not highly perishable. In Costa Rica at that time there was no competition for fine, cured cheeses. These considerations resulted in the establishment of the cheese factory, locally known as *la fábrica* or *la lechería*. Wolf eagerly joined with his neighbors in this ambitious endeavor.

"That first year we had the idea of establishing a milk-processing plant to make cheese. It was a huge community effort and a big commitment for everybody involved, especially in the first ten years. The families united together and agreed to purchase young dairy cattle. We brought up yearling heifers to furnish our future milk supply. We were introduced to Alfredo Volio, who had an interest in improving the herds in Costa Rica and was importing pureblood Guernsey heifers from the U.S. He was willing to help out by selling them to us at a low price.

"Oscar Montein, who had experience at a dairy plant, agreed to be our first cheese maker. He took enthusiastically to the task. First he learned the basics of cheese making, and he struggled on from there. I worked with him at different times, doing anything from steaming up the cans to helping make the cheese. We had to deal with the fact that the plant's electricity, which we got from a water-powered generator, was only available when the sawmill wasn't running. That was a thorn in the flesh for Oscar.

"The dairy plant was run as a Costa Rican corporation whose shareholders were all milk producers. In the beginning there were only seven of us and most of us shared the responsibility of being on the board. At board meetings we had to decide how to manage the plant and how to deal with the many problems that came up as we went along. A lot of times we didn't know what to do about the problems, whether it was mold or transport or the quality of the milk itself. There were many big hurdles for those of us who worked on the board. We certainly weren't as informed or efficient as the board members are today, but we put in a sincere effort.

"In those days we were reluctant to have Spanish-speaking members on the board as we had enough to deal with without having to provide bilingual meetings. We met in the evening, after milking and chores, and the meeting went until whatever hour of the night it took till we couldn't be rational anymore in our decision-making. In the beginning we met at the schoolhouse, in the hub of Monteverde. There was the walk home after that, in my case about two kilometers.

"The plant took a significant amount of money. A few families had enough to invest the biggest percentage, and those of us who didn't have investment money had twenty-five percent of the money from our milk production deducted and in this way we were able to buy into the business. Nobody was doing it to get rich, but having an income was a deep concern. It wasn't until April 8, 1954, that we received the first milk at the plant and opened the door for business. It was at least four more years before the plant was providing us with enough money to balance our own costs on the farm.

"When we got started, shares were available only for milk producers, and you didn't vote according to the number of shares you had. It was one member, one vote. It was that kind of corporation, run as a co-op. We eventually allowed one nonproducer, a teacher at a local school, to buy shares, and that set a precedent. After Hubert Mendenhall left Monteverde in the late 1960s, his shares were offered to some Costa Rican milk producers.

"The Costa Ricans only milked once a day and let the calves run with the cows all morning. We milked twice a day and handfed our calves. To keep the milk cool we would put the cans in cold water overnight until we could deliver the milk to the plant in the morning. It was a problem not to contaminate the milk and to keep the quality good. The quality of milk we had then wouldn't be accepted today, but we were struggling to produce milk in difficult conditions. For many years now we've been able to keep the milk cans in refrigerated water.

"In the beginning we didn't buy milk from the Costa Ricans for lack of a good quality of milk in their dairies. When we started buying milk from Costa Rican families, we soon learned we had to inspect the milking process to ensure that the quality was good. I got involved early on doing some inspections. It was one more way to meet Costa Rican families and promote quality cheese production. Inspecting was an early morning job. We had to be at the dairy farms at milking time, about 4:30 or 5 a.m. The Costa Rican farmers would bring in the calves to prime their mothers. It was quite an operation to see. There would be maybe thirty to sixty cows with their calves, with the farmers making sure the calves got enough milk for their growth. In the bigger dairies they now have electric milking machines, but the power goes out so often an auxiliary power source is needed, usually a diesel-powered generator. Otherwise they still do the milking by hand.

"We always helped our neighbors by hauling their milk. I built a sled to begin with and later built a frame to carry the milk by horseback. As the quantity grew we needed two horses to haul the milk and finally a box on the back of the wheel tractor. One farm still has an oxcart for delivering milk, but mainly the pickup and delivery is done by big trucks. Tank trucks are now used to collect the milk.

"I was on the board pretty much up to its twentieth year. That's when I started working with the Reserve. Our boys took over managing our dairy, along with our hired man, Digno Arce. Eventually our son, Benito, inherited the full responsibility of our dairy farm. I don't play around with dairy cows anymore and haven't for a good many years, but Luck and I still have enough shares in the business to have an active interest in it. Benito has managed to produce more milk than I ever did, from fewer cows! I'm pleased and proud that he kept our family farm alive and productive."

The Productores de Monteverde S.A., as the dairy plant and cheese factory is officially known, celebrated its fiftieth anniversary in 2003. It is an impressive modern operation with a busy retail outlet in

Monteverde and another on the Pan American Highway near Chomes. There are daily factory tours and cheese-tastings for the public. The variety of hard cheeses produced has grown from the original Edam to cheddar, Monterico, Parmesan, Gouda and many more. They also make soft cheeses, sour cream and their famous *cajeta,* a delicious creamy caramel fudge. The decision to expand into ice cream met with great success and several kinds are now available, ranging from classic chocolate and strawberry to coconut, mango, macadamia and coffee, incorporating the natural flavors of Costa Rica. It is also possible to buy fresh milk by taking a refillable bottle to the *lechería* or to other local stores.

As the Quakers had hoped, the business is now very much a part of the larger Costa Rican community. By 1995 only six of the 226 milk producers were in Monteverde, the rest being for the most part *Tico* families residing in the surrounding communities. The milk-processing plant and cheese factory, situated in the heart of Monteverde, has grown to several times its original size. Since 1999 there have been over 100 employees at the plant and another fifty at their other operations.

In 1997 the Productores de Monteverde S.A. developed a pig farm about a kilometer downstream from the dairy plant. Despite being controversial, the expansion into pigs proceeded as a means of dealing with the whey, a by-product of cheese-making, as well as treating the water that exited the milk plant. As the dairy plant had grown, more and more whey and cleaning products used in washing the floors and tanks had been dumped into the neighboring Guacimal River, increasingly destroying its oxygen. Now the whey is fed to the pigs and a system of holding ponds receive the effluent and settle out the chemical waste. This has solved most of the problems and the company continues to study and improve their environmental standards. They now carry a line of pork sausage, ham and other products that are produced at the Chomes plant.

Over the decades the business has had to contend with poor milk quality, falling milk production, spittlebug infestations, waste disposal and community concerns such as odors emitting from the pig farm. Due to new pasture techniques and conscientious farming methods, there has been no more clearing of local forests for cow pastures in the last thirty years in the Monteverde area. However, farmers are now being faced with accelerated land values and pressure by hotel developers to sell their land.

Though the Productores de Monteverde S.A. is a corporation, it runs very much as a cooperative in which no individual can hold more than five percent of the shares. By 2005, of the 500 shareholders, forty-five percent were milk producers and five percent were employees with the rest of the shares being held by local residents. Through community involvement and the constant updating of knowledge and practices, the cheese factory continues to modernize its approach to dairy production and cheese-making. As the dairy plant has grown, it has helped fulfill the Quaker desire to bring sustainable development and an improved standard of living to area residents.

"The dairy plant is one of the things I take a lot of pride in, knowing that the start was an act of faith. There's a whole lot to be said about learning to work together and that was a real part of it. That's what Monteverde is all about. We took the time to hear everybody's voice even though it seemed impossible to take the delays that come with following the process of consensus.

"When we started I was only in my twenties and had loads of energy. During the first ten years when there were no real profits being made it was important for us to work together on the construction of our homes and businesses. Our family probably received more than our share of help. We depended on the other members of the community because we didn't have family here. Among those who never questioned the need but were always there to help were Mildred Mendenhall, Dorothy Rockwell, and Elva and Cecil Rockwell. And the others, well, we always knew where to find them. When we look back to those early years it's amazing, absolutely amazing, the amount of physical work we did and the amount of necessary help we received and the time we spent working out our differences.

"Monteverde felt like it was to be our home right from the beginning and it has continued to feel that way. The economics of it were and still are bouncing on the borderline. There have been opportunities to go into something better economically, but we've made our choices and feel very well satisfied with them. I remember thinking, 'Well, if the dairy plant fails and if Monteverde fails,' and under the circumstances they very well could have, I felt I'd enjoyed the experience and could always start over and survive. Besides, at the time to me it wasn't work, it was just part of the project of this community we were living in."

FIVE

Changing directions

"The work of developing pasture for an expanding dairy was a really big job. That was one I always liked: I enjoyed the art of working with a chainsaw. What with all its dangers and even with the close calls I had, why, nonetheless, it's something that I got great satisfaction from. I loved to hear the trees come down. The *Ticos* would shout *'Al suelo!'* 'Timber!' as my father would say. Although it's true that people may not appreciate land clearing because we're more aware now of the need to protect the forest, the truth is that clearing land at that time was a necessary and important part of rural development." *Wolf walking through his pastures in Monteverde*

The roadmap of life follows the ups and downs and twists and turns of a mountain route more often than it does the flat straight highway of the prairies. The path my life followed in Canada after those eight months in Costa Rica was filled with the emotional uncertainty that can accompany any struggle. I moved back in with my parents in their home in southern Ontario to be closer to my doctor in Hamilton, Dr. Ralph Meyer. My chemotherapy started on the same day in January 1991 that the Gulf War erupted in Iraq. Along with so many others, I was horrified by the televised images of the first bombs raining down on the people of Baghdad. I felt the turmoil of the whole world coursing through my veins along with the toxic medications.

Over the following months I watched fellow patients, familiar bald heads in the waiting room at the cancer clinic, slide down with weakness into their chairs. While many survived, others eventually just disappeared, succumbing to their illness. My doctor understood that I was yearning to return to the north, to regain my health and strength amongst the rock and the pines. In my fifth month of chemo, he arranged for me to continue my treatments in a northern clinic and, with his blessing, I went to work at a canoe camp in the bush of northeastern Ontario on beautiful Lake Temagami. I had spent a lot of time in this area through the 1980s, involved in local environmental and social justice issues. It was the best place for me to be at a time when I needed all the positive energy I could muster.

After nine months of medical procedures, tests indicated that I was cured. Three months later I knew something was wrong. When I was told there were once again pathogens running wild in my body, I was more terrified than I had been following my first diagnosis and gathering my inner strength was much harder. Finally, after completing two more months of chemo and another month of daily radiation, a robustness reappeared in my body and spirit, somewhat tempered by a deeper understanding of my own vulnerability. I began my new life as a survivor, anxious for the day when these feelings of fragility would disappear and my life would start to resemble something normal. I looked forward to returning to Costa Rica, going back up the green mountain and following Wolf down another trail.

Monteverde is reached by a gravel road that starts to climb as soon as it leaves the flat Pan American Highway at just above sea level. Some people would say that it is little more today than the muddy oxcart trail it was in 1950. The truth is that people have been improving the road since the day the Quakers arrived. The sign on the highway at the Lagarto turnoff proclaims a distance to Monteverde of thirty–five kilometers, but this modest number is deceptive. By the time travelers arrive in Santa Elena, the gateway to the larger Municipality of Monteverde, most would insist they had traveled at least twice that far.

For the first while the route is dry, dusty and hot, but as it meanders up the mountain the dust becomes compacted dirt or mud and the greens start to get brighter. The exception is the dry season when the dust coats the roadside houses all the way to Monteverde. In most places the surface is rough, having been rutted by wheels or washed out by rains. As my friend, Jim Oake, said on the occasion of his first trip up the mountain, "On the prairies we'd call this a dry river bed."

In the lowlands, cattle move slowly in the heat and iguanas skitter by. Doorways are hidden behind bushes of hibiscus and bougainvillea in warm hues of red, orange and pink. The road winds up and over steep hills that have been burned or cleared to create pastures, past small homesteads, and in and out of the shade cast by the elegant tropical hardwoods that survived the cull. With the rise in elevation, the jaundice of the deforested land is gradually replaced by a healthy complexion of wooded areas that finally consolidate to paint the mountaintop a deep and vibrant green. There is also a subtle shift in fragrance as you ascend the mountain. The sweet and sour odors of flowering trees and fruit rotting in the sun give way to the heavy organic mustiness that permeates every corner and crevice of Monteverde.

Getting closer to the top, the views stretch further, treating you to the panorama of the vast plains of Guanacaste to the northwest. The pastures and orange groves of the Guacimal River valley sit below to the south while the waters of the Gulf of Nicoya sparkle to the west. No matter which way you look, it is breathtaking. As the road heads higher, its edges drop off abruptly to either side, audible gasps escaping newcomers on their first trip skyward. This infamous route has been a steady if unstable link to the outside world, bringing in the adventurous and inspiring the best-selling "I Have Survived the Monteverde Road" souvenir T-shirts. Through the years vehicles have tumbled over these shoulders, amazingly with few deaths or injuries. For those who keep driving, Santa Elena, Cerro Plano and Monteverde sit waiting near the mountaintop, often nestled in clouds and streaked with rainbows.

There are only a few roads that join the one that begins in Lagarto. The one originally used by the Quakers begins in Chomes. Further up is a newer road and since a good section of it was recently paved it is the route of choice today. It starts at the highway near Sardinal and passes through the pueblo of Guacimal before connecting with the one from Lagarto. Several kilometers farther up, another gravel track heads down into the green valley of San Luis. This tiny farming community is protected by a steep escarpment atop which sits Monteverde, and specifically, the Guindon farm.

It was always an adventure to head down the mountain from Monteverde to the Pan American Highway and beyond. This main transportation corridor stretches from Nicaragua to Panama. For much of its length, the highway keeps to the flatlands on the Pacific side of the country. Just south of the port city of Puntarenas, it detours inland and crawls over the mountains to the central valley of Costa Rica and its capital, San José. In the early years people in Monteverde needing to make a roundtrip to San José could expect to be gone for days, even if the trip went smoothly. Now it is possible to do a return trip in less than twenty-four hours if there are no problems. Buses run daily from Monteverde to both Puntarenas and San José, an improvement over the days when not one bus reached the community and travelers had to get themselves down the hill to Guacimal to catch buses heading south to the cities. They employed whatever form of transport they could find as few families had the luxury of owning a vehicle in those days.

"In the beginning our family's only transportation was by foot or horseback. We had the good fortune of having a real strong horse that had been trained for cattle in Guanacaste. Sam was brought up to Monteverde and that's where I bought him. A valuable thing about Sam was that he could make the turn going through the wire gate. He knew how to turn under my arm while I leaned down to open and close it, so I didn't have to dismount. Sam also let me get out of the saddle, walk along beside him and then swing back on. That was real handy on a long ride.

"I spent many hours riding him to different projects. In 1955, after a period of heavy storms, we had to go twenty kilometers to the Las Juntas area to get provisions. There was a goldmine near there. It was the rainy season and we only had a short time to get through before the weather shut us down. It took several trips with a string of horses to bring up the supplies. Sam made every trip and was the only horse that did. He could recuperate from a long journey.

"We finally had to retire him. He was pretty old by that point. One morning I came across him pivoting round and round on his haunches, having fallen into a hole that had been recently dug. I could see that he was just plain exhausted. It was clear that he wouldn't be able to get back on his hind legs again. I felt real bad about old Sam. I knew it was a mercy to put him to sleep, but I couldn't shoot him myself so I asked someone else to do it.

"We named our farm after our best dairy cow, La Margarita. She also died in a very strange circumstance. One morning I went out to the barn lot and she had her head against a stump. You could see that she had a terrible, terrible headache. And that's the way she died. She must have been hurting all night. I've never seen an animal die like that."

The road that comes up the mountain brings you first to Santa Elena, the busy commercial center of the area. From this hub you can take gravel roads north to the towns of Las Juntas and Tilarán or continue southeast another seven kilometers up the mountain to the Monteverde Cloud Forest Reserve. The boundary lines of the communities of Santa Elena, Cerro Plano and Monteverde aren't marked but local people instinctively know the difference. It generally takes visitors several days to appreciate just which community they are in. In 2007 the main road through the center of Santa Elena and Cerro Plano was paved, a controversial action that greatly reduced the dust that plagued the roadside houses but also immediately increased the speed of the passing cars.

The new pavement ends where the actual community of Monteverde begins. Many of the original buildings that the Quakers constructed still exist but the land between them is quickly filling with homes, hotels, restaurants and stores. Smaller lanes head off to farm properties while footpaths form a network through the forest and pastures linking houses with the rest of the community. For the first few decades, horses, oxcarts, jeeps and tractors kept life moving at a comfortable pace. Since the 1990s, motorcycles, ATVs and four-wheel-drive vehicles have taken over the roadways, but walking always was and still remains an important form of transportation.

Many of the children who attend Monteverde's schools now have the option of getting there by bus, but until recently most children arrived at school by foot. The incredible increase in the number of vehicles throughout Costa Rica, including Monteverde, has made walking along the roads difficult and not nearly as pleasant as it was a few years ago. However, there is still a faithful flock of pedestrians, many of them tourists, going about their business up and down the mountain.

Wolf employed whatever form of transportation was necessary when traveling the countryside, but for a restless, agile and experienced walker, there was no better way to get where he was going than by hiking. Wolf is known in Monteverde and across the Continental Divide all the way to the San Carlos region as someone who might appear on your doorstep at any moment, unannounced except for a celebratory "WHOOP" as he nears his destination. He is known fondly by *Ticos* as *El Lobo*, this time "Wolf" having a considerably more canine than coquettish meaning. His legend throughout the countryside will live on long after his legs give out.

"We always did a lot of walking, clear down to Santa Elena and beyond or up to the pastures I rented where the heifers were. It was just a matter of heading down the road or up a trail.

"I remember when I started walking up the hill from the highway. I was in San José doing business at the embassy as we were getting ready to travel. We had four kids who'd never been registered and I had to get their passports. The documents were ready late in the day and I found out there was a bus leaving at 6:15 p.m. that would get me to Lagarto at around 9:30. So I thought I'd catch that bus and walk up from the highway. I walked up the road in the cool of the night, enjoying the silhouettes of the trees and the stars in the sky. It set the wheel in motion that this was an option I had, a real good option. I pulled that one on other trips, usually at least once a year or sometimes twice.

"Eventually we were able to take a bus heading to Tilarán from San José that would drop us at the bottom of the hill in time to catch the afternoon bus going up to Santa Elena from Puntarenas. That was handier. It made quite a change when we got the second bus that made a roundtrip from San José twice a day. That pretty well cut out any need to walk up the hill. It's probably a good thing because now it might take me two days to hike up the road to Monteverde.

"The thing is, usually I got a ride before I was halfway up so it didn't really count as walking the trip. Some of those rides were pretty unusual, such as the one I had on a truckload of about a hundred bags of sugar. That was a pretty sweet ride. Another time I hung on to the outside of a jeep all the way up since there was no room inside. It still did the trick and got me there hours earlier than if I'd walked all the way."

Gary Diller O'Dell came from California to Costa Rica in 1971. He visited Monteverde and it felt like home, so he stayed and became a Costa Rican citizen in 1977. Gary has been a nature guide in the area for over twenty years. Like Wolf, he has spent years wandering the trails through the cloud forest, often following in the wake of the older but no less energetic man.

"There's a story I heard about Wolf. I don't know that it's true although I'm sure it is. He decided to go to Puntarenas one day. Apparently he went straight, right from his house, down over the cliff edge, up and over the hills, like an earthquake, I imagine. And he can walk up that road, he has many times. He's like one of those snakes that just keeps moving. Once I walked up that same road and it took me eight and a half hours with my knees bouncing about. I was carrying a heavy pack. I stopped for a drink of water part way up and the people there asked me if I wanted to stay. I must've looked pretty bad. No, I said, I want to walk. I kept walking and walking and walking and pretty soon I was just too tired so I lay down by the side of the road and tried to get some sleep. In those days you were lucky if you saw one or two cars go up the whole day. A man on horseback just about ran over me in the morning. I got up and kept on walking and got near the top and my knees just wouldn't take it anymore. But Wolf has always done it. It's part of his constitution.

"He was always a lot stronger than I was, despite the fact that I was lean and tough and much younger. He could carry boards so thick, you know, a few of them could build a good-size house, the boards were that big, three or four meters long. He's one of the hardest-working men I've known in my life.

"Well, one time we had a race. Even though I was in the best shape of my whole life, it was a very stupid thing for me to do, to race with Wilford Guindon, the fastest walker in the world. We were in the Cloud Forest Reserve. He says, 'I'll give you a fifteen- or twenty-minute head start and you take the shortest way, any way you want. We'll race back to the field station.' So I took the steep Chomogo trail because I knew that once I got up on top it would be fast sailing. I got up to the top of that hill and thought, 'Aha, this is the first time that I'm really going to whip that guy.' I was just cooking. I got down the hill and began to hear, way off in the distance, 'WHOOP, WHOOP, WHOOP' and I knew I'd been shot just like an Indian. I couldn't believe it. I think my pace slowed down to a sniveling cry. When I got to the station, there was that guy, sitting on the bench, not even panting, in his usual position with his knee crossed, already holding a great big cup of coffee. 'Where ya been?' he said with a straight face, 'I've been here twenty minutes.' He just whipped me so bad."

Walking was Wolf's God-given talent. On the trail, he was poetry-in-motion. Although he was always willing to set out on foot, he was particularly happy when his hobby could be considered a business venture.

"One time, walking made for a real profitable trip. I got Eston Rockwell to help me 'do a job' on some male piglets for Hector MacLean, a friend of ours out Escazú way. Well, we saw this one piglet that was built to grow into quite the boar. So I asked for the piglet as our pay and the fellow agreed we could have him. It was a fair deal as I wasn't charging anything for the service anyway.

"So, sure, I could have him, but how was I going to get him back to Monteverde? Eston had already gone home with the truck. Well, I knew the lady at the *pensión* in San José real well and I thought that if I got a nice box she wouldn't object to me putting it out in the *bodega* for the night. OK, I thought, we'll play it by ear. I took the first bus out of town in the morning with that little pig in a box on the floor behind my feet. Around mid-morning they dropped me off at Lagarto.

"I started walking my way up, carrying the piglet. It was at that age when it liked to be cuddled so it stayed under my arm, no problem. So I just struck out, trying to keep it happy. If I put it down it would squeal, but every once in a while I had to put it down. I let it follow me, squealing as we walked. By evening I was up by the *lechería* near the bridge. Almost home! In those days you measured a pig's value by how many *latas* of lard it would produce, a *lata* being about four and a half gallons. If you had a pig that would make two *latas* of lard that would be a real good pig and you could sell it for top price. The future for this one looked pretty good so I called that piglet Greasy. He grew to over 200 pounds.

"One of my many projects was using my pickup truck for hauling. There was a demand for hauling freight in to the dairy plant or the *pulpería,* the general store, and sometimes there were passengers or freight that needed to go to San José. A big truck took the cheese out year-round, so I realized that if I wanted to have freight going out I'd have to find my own clients. Purchasing pigs and taking them to market was a good possibility. I did that, and though I didn't make much money at it, I enjoyed the contacts I had with the Costa Ricans and others outside of the community. It was interesting work and brought in some additional income.

"The longest part of the trip was from Monteverde to the highway. It would usually take three or four hours to go down, but sometimes we'd be all night if we got stuck. We'd crawl into the truck when we got cold and get some shut-eye, or we'd dig till morning trying to get out. If it was during the wet season and we were returning at night, we'd often stay at Chalo Zamora's down in La Pita near Lagarto. We'd wait till morning when hopefully the sun would come out and dry up the road. Otherwise it could take as much as ten hours to make it back up the hill. If we were near a house we'd be sure of hospitality, but quite often we weren't near anyone.

"Usually I'd pick up somebody on the road between here and the highway. I'd give them a lift and have a visit. Frequently when they got out they'd say, *'Dios paga,'* which means 'May God pay you,' and they were mostly pretty serious when they said it. That was all the payment they had, to wish you the best and God's care. I always appreciated it. I thought it was a sincere reminder of being in the care of the powers that be. Later, with the public transportation system, people got accustomed to paying for the bus service, and they began to offer to pay me a fare.

"There were lots of things that I was given as payment that were very important, very personal and very much appreciated for services given. Frequently they gave something they'd made or raised, or they'd offer thanks in the form of helping me with one of my projects on the farm."

People who tend to livestock or work the fields growing the food we eat are not prone to romanticizing their relationship with the earth. Farming is a hard-working, weather-watching, do-what-needs-to-be-done, no-place-for-the-squeamish kind of vocation. If you have animals, sooner or later you have to kill them, often out of compassion. If you want to grow crops, you have to cut trees down to have fields to sow. Farmers have a complex connection with nature as well as with the world at large. Society needs them, but their sweat and toil is seldom fully appreciated and never paid for in full.

When the Quakers took over the stewardship of the land they called Monteverde, their goal, regardless of the remoteness of the region, was to create a fruitful existence. They were visionaries, willing to work hard to cut a productive community out of the wilderness. Guiding their decision-making were concerns for their children's future. They were proud and enthusiastic about their mission.

For the most part, today's Monteverdians continue to live a rural life. A few of them still work their land, milk their own cows and raise their own pigs and chickens. Thanks to their efforts and those of their neighbors it is still possible to buy garden produce at the local market, drink milk fresh from the local dairy, enjoy a cup of locally grown and roasted coffee, and eat a hearty breakfast of bacon and eggs supplied by livestock raised on the mountainside.

Wolf was familiar with dairy farming, coming as he did from a North American farming family. In Costa Rica the methods of farming were different, as were other aspects of working the land.

"After I went out and bought some pigs, Howard Rockwell Sr. taught me how to cut them up and how to select the portion for lard and what to do with it. We always had lots of pork for meat and trimmings and enough to make *chicharrones* and scrapple, which is meat boiled off the bone and baked with cornmeal. Raising pigs was a good way to make sure we had plenty of pork and a little cash too. I had learned a lot from my dad about castrating pigs and calves, which came in handy as there were no veterinarians in the Monteverde area in those days. We learned about diseases and what would work and what wouldn't. Our Costa Rican neighbors provided us with information about natural remedies and we gained a lot from their experience.

"When Greasy the boar matured, right away we started to have people wanting his services for their sow and that was a whole new project for me. It usually worked out that when they offered to give me cash or a piglet in exchange for Greasy's services, I got a piglet. I began to see how I often got the runt, and those pigs didn't raise out like they should've. So instead I started going for the twenty *colones*. If I could get a bit of money at least then I didn't have to try to raise runt pigs.

"I did have sows and raise pigs later, but mainly I was always interested in having a good boar to improve the breed. With Greasy I was getting the lard-type pigs. I had him about two years before I sold him. I bought a Yorkshire and had him for a while. Later I got a Hampshire. It got to where the market wanted leaner pigs, so we tried to raise pigs that would grow up fast and lean. Finally I got a Landrace. These pigs supposedly have thirteen ribs...one more pork chop. They're really fast-growing pigs. I had that one for quite a while as other people wanted to use his services.

"When I was hauling pigs it was a good deal to go out at night because of the heat in the lowlands. Even though the pigs survived, they always lost several kilos between the time you loaded them into the truck and sold them at market. I couldn't afford the loss of that profitable pork. Of course, to sell them was a job in itself. It wasn't my strong point to deal with the dealers. It wasn't like an auction in the U.S. with buyers bidding against each other. The custom here was that somebody bid a low price and the other buyers acted like that was a real good price and wouldn't bid higher. Maybe you could get the person to offer more if you really stuck to your guns. I had my good days too and sometimes got better than the average price on the market mainly because I generally had a better quality of pig.

"This occupation seemed attractive but it took some antics to go out on horseback, to find and buy some pigs, or to sometimes take others on commission, to take them to town, sell the pigs and then load up some merchandise and get back home. There were many reasons for leaving that one behind. As the kids got older they were a bigger help, and the dairy was producing more, so I didn't have as much need for the extra income. When the opportunity came I was content to get more involved in going into the woods and having my adventures there. The truth is I was happiest working on the land and in the forest.

"There was a lot of ax work and land-clearing back then. My father had been an ax man in Vermont. We always had an ax at home and that's where I learned to use one. When I came here, I brought along a typical North American short-handled ax. We found out that the axes they use here have a longer handle and a much lighter head. They're much more suitable for the trees here, where you have to reach in through the buttresses to make the cut.

"Many species of trees in the tropics have fins, brace fins, and to cut these trees down with an ax is very difficult. The men would lean wooden poles up against the tree to make a frame to stand on off the ground, high enough to cut the tree above its fins. That's when it's necessary to use the ax with the longer handle. Once the tree came down they'd stand on the log and cut off the round part to make a flat surface that could slide up the tongue of the oxcart. This also required the long-handled ax.

"Tropical trees, even the giants, often have roots of less than a meter in length. Traveling through the woods I've seen many an upturned tree with a shallow root system. It's a wonder any of them stand up. The roots of some species are naturally longer, but I've never yet seen a tap-root on a tree here like I was accustomed to seeing in the United States. I became aware of the danger of leaving trees exposed to the winds after three of my cows were hit by falling trees that I'd left standing either for shade or their attractiveness or sometimes just to save them to cut down later for lumber or firewood. That was a lesson learned in the early years at quite a cost.

"I started out doing my own clearing but in those first two years I had very little time to really dedicate to it. In the end most of the work was done by a young man named Humberto Solano who was more skilled than I was. I didn't have as much money as work for him, but he was very much interested in my rifle, a .22. So I traded it for three *manzanas*, just over two hectares, of tree felling. I still had to pay him some cash because he and his family had to eat while he was earning the rifle. While he was cutting down trees I was spreading the grass runners for pasture and beginning to milk cows. Then I began clearing with a chain-saw.

"Now it's a fact that we begin to look for convenient ways of doing things. My introduction to the chainsaw came from my father-in-law back in Iowa who had a sawmill. He had one of the first Homelite chain-saws with a float carburetor. It was an impressive new kind of mechanical saw. When we moved here it became obvious that clearing land with an ax was going to be very slow.

"Of course, having a chainsaw was a necessity, it wasn't just a gadget. Our Costa Rican neighbors heard the noise and came to see what was happening and they took an interest in getting chainsaws. Following the purchase of my own saw I continued my relationship with the Homelite factory in New York and became the first chainsaw dealer in Costa Rica. You were really somebody when you had a chainsaw. I became well known as I sold saws and taught people how to use and maintain them.

"I learned a lot from the chainsaw business. When I sold a saw I included two or three days of lessons. I thought I'd be teaching the Costa Ricans how to fell trees, but of course, most of them had been cutting down trees all their lives. In the end I was the one who learned the most. I learned about the different tree species and their best uses, whether they were right for firewood or posts or lumber. There was so much to know about working in different weather conditions, whether it was windy or dry or rainy.

"I did a lot of custom chainsaw work in the community and for Costa Rican neighbors. I started traveling to distant communities in developing areas and got acquainted with the regions and the people. It was a real experience working with Costa Ricans who were in the process of clearing land, whether it was training people in the use of their chainsaw or other times doing the work myself by contract. My learning about Costa Rican culture and the people's beliefs and concerns went along with it. I developed a lot of friendships that have lasted over the years. I drank a lot of cups of coffee, but not nearly as many as I did later on when I began to work with the Reserve, traveling over an even bigger area as a forest guard and during the years we were purchasing land for conservation.

"As I was clearing land, I left several trees standing, including a historic one we call the four-legged strangler fig tree. I never dreamt it would last more than a year or two let alone until now. But, fifty years later, it's still here. There's something about the oddity of its stilt legs that's kept it standing in spite of the wind. It now has a terrific spreading top and I'm sure it's doomed to give in to the wind eventually. The other ones I left are all down now.

"The tree felling to develop farmland was some of the most dangerous work I've done. Anybody who's felled trees knows it's pretty tricky. With an ax you have more time to judge the effects of the way you're cutting and notching a tree so it will go where you want it to go when it comes down. With a chainsaw it can happen pretty fast. You aren't able to hear and observe as well and there are dangers that come from not being completely aware of what's happening. A couple times I looked death right in the face and made a jump of a little less than a few feet to one side to avoid having a tree land on me. A large limb coming down can be deadly. Falling limbs have ripped my rubber boots and buried my saw. A tree splitting up is always a real dangerous situation. The first time it happened to me, I didn't realize what was going on until the trunk was falling right over my head.

"I was bringing down trees and there was a fellow with me, a visitor from the States, who was watching and taking pictures. There was one tree I thought I'd cut down real quick. I realized the tree was leaning but I didn't think a thing about what species it was. When I put the saw to it, it split and the trunk shot up about four meters into the air. I saw that it was going to come down right where I was. I barely dove out of the way and while I was doing that I saw the chainsaw go up in the air and do a flip. The fellow came over thinking that I might have been hurt or killed. I got up and said, 'Oh, no, but I had a thought there for a minute that I might've milked my last cow.'

"That was the kind of thing that kept you hopping. I learned a lesson from that, of course. I never had one split like that again that I didn't know just what would happen and was watching out for it. That first one was a big surprise. My father often said that to miss by an inch is as good as a mile. I had many opportunities to test that theory.

"I always figured that the first tree of the day and the last one before dark were the most dangerous, the first one because you wouldn't take it too seriously, the last one because by then you could be careless and have an accident. Another thing I could say about chainsaws is the story about a Quaker farmer who was selling a mule. The buyer asked him if he'd ever been kicked by the mule. The Quaker, who had to tell the truth, said, 'No, I've never been kicked by him but he frequently kicks where I recently was.' That's what happened sometimes with my tree felling. Occasionally it landed where I recently was and I was thankful that I lived to be honest about it."

As the men worked the land and the women bore children, good health care became increasingly important to the community. In the beginning Marvin Rockwell, who was trained in the U.S. Medical Army Corps during World War II, was the person called on to attend to injuries and supply pharmaceuticals. He was able to obtain supplies and necessary medicines from contacts in San José. But over the years people with any knowledge of first aid took responsibility for medical care. Irma Rockwell, amongst others, enthusiastically shared her knowledge and supply of homeopathic treatments.

The Costa Ricans were also generous with their knowledge, although not all their folk medicines were readily accepted. The everyday use of machetes, for everything from clearing land to slicing vegetables, resulted in many serious cuts. The locals put a mixture of cobwebs and coffee grounds or flour into a bad wound to stop the bleeding. This would harden into a cement-like skin over the cut and make it almost impenetrable when it came time to clean it.

Mildred Mendenhall, Elva Rockwell and other women in the community delivered most of Monteverde's babies. It was much safer to stay put with the midwives than attempt the bumpy trip down the road to the hospital. In the early 1970s Silvia Smith, a nurse, came to live in Monteverde. She tended not only to the people in the area but to many sick animals as well. It was with Silvia's arrival that the idea for a proper health clinic for the community was born.

"By the 1960s we had contracted with the Department of Health for medical services, but doctors only visited about once a month. The local people who could afford to went to Puntarenas or San José for medical and dental care. Even Las Juntas and Tilarán had clinics long before we did. Our registered nurse, Silvia Smith, went out on horseback to help women deliver their babies and to attend to other emergencies. The idea was that Silvia could function more effectively out of an equipped building. It was Miguel Valverde who donated the land in Santa Elena where the medical clinic was built.

"I joined the committee when the construction was in full gear. *La Clínica* was completed in 1975. The main financial assistance came from the Ministry of Public Health, but money also came from Canadian Friends. The CARE assistance program in the U.S. furnished much of the equipment for the building. I carted a lot of those supplies up the mountain from San José.

"Silvia worked at the clinic, but when she realized she was overly qualified and wouldn't receive an appropriate salary, she left. The clinic kept on with a small staff, mainly a person who did outreach in the area, registering community members and giving vaccinations.

"At first Bob Law drove down to Chomes to pick up doctors who would come to spend the day. He used the only vehicle the clinic had. It worked out quite well until eventually we got an ambulance. I stayed on the committee until I got so busy with the Reserve that I had to drop out.

"Luck and I look back and realize that somehow or other we raised a family and faced all kinds of accidents and sicknesses. Meeting those emergencies was very much a community effort, which made it so that the problems never seemed insurmountable."

As development continued in Monteverde, the health of the surrounding wilderness was a constant consideration. The settlers had considered the importance of protecting the watershed and that resulted in setting aside those 554 hectares in the first year. However, it was only when biologists started studying in the area that the larger concepts of environmental awareness and protection of endangered species were introduced.

In 1963 the first nature reserve in Costa Rica, Cabo Blanco, was established on the Pacific coast. That same year saw the first biological work done in Monteverde when Carl Rettenmeyer and his assistants came to study army ants. Also that year Wolf's cousin, Jerry James, reported seeing brilliant orange toads in the cloud forest above Monteverde. By 1968 the Organization for Tropical Studies was bringing students into the area to take courses. For these aspiring biologists it was the best kind of classroom.

This was the beginning of a new period in Monteverde. In April of 1970 George and Harriett Powell came to the community to do research for their postgraduate work. They were alarmed at the rate of deforestation in the area and in 1971 started to buy land to protect the forest. The Powells' determination was the driving force that created the Monteverde Cloud Forest Reserve. Among community members it was Wolf Guindon – chainsaw dealer, dairy farmer and land developer – who took up the cause. The union of the young, spirited graduate students and the enterprising, energetic Quaker produced a force that shook the mountainside like an earth tremor. From 1971 on, Wolf would spend far less time in Monteverde working as a farmer and tending to his family at home.

"By this time we had all of our eight children born and being raised. Lucky was occupied full-time caring for the kids and our home. I was on the school board and helping at the school with various projects. Those were some of the years I enjoyed the most, when I was active in community work, and I never imagined that would change. The dairy farm, clearing more land, the credit union and other projects in the larger community, these were the main things that filled my time. So it was a big change in direction when the idea of creating a reserve presented itself.

"During the early years in Monteverde I had an adventuresome role in developing relations with the Costa Rican community. I gathered knowledge and experience that was of good service to me after 1972 when I became involved with the Monteverde Cloud Forest Reserve and the Tropical Science Center that administered it.

"I think that the most important thing I might have done better, and still need to do more of, is to have input in the community and with my family. That was the trade-off. When I took up the cause and got involved with George's campaign I never imagined that it would be a long-term commitment. I thought it might last for three years or so. Now three years have become thirty, but they came regularly, one year at a time."

Six

The path to extinction

"One more trip – *una más* – and it's dedicated to Dr. Alan Pounds and his hopping woodland subjects. It's been a long day because Alan and I sure looked for them golden toads. We shook out every pool. This will be the last official trip this year to see if we might find the toads. It was basically dry on top although there were places where the pools were still full of water. It looked pretty good but there was no sign of eggs or tadpoles." *Wolf in Brilliante, June 1990*

In May of 1986, the same month that a seemingly healthy population of golden toads was being observed in the wet cloud forest high above Monteverde, I was standing under a magnificent tree in the old-growth pine forest of Temagami in northeastern Ontario. The crown of this particular white pine shone like a beacon above the rest of the canopy, an arboreal lighthouse guiding us to its port. I was working with friends, documenting the ancient pines in the area and this was the grandest of them all. It was at least eighty feet high with a five-foot diameter at its base. We estimated that this mammoth pine had survived winds, disease, fire and saws for at least 300 years.

We were collecting evidence to convince the world that the Temagami forest held treasures that needed protection. This tree was our talisman. We were awestruck by its enormity and encouraged by its survival. Three years later, when its presence no longer beckoned from the horizon, we discovered that nature had claimed it for its own. Fallen by what must have been severe winds, the corpse now lay rotting, compost for a future generation. How the earth must have shuddered when it fell! Hopefully, this area will continue to be protected from harvesting by man, but whatever the political landscape, Mother Nature remains the ultimate authority.

Up in the clouds above Monteverde is an area known as Brilliante. Blasted by rains and extreme winds, the forest here, at an elevation of 5,000 feet, is under duress. Gnarled, grasping roots cling to the craggy mountainside. Moss hangs abundantly and woodland debris thickly carpets the damp ground. Clouds blanket this eerie, medieval scene for most of the year. Growth is stunted by the stressful conditions, and thus this ridge of bearded, dwarfed trees is known as an elfin forest.

In May of 1964, Wolf's cousin Jerry James brought a couple of biologists from the Organization for Tropical Studies to Brilliante to witness a spectacle that only those few people who ventured into this high wet forest had previously seen. Masses of brilliant orange male toads were gathered around pools of still water eagerly awaiting the arrival of their female counterparts. One of these biologists, Jay Savage, documented this species for the first time in a 1966 paper, "An Extraordinary New Toad *(Bufo)* from Costa Rica," and named it *Bufo periglenes,* which means "bright toad."

Following the first significant downpours of April and May, depressions along the seldom-used trails fill with water. In those days the male golden toads, as they are commonly known, came out to await the larger, dark olive, scarlet-spotted females. As the females appeared, the males struggled with each other to mount them. The victorious male would stay locked to his mate while the other contenders harassed the couple. Eventually the females laid their eggs and the males fertilized them. Over the next twenty-five years Wolf was one of the lucky few who observed this amphibious orgy.

"The males would come out one or more days before the females, depending on the spell of weather and the amount of water that was filling the pools. That's just about the only time we'd see them as they were hiding the rest of the year. There are hundreds of channels underneath the leaf litter, among the root systems, and that's where we assumed the toads must be when they weren't in the breeding pools.

"They were a real dull golden color but in breeding season they were brighter, almost red-orange. It was difficult to find them the rest of the year although not unheard of. If you could hear their release call, a soft trilling sound, then you might have been able to locate them. But you had to be very near them to hear that. The males were vocal only during the mating ritual when they were telling another male to let go, to 'get out of here, she's mine.' That may have been the only reason for the calls. Male golden toads weren't known to use a call to attract mates.

"I helped Jerry collect specimens to send by air to the herpetologist Jay Savage. I went up to Brilliante to get some twenty-five pairs. We had to collect them, chill them down and get them safely to the airport. That was my first round with the famous golden toads."

The *sapos dorados,* as the toads are known in Spanish, would be the first flag species in Monteverde. Vulnerable, distinctive and attractive, they brought awareness to the area. When George and Harriett Powell set out in the early seventies to establish a nature reserve, the existence of the golden toads was a key factor in getting support from the scientific community and attracting international attention. The interest in conserving the toads' habitat benefited the larger ecosystem and all the other resident species. These exceptionally photogenic amphibians would become the first poster boys for the Cloud Forest Reserve.

"It was important to get people thinking about the golden toads. By 1972 George and Jerry and I had already identified the places in Brilliante where they were seen and we now started working towards protecting that land. They lived in scattered areas in the windswept elfin forest, which sat on an exposed crest of the Continental Divide. The breeding area we identified was maybe five miles along the Cordillera de Tilarán, but seldom more than a quarter mile wide. My Uncle Walter had a piece of land in Brilliante, and Jerry and my sons and I were partners in that land. We'd had plans to develop pastures up there. We stopped clearing and added that property to what was being bought up to protect the toads' habitat.

"There's a tragic story related to the discovery of the golden toads involving Jerry, who first reported seeing them. He was the adopted son of my Aunt Mary and Uncle Walter. They came to Monteverde in the mid-1950s, and by the 1960s Jerry was working for the Organization for Tropical Studies as a driver and field assistant. Although he was based in San José, we still saw him frequently on weekends. On one of these trips he was traveling with his wife, Vicky, on their way to Monteverde. At Cuatro Cruces on the Pan American Highway they didn't see a truck that was turning off the road as it was hidden behind another larger truck. His wife was killed instantly in the accident. Jerry was left unconscious for about a month. Because of brain damage, the doctors said not to expect him to ever be an independent person again. He still lives in Costa Rica though he's never been back to Monteverde since his parents' deaths. His life has been very difficult. The accident took place in April, 1971, just a year before the Reserve was established. But by that time Jerry had already made a great contribution to the future of Monteverde.

"Once the Reserve was started and money began coming in from friends and international organizations, an infrastructure, simple though it was, got put in place. George was working on purchasing border tracts that, in effect, would eliminate public access to the deeper forest and thus help to prevent the destruction of the golden toad habitat. People started coming to see what was going on in Monteverde. There was a small building that we used as a guardhouse and we hired our first guard, Oscar Rivera.

"A male toad was kept in a terrarium at the guardhouse. We didn't want the public tramping around in the breeding areas but felt it was educational to keep a specimen for people to see. Oscar was in charge of our little terrarium. I got reprimanded one time when some people came and asked if they could photograph the male we had in captivity. Requests like that were mostly handled by Oscar and he'd gladly display it, but he wasn't there that day, I was. I told them to go ahead but I didn't stay to supervise because they had introduced themselves as zoologists from England and pledged that they would be responsible. I trusted them. So the next thing I know Dr. Joseph Tosi shows up and finds that the specimen is missing. He was the director of the Tropical Science Center, which administers the Reserve. I was in big trouble. He ordered me to go find the toad and bring it back! So I had to run down the couple, who were Michael and Patricia Fogden. They hadn't wanted to photograph the toad outside the little cabin so they'd taken it up to its natural habitat. I had to make sure they brought it back to the terrarium. They were conscientious and I had no regrets about it. The Fogdens later came to live on a property adjoining the Reserve and became internationally known professional photographers. Their photographs, postcards, picture books and reports brought more attention to the golden toad than probably anything else."

Although the golden toads created a lot of interest in the newly formed Reserve, unfortunately there were few studies completed on them. Wolf felt privileged to have been part of most of the investigative work that did occur. He had knowledge of the location of the pools and acted both as a guide and an assistant to the few biologists who attempted to gather information through the 1970s and 1980s. Wolf served as administrator and then director of the Reserve through two periods during these years. His own concern for the future of the toads and their habitat kept him involved in their protection and searching for new information that would assure their survival.

"Alvaro Ugalde was a director of the newly expanded National Parks system in Costa Rica. I contacted Alvaro when I was the Reserve's administrator in the mid-seventies and requested that he come to Monteverde. We hiked the two hours up to the breeding area together. I was concerned about encroachment into the area where the golden toads were. The property with the known pools was under protection, but the land adjacent to the Reserve was already staked out for future clearing. If the clearing continued, this would dry up the pools and threaten the toads' breeding habitat.

"It wasn't the breeding season when we went up, but in that spot the wind almost constantly blows the mist over and it stays moist year round. We actually found a male toad hidden between the braces of an elfin tree. It helped us at the time as Alvaro assured me that if anyone tried to extend their clearings the government would formulate a decree to create a buffer zone. The government could declare a protective classification for an area of this importance. Fortunately, the clearing stopped before we had to step in. It was a time when I had direct contact with the National Parks administration and got their support. The memory means a lot to me now, even though it looks like we'll never hear or see the toads again anyway.

"Around 1972 John Vandenburg, an undergrad student under the supervision of Dr. Doug Robinson at the University of Costa Rica, came to do a project comparing the *Bufo periglenes* with another species, *Bufo holdridgei,* which lived in a similar habitat. It lived in manmade ditches on the side of Poás, a volcano in the central part of Costa Rica. Dr. Robinson had been involved, along with Jay Savage, in the identification of the golden toads. Those of us working at the Reserve helped John by looking for the presence of breeding pools in surrounding areas. This was when we discovered the toads out near El Valle, an area with primary forest where the streams drain towards the Caribbean. It wasn't elfin woods or an exposed ridge and had more rain and less wind, so we were surprised to find several pools with a small population.

"We started monitoring out there as well as in Brilliante. I did an account of males in proportion to females, covering an extensive area. At that time it was about eighteen to one, really a drastic contrast of males to females.

"The other species that John was studying was more nondescript in appearance, but in general the two species had similar characteristics, breeding in small pools and ditches of nonmoving water filled by rainfall, not from a stream. *Bufo holdridgei* is now also believed to be extinct.

"John was trying to study two species in two areas that are geographically far apart. Of course, you don't know when the toads are going to come out. There were days when he was over in the other study area that it would have been more advantageous if he'd been here. Naturally the toads showed themselves when he was at the other place.

"He studied the comparative growth changes through until the toads metamorphosed. He did a real good write-up, but in the end we didn't have enough data from that particular study. At the time it was enough that they were being investigated.

"In the late 1970s, we hired a new administrator at the Reserve, Walter Timmerman, who was a herpetologist mostly interested in poisonous snakes. In the breeding season he did a good job of marking the pools in Brilliante and noting the location and number of toads. In 1979 Walter went with me to El Valle because we'd seen what seemed like a growing population in that area. We got out there and found that water was seeping from a spring and forming a small pool. There were lots of eggs. I never, ever saw so many eggs as we did there, but the pool was drying up and they were suffering. We took up about seventy percent of the eggs, put them in a plastic bag and brought them down to the field station. We didn't see any adults and suspected that they'd already gone underground.

"Walter spent much of his time the next day counting those eggs. There were two strings of eggs from each female with an average of about 100 eggs per string, for a total of about 200 eggs per female. These lay floating and you could separate them. He figured that there were about 10,000 eggs, indicating maybe fifty females. We went back and found the pool completely dried up. It was questionable that any eggs had survived. We planned on hatching some of the ones we'd collected, studying them and returning them to the area, but none of them hatched. The whole deal that year was without any success.

"Over the years there were attempts to keep some toads in captivity. After we built the *casona* at the Reserve in the late seventies we kept a male or two in a terrarium as a learning exhibit. We'd keep them for a season and then release them and get new ones. We caught insects for them to eat, grasshoppers or whatever. People assumed the toads could be kept in captivity, but we began to have trouble and they'd die. Later George and I tried taking two males to my house. We put them in a different container but they didn't fare any better, so whatever was affecting them seemed to be pretty universal, not the terrarium itself, which I'd thought might be the problem. I was curious as to what was killing them. I mentioned this to some biologists but no one took up the concern to study this problem.

"The first male I collected for the terrarium came from an area I've never been back to. With my favorite hiking companion from England, Leonard Bird, we ran into some pools beyond El Valle on our first attempt to go cross-country to the Volcano Arenal. It was north of anything that the Reserve owned, an area only known by hunters. You can assume that all of Costa Rica has been visited at one point or another by hunters and explorers.

"When Giovanni Bello, a Costa Rican forestry graduate, became co-director of the Reserve in 1984 he took a great interest each breeding season in finding where the active pools were. Some pools were active one year but not the next. Generally we'd find an active pool close to where other pools had been. In that time we saw a lot of juvenile golden toads. Even the little ones, some less than an inch long, were easy to identify. When you turned them over they'd have black and white polka-dotted bellies.

"We were working on expanding the Reserve and establishing boundary lines and surveying the property that we'd purchased. We were working southeast of any of the known breeding pool areas, on the Continental Divide a good day's hike beyond Brilliante where the streams flowed south to the Aranjuez River. Even there we found a sizable population. This would turn out to be the last place that any were spotted, several years later, by two of the Reserve's forest guards.

"In 1985 the Metro Toronto Zoo was interested in doing a study on breeding ecology. They requested permission to take at least three pairs to do captive breeding at the zoo in Toronto, Canada. They also wanted to set up a unit outside the field station in Monteverde that would demonstrate the breeding cycle using the information their study had gathered. It was to be a more extensive terrarium, you might say a self-sustaining exhibit. This didn't happen because nobody at the Tropical Science Centre would agree to have any of the toads exported to Canada.

"I've often wondered about this. I've been in Toronto and visited their zoo. They've collected species of toads from Africa and successfully bred them in captivity and released the young ones back into the wild. Who knows if we could've sustained the golden toads by having them raised somewhere in captivity. A lot of animals kept in captivity are reproducing. It's proven to be an acceptable method to amplify a small population and sometimes to help save a species. Of course, now we realize that transferring a species from one country to another might spread a virus, fungus or other disease.

"There's practically no end to golden toad stories. The only person we ever caught taking a specimen, a male from a breeding pool, was a little girl who'd been with her parents in the Reserve and cried to have one of the brightly colored males to take home. They'd gotten as far as Irma Rockwell's *pensión* before Irma reported them to us. We worked out an agreement that they'd bring it back and deposit it in our terrarium so that other children could observe and appreciate it. There's no way they could've taken it home and kept it alive. That's the only one we ever caught, but who knows about professional or even nonprofessional poachers?"

The last study of the fated toads before they disappeared was conducted by Dr. Martha Crump, a professor and herpetologist at the University of Florida in Gainesville. In 1987 she arrived in Monteverde to do research on tree frogs but was sidetracked from her plan when Wolf arrived on her doorstep and told her the golden toads were breeding. He led her through the mountainous chill and steady rain up the long, muddy trail to witness a scene that only a fortunate few had witnessed before her.

"When Marty Crump endeavored to do a thorough breeding ecology study of the *sapos dorados* our hopes were high that a herpetologist of Marty's experience would be successful at getting more complete data. This was to be a two-year study. There being three of us, Marty, her assistant and myself, we planned to look at six pools. We'd take two pools each, identify the population in the area, and follow the toads from the time the females arrived through to when they laid their eggs and the tadpoles metamorphosed. Marty had a lot of questions and hypotheses to work out. We hoped to find out once and for all where they came out from, where they went during their inactive period and more about their breeding ecology and their predators.

"We knew there were predators. Every year we'd see a few adult males that had been killed, the stomach ripped apart or the back opened up. It seemed to show there were poisonous glands in the skin and the predators instinctively knew not to eat it. George Powell and I found some like that and we didn't know what animal had done it, perhaps coatis. Marty observed that the main predators were the freshwater crabs you see along the trail. When it was egg time, the crabs would be in the pools.

"The first year that Marty saw the toads was a normal year at the breeding pools. She proceeded to get funding and started the two-year study in 1988. But Marty had other work on the go and she couldn't be sitting here two or three weeks waiting. So we decided I'd keep a lookout and phone her when the first male came out. The Tropical Science Center, which was paying my wage, allowed me the time to participate in the study. I was really excited about the project!

"1988 was an El Niño year. When the toads didn't come out en masse in the first weeks of May we didn't know if we'd see them later. Then the rains brought the water, but the toads still didn't come out. In the second year, when the big work of the project was to be done, we saw only one male in one area. We looked where we thought they'd be but they weren't to be found. We searched underneath the channel openings, under the leaf litter, but we didn't find them there either. So that's where it ended."

In 1987 Reserve personnel counted more than 1,500 golden toads. In 1988 ten golden toads were seen, only one of them in the main study area in Brilliante. The next year was wetter, which was cause for optimism, but when Marty returned only a single toad was found. That same year Eladio Cruz and Erick Bello, patrolling the trails a day's hike beyond Brilliante in the Miramar area, reported seeing ten adults. These would be the last golden toads ever observed.

The swift decline of *Bufo periglenes* shocked everyone who had been monitoring them. Researchers asked themselves if they were in any way responsible. Did they track in a pathogen that affected the sample populations? Did they disturb the natural habitat or foul it in any way? Despite their best efforts, did they over-collect and thus contribute to the declining population?

"You can't help but wonder if you're responsible when something like this happens. All these years, you're told 'don't touch, be careful,' but the only way to gather understanding is to do the studies. In my experience professional researchers take every precaution and proceed with care and foresight. I don't feel responsible for the loss, but I do feel regret for not having insisted that more studies be done. It may seem that we gathered a lot of toads but that isn't the case. Considering the thousands of toads we saw over the years, we took very few, and the heaviest collecting was in the 1960s and 1970s. This was a seemingly healthy population that just basically in one season withdrew from the planet. We don't know what caused the disappearance. Was it from something we did or didn't do?

"There's a theory, at least people have wondered aloud, that human contact got to them, that stepping on them, handling them and taking them caused the drop in population. It's not likely. The toads were in remote areas and only easily seen for one or two weeks a year. On top of that the population was so scattered that in any one season people couldn't possibly have collected them to extinction.

"There's no question that to observe or investigate them was a matter of perseverance and chance because their breeding season was so short and so dependant on weather conditions. When word got around to the tourist population, then we did find that people came in to see them. We had to monitor by patrolling the area and take measures to prevent people from walking off the trail and doing harm. Occasionally it was necessary to check packs before people left the Reserve. I know there was some material taken out, mostly plants for gardens and collections. But we don't have many big flashy orchids, so the big attraction was the golden toad. It was a hard one for collectors to hit at the right time.

"I was told that dealers of exotic frogs had advertised them for sale in both Germany and the United States. Apparently you actually could buy one for five dollars. Well, they surely aren't offering any for sale now when we'd really like to have them. We'd at least have another chance to see if we could keep the species alive."

When Marty discussed her findings with colleagues at a conference in 1989, the problem of disappearing amphibian populations worldwide was acknowledged by many fellow researchers. Scientists responded by forming the International Task Force on Amphibian Declines and Deformities to continue studying the phenomenon. Today the loss of amphibian populations is widely considered to be a warning sign of ecological degradation. As a result, biologists around the world are studying the sensitive nature of the relationship between amphibians and climate change.

For several years following the last golden toad sighting in 1989, Wolf and others, including local herpetologist Alan Pounds, made regular trips through the known breeding areas in search of the elusive toads. To this day there are some people who feel they may reappear, having somehow survived in small numbers and evaded the searchers. But like many other species that have disappeared, tales and photographs may be all that is left of their once brilliant existence.

Alan Pounds continues searching for answers to the problem of diminishing amphibian populations. Throughout Central America, since the early 1970s when populations started to be recorded, declines or disappearances have been documented in dozens of frog species. In some areas half of the known amphibian species have disappeared. Most of this has taken place since the late 1980s in pristine forests at altitudes higher than 800 meters.

Possible causes of amphibian declines include climate change, habitat modification due to deforestation and development, fragmentation of habitat, introduced species affecting indigenous species, overexposure to UV radiation, chemical contamination, acid rain, over-collection, disease or some combination of factors. A common denominator in many areas where species loss has occurred seems to be the presence of a chytrid fungus, a phenomenon currently under study.

In Monteverde, Dr. Pounds has provided one possible explanation for the mysterious loss of the golden toads. Global climate change may have caused the cloud cover over the Tilarán Mountain range to lift slightly, leaving areas once heavily watered and protected by a blanket of moist clouds now exposed to drier, warmer conditions. This could explain why birds and bats normally found at lower elevations have been appearing in the cloud forest over recent years. But earthbound species cannot move like birds can, and the toads were already as high as they could go on their mountain. Affected by this climate change, the toads could be more vulnerable to pathogens, parasites, virus and fungi. In the case of the golden toad, there are no specimens to study, no corpses for forensic analysis, no evidence to provide a definite answer.

"I've visited pools over the years since the toads were last seen, but I haven't seen a single toad footprint. You know what we say in the woods: if you don't even see a footprint, you sure won't see the animal. But people still come to look for the toads whether we have them or not. All in all, their existence worked to get conservation organizations to expend time and money to save this area and to consider the future of all rain and cloud forest habitats. What super good fortune to have enjoyed their uniqueness and benefited from their contribution to our Reserve. I would call it a miracle because, after all, it's something we can't explain or repeat. Those beautiful, photogenic toads just appeared when we needed them to. Since we didn't have gorillas or elephants, we needed something to stir up people's interest in saving this cloud forest."

SEVEN

Walking softly

"I guess if we're going to dedicate this day to anybody, we're going to dedicate it to the Fonseca brothers. In the late 1960s they came in and started working on the old abandoned clearings. Then they began widening a trail to El Valle to let the sunlight in and dry up the mud. By cutting down a lot of trees they really began to stir things up. The Monteverde community owned the area that the trail went through and the cutting concerned us so we filed a *denuncia* against them. The Fonsecas stopped cutting trees to prevent having any more problems with us. Then George got enough funding to make this land part of the Reserve. The Fonseca's work out this way made it easier for those of us who are trying to patrol and protect on these trails. So we'll dedicate this to you, my friends, Señores Edwin 'Zapatillo' and Bolivar Fonseca." *Wolf wandering through El Valle on a dry trail*

In 1989 I was one of the organizers of the blockade of a logging road extension in Temagami, Ontario. The action brought hundreds of protestors into the northern wilderness, joined together by our mutual objection to the construction of a link between the two existing logging roads. If completed, this industrial highway would have facilitated the destruction of old-growth pine trees as well as trespassed on land the Teme-Augama Anishnabai First Nation was struggling to reclaim their rights to in the courts. During those seven weeks at the blockade camp I represented the board of the Temagami Wilderness Society, mediated group discussions, talked to the press, listened to the local natives, supported nonviolent civil disobedience and helped maintain a strong, united presence against the machines. In the end the roadway was cut through, but continued opposition by the indigenous community and a somewhat sympathetic government prevented it from being finished or used to carry out arboreal bodies.

One of the visitors to the camp was Bob Hunter, a founding member of Greenpeace in Canada and an environmental journalist in Toronto until his death in 2005. On our first night in the bush we were gathered around the campfire, the circle of eyes reflecting the flames along with our passion and conviction. Bob put forth a scenario that inspired great discussion that evening and would return often to our nightly conversations. You're on a boat and in the presence of the last known individual of an endangered whale species. As you look in awe at the beauty of the vulnerable beast, a whaling ship appears, spear guns at the ready. What do you do? What are you prepared to give for the life of the endangered animal? Would you hurl yourself onto the back of the whale, placing your body between it and the hunter? Would you feel righteous in killing the potential killer in defense of the defenseless? Do you accept violence as inevitable in the quest for an improved world? Do you place your faith in the power of words, believing that more discussion will change the course of an action already set in motion? Or do you simply place your faith in God and pray for us all?

Everyone responded differently, often changing their thoughts from one night to the next. It requires a lot of introspection and honesty to make and then adhere to a personal commitment to nonviolent action when supporting positive social change. The issues are so often complex, the answers usually requiring us to sacrifice some of our comfort zone in one way or another. Are we not just delaying the inevitable if we save a tree without equally nurturing the community that lives in its shadow? Experience and instinct tell me that, at its most beneficial, activism must be inclusive and holistic.

The Quakers came to Costa Rica and founded Monteverde as peace activists, believing that people, both individually and communally, should walk softly on the earth. For the first twenty years the harsh realities of pioneering on a remote tropical mountain demanded the pragmatic development of their farms, businesses and public institutions. Their political, social and spiritual beliefs always provided a touchstone from which to measure their progress. Since it was established Monteverde has attracted a steady stream of inquisitive, thoughtful people, many who have stayed on to donate their own talents and peculiarities to the social stew. The result is a powerful, creative spirit within the community that captures the imagination of those who visit and an evolving problem-solving process that is inclusive of all community members. As in any small town, difficult personalities and disagreements among neighbors have sometimes threatened community unity. Yet the Friends' strong convictions about peace, spiritual growth and truth have imbued Monteverde with curiosity, purpose and a receptiveness to changing sociological influences and the evolution of scientific knowledge.

Monteverde townsfolk spend a phenomenal number of hours in meetings. Organizations and committees exist that monitor water, schools, roads, the dairy plant, environmental interests and just about every other aspect of the community's life. To be the dynamic center that it is today, attempting to keep its soul intact amidst the rapid changes in population growth, technology and tourism, Monteverde has needed to balance tenacity with flexibility, conformity with individuality, and enthusiasm with patience.

It was within this rich context that the Monteverde Cloud Forest Biological Preserve came into being. Known locally as the Cloud Forest Reserve or simply the Reserve, or *La Reserva* in Spanish, the MCFP has never been wholly funded by any large international conservation organization, though the World Wildlife Fund, The Nature Conservancy and several other groups have made significant contributions over the years.

It was George and Harriett Powell's own money that bought the first properties in 1971 and financed the initial funding drive. Since then, monies have been collected from visitors to the Reserve as well as from around the world to build, maintain and increase the infrastructure and scope of the Reserve's physical holdings and resources. Monteverde is a showcase for how individuals, collectively, can make a difference. While many people have contributed their energy, time and money to the Reserve, without a doubt Wolf has donated the most sweat.

Jerry James played one more role in the transformation of Monteverde before his tragic accident. When he was working for the Organization for Tropical Studies he met an American biology graduate student, Bill Buskirk, and impressed him with stories about Monteverde. Bill and his wife Ruth were friends with George Powell and Harriett McCurdy. The four had met at Earlham College, a Quaker institution, in Indiana, and were now enrolled in postgraduate studies at the University of California at Davis. The Buskirks and George had done a short study of highland mixed-species bird flocks in Panama. George and Bill decided to expand that work for their dissertations and were searching for a new site. Gary Stiles, a professor at the University of Costa Rica who later wrote a field guide for the birds of Costa Rica, highly recommended Monteverde for this study. Sight unseen, the young biologists decided that Monteverde was the best choice for their PhD work.

When the recently married Powells and the Buskirks arrived in 1970, they found a modest rural community surrounded by expanses of forested wilderness that was steadily being cleared for farmland. Even then Monteverde was receiving its fair share of visitors, mostly friends and family of the residents, but also the first scientists and student groups. The two couples took turns switching monthly between a cramped bedroom in the main building of Irma's *pensión* and a small but comfortable cottage on the property. This inconvenient living arrangement led to the first of many dealings between George and Wolf.

"The first time I met George Powell, he and Bill Buskirk were coming along the road, dragging bamboo poles, preparing to set up nets in their study area in John Campbell's woods adjacent to my own farm. George was a thin young man and very outgoing. He had a real boyish face and people found it hard to believe that he was working on his doctorate. These guys were nothing if not enthusiastic. I was wondering why in the world they were hauling these long bamboo poles, obviously imported from down in the lowlands as we had no bamboo for fifteen miles around. In those days we weren't worried about strangers, unlike today when you tend to take note of unfamiliar faces near your property. I didn't pay them much mind and certainly didn't see that there was my destiny walking up the road.

"Their situation at the *pensión* was less than ideal. George approached me about living in a small house on our property that he'd fix up in exchange for rent. It'd be closer to his project site and give the two couples a bit of space. Lucky and I were pleased to have this interesting young couple living close by. At some point we invited them to join our family's Sunday evening gatherings. That's when we really began to get acquainted with them.

"We were neighbors for almost two years while they were doing their research. George and Bill were busy out in the forest, netting and banding birds. They got to know those woods and had a better under-standing of its scientific value than we'd ever thought about. I knew about the golden toads because they were first discovered in Brilliante where my cousin Jerry and I were developing pastures. We took for granted the presence of the resplendent quetzal in Monteverde and were aware of the bare-necked umbrellabird down in Peñas. I don't think we considered that trying to chop a clearing out of this forest could ever seriously affect the survival of any of these species. In fact, we were the species that was trying to survive by clearing pastures and homesteading.

"Then the sound of the chainsaws got to George. He started to talk seriously about what could be done to protect the forest. I didn't agree with him in the beginning. There was a need for working farms and pas-ture and crop production. As he was talking about the whole area being protected, I thought he was in the wrong country. Costa Rica wasn't the place to be creating large protected areas. It's a very small country and you couldn't expect people to make a living when they couldn't develop the forest for lumber and clear land for farms and buildings. I suggest-ed that the idea might work in Brazil or Africa, but not here. A lot of people told him he should go away.

"If it hadn't been that George and Harriett moved onto our land and I saw them often over a two-year period, I may not have been detoured into this lifetime project."

The success of Monteverde's cheese factory had encouraged more people to try their hand at dairy farming. High up the mountain in Brilliante, where the golden toads had been found, adventurous souls were trying to cut out pastures to keep cattle. However, Brilliante was brilliant in name alone. Wolf already knew that the dream of having fer-tile pasture at such a high elevation where the mountaintop is so often shrouded by clouds was just that, a sweet but unrealistic dream.

"In the late sixties my Uncle Walter financed his son, Jerry, to pur-chase a property in Brilliante. Uncle proposed that we could join in so my sons and I got an interest in what Jerry was doing. We had a deal that whatever forests we developed would be for my family and me, so we started going up to Jerry's property and, under almost constant cloud cover, clearing land.

"I looked at the whole forested area beyond Monteverde as having a lot of potential for exploring and for clearing land and growing crops we couldn't grow on our farm. However, I soon knew that Brilliante wasn't the place this was going to happen.

"I remember going up with my son, Tomás, and working three days and not seeing the sun until we were headed back down from the Continental Divide in the late afternoon. Add to that the fact that the grass reacted negatively to so much cloud cover and the soil wasn't fertile enough to grow a healthy crop of anything but ferns. I was soon convinced that that area wasn't the place for clearing pasture. I was glad to head into Peñas Blancas, deep in the valley, which to me was a much better prospect for homesteading, with a better climate for corn and fruit crops, warmer and with more sun.

"I was approached by Manuel Solís, who also owned land in Brilliante, and he offered to buy our claim. It turned out that he was acting as an agent for a couple of men from San José. They were interested in making a big dairy operation up there. Manuel had already sold his piece and was starting to ask the other homesteaders about selling their properties, all of it destined to be part of this big dairy project. I mentioned to George that someone wanted to buy our Brilliante property. When George found out who was looking to buy and what they planned to do with the land, he decided he'd buy those properties first since this was the primary habitat of the golden toads. Right away Jerry and I agreed to sell our piece to George. He then asked me to go with him to talk to Luis Chavarría, who was another squatter in Brilliante. George wanted to get to him before Manuel Solís did. The year was 1971 and these five properties in Brilliante would be the first that were purchased for the Reserve. So that's where it all began, though George may remember it another way."

In Costa Rica there exists a system that allows squatters to legally mark out a piece of national forest no greater than 300 hectares, make improvements on it and claim it for their own. Whether driven by a pioneering spirit or by poverty, *Ticos* sometimes would also invade unprotected private land and illegally establish a claim. Squatters could claim a right of possession on private forested lands unless the landowners could get the invaders removed.

First a boundary would be cut and a clearing made, then a simple structure would be built. After one year the squatter could claim rights to the property. After ten years the legal title could be obtained. Before being sold a piece of property had to be evaluated and the location of the property, its boundary lines and its neighbors had to be identified. At this time maps and surveys were unavailable for most of the forested areas of Costa Rica, and as a result there were often great discrepancies regarding boundary lines. Finally a legal document called a *carta de venta* would be produced that had to be validated by a local policeman or lawyer. The system gave people the possibility of owning more than they could afford to buy and at the same time promoted the development of Costa Rica, clearing by clearing.

"When George decided to buy out properties to stop the clearing of the forest he was bringing a whole new idea to the area. The National Parks system was just evolving in Costa Rica, introducing a different way of looking at using and protecting the land. In the meantime there was this system of *mejoras* that rewarded farmers who 'improved' their land by deforesting it. George was now not only approaching people to buy their pieces of land but was talking about turning this forested area into a preserve. Instead of 'making improvements' meaning cutting down the forest, in the Reserve improving the land would mean leaving the forest intact.

"How was this going to help the people? How could uncut forests supply the lumber for the development of the local communities? Many people were willing to sell to George to get the money, but it took a long time for people to truly understand the value in the whole idea of the preserve.

"George needed someone to help with cutting trails, contacting land owners and establishing boundary lines around the area he'd decided to purchase and protect. At the time I was paying my hired hand, Digno Arce, three *colones* an hour. George offered to pay me five *colones* an hour against the three. I knew that our boys, with Digno's competent help, could handle the dairy themselves. The economics of it meant extra hours of paid work for me. It was that big difference in wage that brought me into this life.

"I was influenced by the Powells' great concerns, whether I agreed with them or not. I was myself clearing forest at that time. I got involved with George in a neighborly way, but the real truth is that I took on the work because of my love of working in the forest, which I was doing for nothing anyway, and the offer of a cash income. So I started out on the tough one which was my going away from chores and the community and leaving my family, along with Digno, to take care of the dairy."

It seemed impossible that they could buy all the surrounding forest, so George's focus was to buy the pieces that would protect the known habitat of the golden toads as well as boundary pieces that would restrict access to the greater forest area. By putting their resources towards purchasing these significant properties, the Powells could provide protection to a larger area than they could afford to buy with their limited funds.

"George and Harriett were actively trying to get donations that would help finance the purchasing of land. They put in their own savings and convinced their friends to contribute. They started a full writing campaign to get international organizations interested in investing. It was a real team effort, Harriett writing and typing the letters on our old antique typewriter, George running around talking to anybody and everybody. They worked hard at building confidence in the idea that this area should be protected as a preserve. It's truly amazing what they were able to accomplish, but that's what hard work and dedication will do.

"When George purchased the five properties up there in Brilliante, we found that most had only partially defined boundaries. This would be the case over the next twenty years of purchasing land. I started heading out with George, finding the owners of the properties, negotiating with them and then measuring the outside boundaries.

"In Brilliante the title to the land was owned by the GLC, the Guacimal Land Company. After paying for the homesteaders to leave and measuring the outside boundaries, we had to deal with José Pacheco, the lawyer who held the title for the GLC. He said that if George could find a nonprofit organization to hold the title to the land, the GLC would donate the title. George was relieved to find that such an organization already existed: the Tropical Science Centre based in San José. He immediately got the interest of the director, Dr. Joseph Tosi, who had visited the forests of Monteverde in 1968 and recognized the need for their protection. In April of 1973 the 328 hectares that George held in his name were transferred to the Tropical Science Center.

"George used a system where he bought land in his name first and then transferred it to the TSC, giving it more legality. The *carta de venta* didn't really make things legal unless you'd developed the land for more than ten years and had received the title for it. Transferring the property one more time, from the original landowner to George and then to the TSC, gave it a more officially recognized ownership.

"By the time all the property bought by the Powells was ready to be measured, Eladio Cruz, a hard-working young man from San Luis, was helping as well. We started to spend long days in the forest cutting trails, surveying boundaries and patrolling against poachers. There arose a great need for a shelter in Brilliante for our work crew. We constructed a small building using the materials from a few floorless rustic huts that already existed there. It was a nice little house, but Brilliante was always cold and wet, and the firewood was damp and spongy and would produce more smoke than heat. There were some pretty sad times overnight in Brilliante. We had platforms that four people could sleep on, though three people would sleep better. As it was, we'd all crawl in and hope that everybody slept and didn't roll around or snore all night.

"That's what we did for the best part of a year while we were measuring the outside boundaries. George hated it and tried to get us to commute. He didn't like the dense smoke from the smoldering fire, being constantly wet, elbows poking in your head while you're trying to sleep. Neither did we, but we were more accustomed to the conditions and since it meant a two-hour hike home, we often argued to spend the night, uncomfortable though it was.

"The surveying part was done by George, with myself and others as the crew. We plugged away at measuring the property. The way we were doing it was with a compass mounted on a pole and a tape measure pulled tight and a sighting gauge to get the angle of gradient. We took each measurement with a 100-foot tape. We very seldom could make a straight shot of more than 100 feet. We gathered the measurements and lots of data that George very conscientiously and capably put together. He got a registered engineer to use the data to draw up an official map, what they'd now do by computer. We still use that same map today.

"Once the Tropical Science Center was on board, George and Harriett's efforts took off. From the beginning biologists donated money, as did students and others connected with the Organization for Tropical Studies and the Audubon Society. Then, once the TSC was involved, George wrote up a funding proposal for the Monteverde Cloud Forest Biological Preserve. That proposal got us money from the World Wildlife Fund to buy three more vital properties plus enough to cover three years of administrative costs. The administrator would be the Tropical Science Center. More money came in from the Explorers Club of New York and the German Herpetological Society, among others, which allowed us to continue buying land to place under our care and protection. I was officially hired by the Tropical Science Center as a half-time employee in October of 1974.

"We started out in Brilliante pretty small and pretty humble. Then we were able to purchase the Fonseca property when it came up for sale. This property was on the eastern side of the Continental Divide, part of a large area that at that time was known as Chomogo, which was a local name that meant swamp. Actually, Chomogo is a large catch basin where the streams drain into the Guacimal River, which flows west to the Pacific. However, where the Fonseca property was, the streams drain into the Peñas Blancas River, which flows east to the Atlantic. It's a different watershed with a different terrain. It wasn't logical to call the total area Chomogo and we felt the Fonseca property deserved a more descriptive name. George was inspired to call the area *El Valle* and I certainly agreed, so we did.

"During the early years roaming through the new Reserve, George and I had our adventures. On our first cross-country trek, heading out with our compass and our faithful machetes, we started on what was scheduled to be an afternoon excursion of two kilometers from El Valle heading down to the trail by the Peñas Blancas River and home another three kilometers on the horse trail. All went well until we had to slide down into a steep draw, which led to the top of a waterfall. We considered tying a vine to a small tree to let ourselves down but decided to tackle the landslide that was sloping in the direction we wanted to go. George informed me that a rope wasn't needed as long as there was vegetation to hold on to. At first this seemed logical as there was bushy growth at the top, but near the last bit there were only short ferns and I had to question whether this was considered vegetation.

"Once off the slide it was just straight through the forest for a couple of hours, then an hour in along a small stream. About then the sun left us and we pulled out the flashlights we'd brought along more as a joke than thinking they'd be needed. Fortunately, the terrain became easier to walk on and one more hour brought us out to the Peñas trail.

"The trick then was to climb the steep muddy path up to the Continental Divide. There we had a stroke of lifesaving good fortune. As we approached Marcos Vargas' humble cabin we observed that a candle was shining through the cracks in the wall and a cloud of smoke indicated food and coffee. After a bowl of hot soup and an hour of visiting, the trail didn't look so steep. At 8:30 p.m. we gladly headed home and at 10 p.m. sharp we landed there. Yes, our wives were already wondering when they should start asking for a search party, a question my wife has had to consider many times."

After two years in Monteverde, the Buskirks returned to the United States, where Bill, now an ornithologist, still teaches biology at Earlham College. He fondly remembers hiking with Wolf in the early 1970s, attempting to keep pace with this man who was twice his age.

"A few of us arranged to go from Monteverde over the mountain and down Peñas Blancas to visit the middle elevations on the Caribbean side. At that time there were hardly any visible trails below the first pastures at the foot of the *Ventana*. Wolf was leading us, clearing a trail with his machete as we trudged along. In his inimitable way, while swinging the machete, he was telling stories a mile a minute, telling us where someone had hunted a tapir, pointing out where this or that had occurred. The rest of us were muscling our backpacks and plodding through the deep mud. Wolf was doing all that plus whacking and talking. We all began to lag behind. It finally got to the point where we'd be topping one ridge between streams while Wolf was already at the top of the next one. There he'd be, cleared trail behind him, machete swinging and pointing, talking in rapid fire with no audience within earshot! What a remarkable energy and investment in the wilderness he has."

In 1975, after having started the Reserve, secured funding for three years and spurred international interest in the project, George and Harriett returned to the United States. During their time in Monteverde, besides carrying the expenses of their education and postgraduate work, they had poured a significant amount of money into the beginning of the Cloud Forest Reserve. Their contribution to the future of the Monteverde area was immense and their dedication inspiring.

Since then George has become an internationally recognized field biologist and conservationist. He has conducted numerous research projects in Costa Rica over the years, most notably studying and tracking birds using mini-radio transmitters. Through his many projects he has contributed a wealth of knowledge about the natural history of the resplendent quetzal, the three-wattled bellbird and the great green macaw. George still maintains a cottage on Wolf's farm near the Reserve. Although he is very busy with research throughout the world, the discovery in Monteverde of three dead quetzals in February of 2004 caught his interest. He was immediately in contact with the Reserve's director, his concern for Monteverde's environment as strong as ever.

While in Monteverde, Harriett taught science and biology at the Quaker school, influencing many students to pursue these fields. After she left the community she went on to teach all over the world. Although her now ex-husband George is considered the founder of the Cloud Forest Reserve, Harriett is respected and admired in the community for her own strong spirit and generous involvement in ensuring the protection of the local wilderness.

With the Powells gone, a small crew of dedicated workers, including Wolf, continued maintaining the *carril* lines and keeping watch for poachers and squatters.

"The early years were spent working a small amount of land, relatively speaking. But this land was very significant, and it was important to stay on top of things. The Tropical Science Center board needed to provide leadership because there was no income to hire professionals. Monteverde citizens were too busy using their energies for their own community necessities. There was no local interest in establishing or administrating the Reserve so it was almost impossible to get enough people to sit on a board that would be committed enough to be effective. In 1975 the piece of community land known as Bosqueterno S.A. was turned over to the TSC for a nominal amount of money to become part of the Reserve, bringing the total land area under protection to 2,000 hectares.

"When George left, Roger Morales, a Costa Rican naturalist, became the first administrator of the Reserve. My son Tomás, Eladio and I were cutting *carril* lines and making and maintaining trails. We continued doing land purchases with Roger supervising and me working with the people in the area. We dealt with Miguel Leitón to get the San Luis waterfall property, with the Cambroneros to get a larger piece in Peñas Blancas that they were developing, and with the Mendenhall family to buy an adjoining property that extended from the Monteverde community holdings to the Continental Divide. There were many pieces. I took the responsibility to go see one over in Vera Cruz, on the far side of San Luis, which turned out to be quite significant. That piqued my interest in that area, and with Roger's help we got protection for the habitat of a population of Baird's tapir. We did lots of outreach, going beyond Brilliante. As funding came in we evaluated different properties we could buy.

"There were people who wanted to use the Reserve as a study area while completing their thesis for a doctorate. The TSC got a little income from that as they charged a percentage to use the Reserve, but it wasn't nearly enough money considering what it took just to maintain a *carril* line year round. And once we had visitors coming, we needed better trails as well as someone to supervise their activities in the forest. There were also costs that arose from squatters and hunters threatening to invade. Protection work was all expenditure with no direct financial gain. As we expanded the infrastructure to accommodate the administration and student groups, there were always more costs than income. With the international community's growing interest in protecting tropical forests, we were number one with our foot in the door to get that assistance.

"More people started coming and we began charging them a walk-in fee. That's when Oscar was hired. His job was to talk to people about what we were doing and to collect a small amount at the entrance, twenty *colones*, which was about $2.50. This was only pocket change for foreigners, but it helped us earn a bit of money and keep track of how many people were coming in. Oscar controlled the entry, watched over our golden toad terrarium and went out patrolling, keeping an eye out for poachers.

"Roger Morales had been here for over a year when the Tropical Science Center asked him to go to the Osa Peninsula in southern Costa Rica to establish what is now Corcovado National Park. I was called on to be the interim administrator of the Reserve for the last months of the three-year period that was being financed by the World Wildlife Fund. There were serious problems trying to protect land in Corcovado from miners panning for gold there. Roger's assistant, a farmer in the Osa, got into trouble with the miners by furnishing information to the TSC, which was guiding the purchase of land in that area. He was threatened and the TSC brought him here until things cooled off. He became our administrator and I accepted the post of Head of Vigilance. As it turned out, it wasn't long before he was in trouble here. He threatened a tractor driver who was working on the road that was being extended into Peñas. He was in turn threatened by area people and warned never to appear in Santa Elena again, so he left in the middle of the night to avoid any more conflict.

"I took over as the administrator on a full-time salary. I was going to San José each month to get the paychecks for those of us working as there was no bank yet in Santa Elena. I was still involved with procuring land. With the early purchases, it was a matter of transferring the *cartas de venta* here in Monteverde, but soon it became necessary for the papers to be signed in San José. The lawyer for the Tropical Science Center at the time was Oscar Herrera and his office was right beside the TSC office, and that's where the business was done. It was no small thing for local people to get to San José, and then they would have to spend the night there when many had never even been to the small town of Puntarenas. For most people it was difficult to go through the business of transferring property.

"At that time I was on five different boards: the Medical Clinic, the Reserve, the Dairy Plant, the Quaker meeting and the Co-operative, which was the general store. I was also a member of ASCONA, a conservation organization consisting of young biologists and university students. We were concerned about conserving forests. By now I was peddling the idea that no matter what, the land was being rented, kept intact for the future. Even if it wasn't financially benefiting anyone directly, it was being held for the next generations.

"It was during this period that Luck and I had the hardest time. I was deeply involved with the Reserve, though I always felt that someone would come along who could do the administrative job better than I did. Management wasn't my bag of tricks, nor was organizing and handling a business, nor did I have a strong knowledge of natural history. I accepted the position but I thought it wouldn't be for very long. We never thought that the Reserve would be more than a protective buffer zone around Monteverde. I never imagined that Peñas Blancas, which at the time was still being developed, would become part of the protected area."

The idea of a reserve was difficult for people in the area to understand. They failed to see how it could be economically viable, and there was some suspicion that George Powell would be the one to profit. Many locals took issue with the fact that Wolf, who was until recently enthusiastically clearing land, was now talking about protecting the forest. If the land were to be protected, meaning no tree cutting and no hunting, then how would the community get anything out of it? As the Reserve's small crew worked at purchasing land and defining boundaries, they followed ridges and streams in search of natural land divisions that would make the most sense for their property lines. Some perceived this as an attempt on the part of the Reserve to push property lines beyond the purchased area. The Reserve had a lot to prove before it would be truly accepted by more than biologists and conservationists.

"All the boundaries were beginning to take shape. We were getting into land purchasing campaigns that were time-consuming. I think that's when I got to wandering cross-country, here and there and everywhere, trying to find the logical place, and hopefully the easiest place, to make a division of property.

"I got a lot of help from biologists and others interested in the Reserve who made suggestions about what we might do to better protect the area. We also benefited from information that biologists were gathering on the flora and fauna of the area, which helped promote the Reserve and enabled us to provide protection for nesting sites and other sensitive areas. Many student groups, initially from the Organization for Tropical Studies, came to study tropical biology. All this helped to attract more interest in the Reserve.

"Gary Stiles brought in the first student groups from the University of Costa Rica. He had several projects going. One of them happened each year and might seem a little out of place now. Gary would take a group of students into Peñas Blancas, cut a small tree that was loaded with epiphytes and vines, and strip off the vegetation. They would analyze what they could in the forest and then take the plants to study them in our schoolhouse, which was the only building big enough for them to work in at that time. I went with Gary and his assistant to Peñas to collect bird skins and eggs to mount at the National Museum. The way things were done then is very different than what is permitted now.

"More than anything, the biologists and students stimulated real interest in the area. The reports filed by researchers enticed bird-watchers to come. This was the beginning of what became known as ecotourism, and that's been the main economic benefit of the Reserve."

In the late 1970s Bob Law, a resident of Monteverde, oversaw the construction of the *casona,* which was built to hold offices, a field station, a dining room and a second-story dormitory. He also held the position of administrator for a time. In 1979 Walter Timmerman became administrator for one year and his wife Karen managed the reception. By now Wolf was cutting and maintaining trails with Eliezar Mejías, a local machete hand, though he continued to be involved with land purchases and patrolling within the Reserve. Wolf also became a representative on an international Quaker committee and spent some time traveling outside of the country.

In the late seventies the Reserve faced a number of serious challenges. Since the 1960s the government of Costa Rica had been issuing mining concessions for exploration in the Peñas Blancas valley. At the same time there was a concerted effort by homesteaders in the valley to establish viable farms within a functioning community. Wolf's own son Tomás and his wife Lindi had a claim in Peñas and were considering living there. They were talking about opening a school for the homesteading community. However, the Tropical Science Center was firm in limiting access to the valley through the Reserve, announcing that the road that existed was not to be extended or improved. This created friction between the TSC and the Peñas homesteaders.

Closer to Monteverde, the government threatened to expropriate Bosqueterno S.A., which encompassed Cerro Amigos, the highest peak in the area, to install communications towers. In November of 1979 the *casona* at the Reserve was inaugurated and shortly after the Timmerman's left. Wolf, while continuing in his post as Head of Vigilance, once again took over the administration of the Reserve. In 1982 he was officially named the director of the Monteverde Cloud Forest Reserve.

"In Peñas Blancas people realized that although they still had the use of the road, it would probably never be extended. They started feeling self-conscious about going through the Reserve to go down to their holdings. It was a tough one for me because I had a lot of sympathy for the people who were trying to develop small parcels there. Our family had worked on three different pieces.

"We got into doing *denuncias*. Government guards based in Santa Elena started patrolling and enforcing the laws against poaching and cutting down trees. I would go with them when they needed a witness or someone to help out on behalf of the Reserve. Then Eliezar Mejías and I would be required to go to Puntarenas to testify in court, hoping the people would be fined for their illegal acts. The amount of the fines was insignificant but the hope was that it would be enough to convince the violators to stop what they'd been doing. It was really time-consuming and was creating negative feelings towards the Reserve.

"Around the same time, the government put in the radio repeater towers on Cerro Amigos. It was a big job to oversee the bulldozing being done on the site and to restrict the destruction as much as possible. The government's intent was to expropriate the land but the laws on expropriation weren't simple. The government eventually signed a contract with the TSC to sublease the land from Bosqueterno S.A. The agreement we had with the TSC was that they'd handle the leasing of contracts and receive the financial remuneration for use of the site. One of the contentious issues was who was going to benefit financially from it. That was another big lump of our energy, going up and down the steep road to the tower site, my record being two trips to the site and back in one day.

"That was a time of conflict and I was expecting that things would escalate. Some of the people going into Peñas would show that they were carrying a knife in a sheath inside their boot. Once or twice men were denounced for some violation and you didn't know what they might do in retaliation. It would be many years later, in the late 1980s, after the families had sold and moved out, that the Reserve got the Ministry of Public Roads to agree to have the road limited. After that it was closed off by a locked gate.

"Anyone who didn't sell out their piece was allowed a limited right of way through the Reserve to get to their property. The only person who wasn't bought out and actively used the road was my old friend

Eston Rockwell. Part of his reason not to sell was because he wanted the road to remain public. The agreement with the Road Department was that we had to give Eston a key to the lock on the gate so he could access the road, but others weren't allowed to use it. The lock is still there. After all these years the TSC has never bought Eston's property, which was transferred years ago to his son-in-law, Tom Dixon. My friend Eston passed away in 1999.

"The only protection against land being invaded by mining exploration and development was to designate it as a national park. I've always felt that private nature reserves should have this same protected status, however, if that wasn't to be, then I was sure that one day the Cloud Forest Reserve would become a national park and have full protection. In George's original funding proposal to the World Wildlife Fund he stated his expectation that if the National Parks system developed as anticipated, the Reserve could one day be incorporated into it. By the end of the funding period I felt that Costa Rica's National Parks had developed significantly and certainly had the ability to finance and manage the Reserve. I also thought this would put an end to the feeling of some local people that the Reserve was just another business run by foreigners. However, the Congress didn't approve the funds that were required to purchase the land. In general, Costa Ricans take great pride in their national parks, but they never felt the same sense of ownership for our private reserve in Monteverde.

"As the Reserve grew in size we added more personnel, and more people started visiting, including student groups. Monteverde needed additional lodgings. The first proper hotel was the Hotel Montaña and with that began another conflict. Should the Reserve encourage people to vacation at the Hotel Montaña? On the other side of the coin, should the hotel take the initiative to put out brochures that publicized the Reserve? As I went back and forth between the two, I caught flack from both sides. On top of this, some people in Monteverde weren't happy that tourism was being promoted at all."

The Monteverde Cloud Forest Reserve grew from the original 328 hectares that the Powells had purchased to approximately 10,500 hectares in the 1990s. In the beginning there were fewer than 500 visitors a year. 2005 saw close to 80,000 visitors, the largest number ever. The Reserve is roughly ninety percent pristine forest, with a wealth of biodiversity: more than 3,000 plant species including 900 species of epiphytes and 500 species of orchids, 100 species of mammals, 400 species of birds, 120 species of reptiles and amphibians, innumerable insects and countless shades of green.

Although Wolf was responsible for administration and on-site coordination in the early 1980s, these were not his strengths. His preference was always to be outdoors, involved in protection and trail maintenance. Being on the go, clearing boundary lines and patrolling what had become his forest sanctuary were activities that fit his restless soul. His involvement in all aspects of the development of the Reserve ultimately took its toll.

Through these early years of the Reserve, Wolf was often short-tempered on the job and irrational in his reactions to many situations. By 1982, under intense pressure from his job, which often led to conflicts with authorities, his bosses, community members and his wife, Wolf became increasingly unwell. Lucky and Wolf knew that things had reached a point where something had to be done. In 1983 the Reserve hired Vicente Watson as temporary director and Wolf took five months off to deal with his health.

Eventually Wolf was diagnosed with bipolar disorder and prescribed lithium, which properly addressed the chemical imbalance in his body and allowed him to get back to work full-time. In 1984 Watson left the Reserve, Giovanni Bello was appointed as director and Wolf became co-director and advisor to the Reserve. Since the end of Giovanni's term in 1988 the Reserve has gone through a number of directors, including William Aspinall, Francisco Chamberlain, Bob Carlson, Rafael Bolaños, Ricardo Rodríguez and Carlos Hernández. By the 1990s it was employing close to fifty local people.

Until his retirement in 2003 Wolf advised on the development and maintenance of the more than ninety kilometers of trails that crisscross the Reserve. He also held the position of Head of Protection, coordinating the forest guards while happily continuing to patrol the trails himself. Although Wolf's devotion to the forest came at a cost to his family life, it was fed by his enduring love for the jungle.

"I always felt like I kind of helped to conceive it, maybe in some ways negatively, but somebody had to do something to get people thinking in a positive way about saving the forest. It didn't really amount to much, just a smudge on the map. I mothered it when protecting the forest didn't bring in any income because nobody thought the Reserve was worth paying anybody to do a really good job of looking after it. Even though I'm officially retired from my duties, I still feel pretty protective of it."

From these humble beginnings the idea of conservation spread across the country, and the community's involvement in preserving forests also grew. In 1992 the Santa Elena Cloud Forest Reserve (SER) was founded on the northern side of Cerro Amigos, the hill that now holds the communications towers. Dedicated to conservation and local education, it sits six kilometers northeast of the town of Santa Elena and is administered by the Santa Elena High School.

"The money collected at the entrance to the Santa Elena Reserve goes to support projects in the public high school. It's another project in this area that's benefited directly from Canadian support in the form of volunteers raising funds and working to develop the trails. When SER started it reminded me a whole lot of the Monteverde Reserve thirty years ago, before tourism was on every corner and the packaged tourist became a big factor in the area. The secondary growth forest in SER, where the tourists walk, is very similar to what we had in the 1980s in the Monteverde Reserve. People aren't aware of the fact that they're walking across old cow pastures where the forest has regenerated and is now probably thirty feet high.

"In the Santa Elena Reserve there's a whole other climate. It's a slightly higher elevation, but they have a little less wind than we have, which gives you another feeling. Their views of the Arenal Volcano make it different from Monteverde, but their beautiful cloud forest is the same. From my point of view, the more forest being protected, no matter who's in charge, the better it is for all of us."

EIGHT

Into Peñas Blancas

"Well, what a great place to be! We're at the lookout near the waterfall, on *El Sendero de Mil Miradores,* about to head straight down the ridge all the way to the Peñas Blancas River. Between the dips and bumps in the valley I can just make out some of the clearings that were made when man was playing around in here. You're not as likely anymore to see the white specks that used to be cows and horses. I can still see the big *higueron,* the old strangler fig tree, sticking up above the tree line on the other ridge. If it ever goes down it would open up a gap big enough to see the better part of Costa Rica." *Wolf on the Catarata Trail*

Following my successful cancer treatments my body slowly regained its strength and my feelings of vulnerability began to subside. I was finally able to return to Costa Rica in 1994. Wolf's infectious laugh and his warm hug of welcome were long-awaited tonics. He presented me with the more than twenty tapes he had recorded since 1990, the last time we had seen each other, and I resumed transcribing his stories. Over the following years we took as many opportunities as we could to go hiking, using the time on the trail to discuss our oral history project. Our destination was often the rustic *refugio* at El Valle, an easy two-hour walk through the Reserve. Sitting on the porch, steam rising from our cups of coffee, clouds of mist encircling us, I would lean back against the shelter's damp wooden wall as Wolf's memories took us on past adventures through the verdant landscape. The little black box recorded for as long as the batteries held up. While the howlers settled down and the night creatures started up, the conversation and laughter continued until we would finally drag ourselves to the thin foam pads waiting inside.

It was from that humble abode that Wolf led me down one of the most dramatic trails in the area, the Catarata Trail, named for the waterfall that is visible across a high ravine, a powerful ribbon of water that pours out of the mountain and is absorbed into the thirsty vegetation at least 200 feet below. At each bend in the path a different view of the Peñas Blancas valley presents itself, inspiring Wolf to nickname it "The Trail of a Thousand Lookouts." Quite often as you are admiring the distant ridges through gaps in the vegetation, low-passing clouds will suddenly move in, completely obscuring the view and filling the forest with a somber light.

The Catarata Trail winds along the narrow, twisted spine of a ridgeback. The land falls away sharply on both sides and is quickly lost in a jumble of arboreal roots and shadowy foliage. Hiking in the slippery jungle always demands careful footwork – here, a single misstep and you could disappear into the forest's depths. It is truly amazing that Wolf has walked this trail in the black of night, not once but on several occasions. Even he shudders at the thought of it.

On this day in 1995 an almost constant drizzle accompanied us until the hope of remaining partially dry was totally abandoned. After three hours of slow walking down the steep slope we met up with the relatively level river trail. When we were close enough to hear the rushing water of the Peñas Blancas River we took a short break to fortify ourselves with more coffee. Wolf ran off to a meeting in Monteverde and I continued on my own for a couple of hours to the *refugio* known as the German's. I was meandering along happily, contemplating my solitude, when I came to a grassy part of the trail and found myself face-to-face with an enormous snake: flat-nosed, black and shiny, drying its long, thick body by the side of the trail now that the sun had decided to appear. The startled serpent shot up into a strike pose. I retreated down the trail, grabbed the biggest stick I could find and cautiously returned to the clearing, loudly negotiating with the snake. I didn't want to disturb it and I wouldn't have killed it even if I'd had a machete with me – all I wanted was to get by. To my great relief the snake slid away, but after that I approached every sunny clearing with my senses on high alert and my stick held at the ready. As I have observed every time I venture into the mossy, mysterious world of Peñas Blancas, its greatest beauty lies in the moments when its hidden treasures choose to reveal themselves.

Pre-Columbian civilizations in the Arenal area to the north and the east of Monteverde left enough evidence to suggest that they constituted a major population dating back to at least 10,000 B.C. These indigenous people supported themselves by agriculture augmented by hunting and gathering, traditional practices that were still followed in the mid-1900s by the descendants of the Spanish conquistadors. It is safe to say that the Peñas Blancas valley, which cuts through the southern part of the Arenal area, has been sharing its wealth with hunters, explorers and homesteaders for millennia. Compared to Monteverde, the valley is several hundred feet lower in elevation, providing a warmer climate more suitable for growing tropical crops such as bananas and sugar cane.

Before the idea of conservation was introduced, men headed into the lush valley to hunt tapir, peccary, deer and anything else that would provide protein for their families. They came from the surrounding settlements of Santa Elena and San Luis in the west, Palmital and San Ramón in the south and San Miguel and La Tigra in the east. Many were inspired to make small clearings in this forest of abundant game and timber and set up camp, taking advantage of the Costa Rican homesteading laws. Since the 1980s the valley has entered a new phase. Now the hunters are armed with cameras and the gatherers are working on scientific theses. For the foreseeable future the mountain lion can sleep more soundly in Peñas Blancas.

Rio Peñas Blancas was probably named for the white clay outcropping that stands guard near its headwaters. The stream flows out of the mountain on the Atlantic side of the Continental Divide, near Brilliante, gathering momentum as it cascades eastward, descending 500 meters in elevation over ten kilometers. The largest river in the area, it drains the central Caribbean slope of the Tilarán Mountain range. Dozens of feeder streams, *quebradas,* join the main river, funneling the area's substantial rainfall back to the Caribbean Sea. These streams were named after memorable animal sightings – *La Leona, La Mona* – or distinct physical characteristics – *El Portal, Gemelos, Azufre* – by the same adventurers who built the simple cabins that until relatively recently were home to the settlers of the region.

The path that begins at the entrance to the Monteverde Cloud Forest Reserve winds all the way down to the Peñas Blancas River. About halfway down, on a flat plateau and overgrown with vegetation, is Dos Aces, the first of the area's several *refugios* where forest workers and wanderers have found respite over the years. The path continues eastward to the German's, at which point the land becomes part of the Children's

Eternal Rain Forest (BEN), which is under the care of the Monteverde Conservation League. The trail roughly follows the river, passing a series of original homesteads with names such as Rojas', Alejandro's, Eladio's, and the more recently built Portland Audubon Center. At the eastern limit of BEN is Laguna Poco Sol, a tiny lake that sits to the north of and 200 meters above the Peñas Blancas River. From Poco Sol a dirt road heads east through the *pueblo* of San Miguel to the highway near the village of San José de La Tigra in the San Carlos region. Here it is possible to catch a bus north to La Fortuna near the base of the Arenal Volcano or south to the cities of San Ramón and San José.

East of Poco Sol, the river has had its water redirected via a canal to a hydroelectric turbine several kilometers away and is now a different version of its former self. What was once a cascading, rocky, white-water river has been reduced to wide pools of water waiting to be employed in the country's never-ending search for more hydroelectric power. As is the case with many of the large waterways in Costa Rica, further damming of the river is likely. The conservationists may control its beginnings, but the demands of consumption control its future.

Wolf's first trip into the Peñas Blancas valley was in 1952 when it was largely unexplored. As he readily admits, it was "love at first sight." This vast wilderness, extending down the east side of the same mountain that the Monteverdians were developing, enticed some of the young, adventurous Quakers to venture into its depths.

"This little speck of creation was considered a 'dreamland' to be developed and populated by pioneers. Who could say no to visiting the land of spider monkeys and wild pigs? Or to following the tapir and jaguar trails down to the river, reported to contain not only fish but gold! The tales we heard from the few hunters and adventurers who'd followed the trails down the steep cliff were bait enough to lure the community's younger set into organizing an excursion.

"The rutted cart trail led us uphill from the community center, past the upper holdings to the Mata brothers' pastures. Then the wider cart trail ended and the untamed forest began. We took a freshly cut foot trail that, after a series of climbs and dips, led to the Continental Divide. To this day I remember our surprise at moving along these trails, no doubt cut by hunters and explorers, which suddenly disappeared, leaving no trace of where the person who had created them had gone!

"Arriving at the cliff edge that marked the Continental Divide, we were disappointed because there was no view, rather a mass of drippy, plant-covered trees and clouds that were drifting up through the tangle of vegetation. For the next hour we slowly lowered ourselves down the slope, hanging on to shrubs and small trees, mostly descending a narrow ridge, but occasionally crossing rocky, nearly bare landslides. Upon reaching the plateau at the base of the cliff we received our next surprise, an area of marshy swamp directly in front of us. We circled around it to a small clearing that belonged to Rafael Vargas, where we stopped to rest and eat our lunch.

"We headed back by the same route and as we ascended the clouds magically cleared away. At each opening in the tree cover we rested and got a peek at the rugged forest-covered ridges that surrounded us. We all agreed that these views were the highlight of the excursion. The real payoff was that we had raised our status to that of the elite few who'd been to Peñas Blancas. I consider myself fortunate to have had such a memorable adventure in this wrinkled valley before all the changes came.

"Don Ricardo González was one of the old-timers who was a pioneer in Peñas Blancas. He and Rafael Vargas had the first squatter claims, but he also worked in the community for Hubert Mendenhall. We became neighbors in 1954 when I purchased a claim on a parcel we now call Dos Aces, on the last shelf before you cross the ridge and go down to the river. When I went into Peñas I would stay in the *rancho* Don Ricardo had built. I learned a lot from his colorful stories about pioneering. He was raised near San Ramón, in coffee country. As a young man he worked as a *boyero,* delivering coffee beans in his oxcart to the port at Puntarenas and hauling salt on the return trip. Don Ricardo was a true adventurer who had gone into Peñas as a hunter and fallen in love with its charms. Without a compass, without any maps or anything else, he learned his way around the valley.

"At that time each trip into Peñas stirred up our awareness of the uniqueness of the area and the vastness of the jungle. It was an adventure to follow the ridges, always watching for animal trails that would lead us the best way through the forest. Sometimes we were able to walk following the streams all the way down to the Peñas Blancas River. We'd then work our way along the river, seeing no signs of development but many signs of animals. We did that for a couple of years, having a look, often taking a dip in the river, before homesteaders started establishing claims and making formal trails.

"I think it must have been about 1958 when I first slept out beside the old river and listened to its roar. Luis Antonio Zamora and I started out, having set our goal of going through Peñas Blancas all the way until we hit civilization. We came clear down to the river and went as far as the last shack and spent the night. The next morning we set out at daylight and hacked our way through the greenery. We would chop as little as possible as we moved through the tangle, never sure that we were going the best way, knowing that we might have to retrace our steps at any point. We kept heading along the edge of the river until we couldn't do it anymore. At the rock chutes we knew we were done for, so we started looking for our way back. We didn't expect to be able to follow the exact same route by which we'd come and therefore the going was still tough. We finally made it back to the shack by moonlight. That was as close as I got to going all the way through until the mine company came in 1964. That was when people from the mining camps near San Miguel made contact with those of us from the communities at the west end of the valley who were establishing claims in Peñas. The pity is that I was confident Luis Antonio could lead me all the way, but that was one of the last times he trekked in the woods. He was a sawyer and one day slipped and stuck his foot in the circular saw. He never hiked comfortably again."

In 1964 the Peñas Blancas valley was opened up to mining exploration. A Canadian branch of the U.S.-based Gypsum Mining Company, bent on finding mineral and sulfur deposits, established a series of mine camps. They cut a wide trail through the forest on the south side of the river, heading west for several kilometers from the community of San Miguel. The heart of the mining interest was at Camp Three, from which a horse trail climbed in a westerly direction up the mountain to Camp Four, a distance that could be covered by foot in a couple of hours. Camp Three was on a knoll with a view overlooking the river valley. The elevation of the camp was 1,000 meters, the river below sat at 540 meters and behind the camp, two peaks thickly covered in rainforest vegetation rose to about 1,600 meters. The sites for Camps One and Two were on the north side of the river but were never developed.

At the peak of activity, which lasted from 1964 to the company's withdrawal in 1968, there were five buildings and a helicopter pad at Camp Three. There was an administration center, dormitory, storage depot, equipment and repair shop and a kitchen-dining hall. Equipment was brought in to make core borings and determine the quantity and quality of the sulfur deposits.

"The mine company was intent on doing exploratory sampling in every stream in the area, many of which smelled strongly of sulfur. The company built a trail that wound all the way up to their camp from the village of San Miguel. First it was nothing more than a scrambler trail that followed the old hunters' trails, but then they had a crew go in and widen it on a better grade and build what became a pretty fancy trail. Lumber came in on it as well as supplies and equipment for the over eighty people who worked in the camps. Two big stoves and a boring machine were stripped down and carried in in pieces. The machine's engine on its own weighed 400 pounds and took four people on each side to carry it.

"This was when people on the Pacific side of the Continental Divide met up with people from the Atlantic side. The first contact was made when some men from San Miguel, scouting for the mining company, arrived with a turkey at the little cabin that belonged to Acilino Trejos and Miguel Salazar, two hunters from Santa Elena. Their clearing was the furthest one down the valley that anybody from the Monteverde side had ever developed. Acilino was one of the first in the valley to have a cane patch and a still.

"Well, the story goes that everyone was set to have a fiesta. Wanting to be a good host, Acilino took the turkey they'd brought and turned it into a big pot of soup. It was late in the day and he wasn't at his best, no doubt he'd been dipping into his own brew. He added some potatoes and whatever else he had around, and some salt to flavor it. A little later he tasted it again and noted that there wasn't enough salt, so he added a big amount more. It still didn't taste quite right but he served it up. It turned out that he was putting sugar in, not salt. Anybody hungry enough could rinse the sugar off and still eat the turkey, but most people had a problem eating it. So that's the famous sugar turkey soup that's still being remembered by those of us who were in Peñas Blancas at the time!

"Adventurous people started traveling by foot through the valley. Mostly they'd come up to Monteverde because they'd heard about this strange Quaker community from the workers at the camps. People from this end went down to get work. They were paid forty *centimos* a pound for carrying in freight on their backs. They'd carry about 100 pounds in, maybe a little less if they were making two trips a day.

"For about four years there was a lot of activity around the camps. For me, it was always fun to go down there because they had real good cooks and they'd always serve you up a big meal. It got us thinking that we could make some money supplying meat or food crops. In 1965 Eladio and his brother José Angel built a small cabin that I used as a base for many years. Eladio still has a cabin there, a couple of hour's walk from Camp Four. We really thought the mining company was going to exploit some of the sulfur and would develop the camps into something more permanent. But the Vietnam War was slowing down and less sulfur was being used for defoliation over there, so prices fell and everything ended. Quality sulfur was more easily available in large deposits near the volcanoes.

"Supposedly there was a small area around here that held copper, and it's possible, but less likely, that there was gold, but I don't know what they found. It didn't work out and we were glad. They would have destroyed that big chunk of tapir country. It's all under protection now, but it wouldn't have been if the mineral deposits had been valuable enough.

"It was a great time, though. Of course, people who came to work at the camps were introduced to the valley, and that spurred their interest in cutting out a clearing for themselves. When the mine company closed up in 1968, it sold off some equipment. I bought sleeping pads and other things we used later in the shelters on our clearings. At Camp Four a good bit of pasture was planted and several of the buildings were relocated and used as squatter's cabins. The rest of the buildings were stripped down, and then, one by one, what was left fell down. Everything of value was carried back out on a much better trail then it had arrived on.

"During the sixties I became good friends with José María Corrales, who lived over in Tanque in San Carlos. He's known as Carmelo by all his friends. He worked for the mine company as one of its field directors and was in charge of the camps' operations. The land the camps

were situated on and the concession rights were owned by three partners: Mario Echandi, an ex-president of Costa Rica; Estella Quesada, a
congresswoman from Ciudad Quesada; and Doña Teresa Ugalde, an
area businesswoman. Carmelo received a large portion of this land as
severance payment for work he did with the mine company. In 1969
Marcos Vargas and I purchased about 100 hectares from Carmelo near
Camp Four. I was also developing a seventy-hectare piece that adjoined
Eladio's land. Even though the mine company pulled out, the relationship between the communities at the opposite ends of the Peñas Blancas
valley continued.

"It takes a big stretch of the imagination to remember back to when
families were living there and horse trails were everywhere. Alejandro
García was one friend whose home was in the heart of Peñas. He would
always give you a cup of coffee. I can remember him talking about his
trapiche and the several varieties of sugarcane he was experimenting with.
He always had a sincere interest in developing the community of Peñas
Blancas. Tragically, Alejandro's first wife and four of his children were
lost in a mudslide there in 1973. They'd built a new house between two
small streams. In a real hard rainstorm, mud and logs blocked a larger
feeder stream above the house and when the dam let go, a head of water
came down upon the house. Alejandro and one of his sons survived
only because they weren't home at the time. I delivered medication to the
mudslide's survivors and joined others who made the sad trip down to
bring out the bodies. It was a tragedy for all of us in the Peñas Blancas
community.

"Eladio Cruz and I have spent more hours than I can count moving
around the woods, from the early days of working for the Reserve and
over the many years of hiking through Peñas and beyond. We stayed
with adventuresome families living in remote places, slept on a variety of
floors and listened to a lot of stories. We told our share as well. One time
we left Monteverde, digging to get to San Miguel by sundown. We just
made it and stopped by the home of a friend of Eladio's. I was feeling
sort of sick to my stomach, so the man offered that we spend the night.
The only place to sleep was on a tarpaulin out in the *bodega,* which I did-
n't look forward to since I wasn't feeling all that great. He sent his daughter, who couldn't have been more than twelve or thirteen, to fix us something hot to eat. The gal cooked us up some green bananas, which did
nothing good for my stomach.

"While she was cooking he shared his sad story. He explained why his young daughter had to do the cooking. With his head hung low, he said that his wife had died not too long ago, and as if that wasn't bad enough, he'd gone up to the pasture and found his steer dead. That in itself was another tragedy. He continued on, shaking his head, and with real pain in his words, said, 'And then, when I came back to the farm, I lost my mule.' Well, the loss of that mule was just too much for him!

"We had to get up early in the morning to walk a good hour down to the bus stop beyond San Miguel where the bus was scheduled to come at 5 a.m. The only thing the man had for an alarm clock was his radio, which he'd set on Radio Musical, a lively Costa Rican station that played pleasant tunes and gave you the time twenty-four hours a day. At about one in the morning he turned on the radio and listened to find out what time it was, waking us all up in the process as the sound easily carried out to where we were trying to sleep. He found that it wasn't the right time, so he turned it off and went back to sleep. It seemed that every half hour after that, the radio was turned back on. At the same time there was a small child who was sick and whooped and coughed all night long. Between that and the yo-yo kind of alarm system, we were more tired when we got up than when we'd gone to bed. I shouldn't complain as, after all, the man provided a place to spend the night.

"My son Tomás and Lindi Maxson were married in August of 1975 and honeymooned in Peñas Blancas. That was when the people of Peñas were getting excited about starting a school in the area for the families that were homesteading there. Tomás and Antonio, one of my other sons, were developing a piece of land on the south side of the river. It was very difficult for the ones who were trying so hard to homestead in Peñas Blancas. The climate was too wet for successful farming. The rain would leach out the nutrients from the soil, leaving land that was only productive for five years or so and was vulnerable to erosion. In the late seventies and into the eighties, the priority for the homesteaders was to improve the road that went through the Reserve into the valley. At the same time it was a priority for the Tropical Science Centre to close the road. They wanted to prevent people from cutting trees and extracting timber by limiting the road access."

As settlers in the valley continued to make clearings and build simple houses, higher up the mountain a new approach to the land was becoming a reality. The seed of conservation had germinated and its green tendrils were spreading throughout the forest. During the 1970s the Monteverde Cloud Forest Reserve was committed to buying up land to prevent further cutting. As Wolf worked with the Reserve, measuring properties and clearing trails, he spent more and more time hiking through the Peñas Blancas valley. He had a good rapport with the settlers in the area, though they weren't necessarily in tune with his new ideas on conservation. But who could resist this friendly, enthusiastic visitor who announced his arrival with a "WHOOP, WHOOP" and was happy to share stories and laughter in exchange for a cup of coffee?

"The mine company had explored as far as a large pond called Laguna Palmital that was to the south of Camp Three. We'd heard enough stories about it, so George Powell and I packed up one day in 1973 and took a trip to see what the area looked like. It was quite a hike. We spent the first night in one of the buildings at Camp Three that was about to fall down. By the next night we got all the way to the *laguna*. It was very impressive and we felt lucky to be there. This was tapir country. There were sure signs of tapirs all around the area of Camp Three and near the headwaters of the stream we call *El Portal*.

"On the way in to the *laguna* we heard dogs chasing an animal. George wanted to see if we could head them off but in that terrain we had no success getting near them. We spent the night at the little lake, followed by a hard day of scouting around. We hiked until nightfall to get out at San Miguel. On the way we went by a house where a tapir had been recently killed and the meat was hanging up, the hooves and hide still evident. It turned out to be a pregnant female who'd gone into a small pool to defend herself and was easy to shoot. That was a very sad way for us to end our adventure.

"In 1976 I went for the first time all the way through the Reserve and the Peñas Blancas valley to Laguna Poco Sol, which at the time was part of a working hacienda. I was accompanied by Chico Mata, who was working for the Reserve. We followed the trail on the south side of the river through what was left of the mine camps to San Miguel. We spent a night with the Castro family, who lived a few hours' walk beyond Camp Three. They told us that there was a family fiesta going on over at Poco Sol on the other side of the river. Near San Miguel there was a narrow cable bridge that crossed over the Peñas Blancas River. The *laguna* was a good walk back up the slope on the north side. We met up with a fellow going to the fiesta and he led us across the pastures and up a trail that was the shortest way to the party.

"We were too early for the main event, but the pig was already skinned and the home brew arrived with our companion. We decided to stay until the first *chicharrones* were ready. We learned a little of the history of Poco Sol through the stories that were told, but we had to leave before the party really got going, when the local families would arrive with their music and drink and no doubt plenty of food.

"I had heard about Laguna Poco Sol, but that was the first time I visited it. I immediately appreciated the size of the lake, which was about four hectares. I realized then the potential it had to attract people who wanted to take a dip. It had already been stocked with tilapia, but they'd stocked it with both males and females so it was overrun with small fish. Not many people had the patience to fish there. At the time the hacienda was owned by an individual living in Ciudad Quesada who wasn't doing much with the pasture. And there was still a lot of forest. It made quite an impression, one that would come back to haunt me."

Besides the restrictions the Tropical Science Center had placed on the road into Peñas Blancas, a further damper was put on development when the Costa Rican government established the Arenal Forest Reserve in 1977. The purpose of the reserve was to protect the watershed that supplied the lake that had been created in the mid-1970s when a hydroelectric dam was constructed on the Arenal River just to the north of the Arenal Volcano. As well as supplying hydroelectricity, Lake Arenal provided water to an irrigation system that nourished the arid Guanacaste lowlands. With the establishment of the Arenal Forest Reserve, 18,000 hectares of forest surrounding the Peñas Blancas River and extending to the north were subject to stricter forestry laws. This was good news for conservationists, as was the government's promise to buy out the squatters who had established claims in the area. But the government didn't fulfill its promise and by the late 1970s many of the valley's absentee landowners had abandoned their claims while others continued to cut trees illegally. Hunters still followed the tapir tracks, and in *Semana Santa*, Easter week, people poached palm trees to collect *palmito*, a traditional Easter food.

Biologists were now studying beyond the borders of the Cloud Forest Reserve and becoming aware of the great diversity of bird and plant species in the Peñas Blancas valley. As they published their reports, the scientific and bird-watching communities became more interested in seeing for themselves the incredible flora and fauna of the area. Peñas Blancas was set to become the center of a tug of war between development and preservation.

By the early 1980s the community in Peñas Blancas was pressuring the government to improve the road or buy them out. At the same time the Tropical Science Center had slowed its acquisition of properties outside of the borders of the Cloud Forest Reserve, leaving the Peñas landowners frustrated. People were also clearing land illegally in the area of San Gerardo, a small settlement on the Atlantic side of the Continental Divide that was several kilometers north of the Peñas Blancas valley but still within the Arenal Forest Reserve. Meanwhile, land was being cleared near Monteverde for agricultural development, leaving smaller and smaller forests on the Pacific side of the Continental Divide.

In June of 1985 a group of concerned Monteverde residents, including biologists Bill Haber, Willow Zuchowski, Alan Pounds and Richard Laval, and landowners John Campbell, Bob Law and Wolf began discussing how to respond as a community to the continuing development in the area. Among their concerns was the future of their water resource as Monteverde continued to grow.

On December 27 of that year, following a series of meetings, the Monteverde Conservation League was formed with twenty-two charter members. The mission of the group was to preserve the Pacific slope forests, to cooperate with the Tropical Science Center to save threatened portions of the Atlantic slope forest, to promote reforestation and environmental education, and to promote political action leading to the protection of area forests. The League immediately began a campaign to raise funds for land purchase, the original area of concern being the Peñas Blancas valley.

"Just the fact that the Conservation League got off the ground was a miracle considering the personalities involved and the great amount of time and effort it took to get it going. There was a combination of factors that came together, including international interest in saving the rainforest at the same time that rampant development was occurring in our own backyard. A community meeting was called by local biologists who wanted to see what people in the community could do to ensure the protection of animals and water in the surrounding countryside. Restricting tree cutting was also a priority. Once it got rolling the League became an important part of conservation in this community.

"With the first discussions, I thought I would stay out of the League. It looked like it was going to be mostly biologists involved. I don't think or act in as focused or disciplined a way. I'm prone to broader philosophical views as opposed to what I might say was sometimes tunnel vision on the part of the scientists. For instance, some of the academics felt that the protected forest should only be accessible to university folk who would be conducting studies. I've always felt that all the land should be protected but open to anyone who would enjoy it, especially the Costa Ricans. But I did feel I could help out because I'd been involved in setting up other organizations and had many contacts in the area as well as in San José.

"I was impressed with the emphasis that the League was placing on reforestation. They were interested in helping dairy farmers and coffee growers to get better production off their land. This involved planting windbreaks as the land here suffers from heavy wind and rain, which causes serious erosion and stresses the crops and cattle, resulting in decreased production. There was also a plan to undertake environmental education in the surrounding areas. I liked that these were helpful things for the broader community, so I threw my support behind the League and became its first vice-president.

"The idea of purchasing land in Peñas Blancas came directly from the very real concerns of Michael and Patricia Fogden, our famous photographers. In the mid-1980s they were studying sunbitterns down in Peñas. During the several weeks that they were patiently spending their days in their blind monitoring a sunbittern's nest, they were spending their nights at Eladio's cabin. They had the small one-room addition because a homesteading family was occupying the main room. This family was busy taking over abandoned homesteads, cutting secondary forest and enthusiastically working towards the development of the community in Peñas Blancas. On a daily basis the Fogdens could see how all this development was putting pressure on the surrounding forest. One day the family produced a dead umbrellabird and served it for dinner, aggravating the Fogdens with the knowledge that people were willing to kill these species despite the fact that the Fodgens and others were studying them.

"When the Fogdens returned to Monteverde they reported on the amount of tree cutting that was being done and expressed their concern about the future of bird species if the development continued. Because I'd seen the situation firsthand, I was able to back up their fears to the members of the Conservation League, and as a result the League started focusing on protecting the forest in Peñas Blancas. The importance of the Fogden's study, and particularly their photographs, can't be underestimated. I credit them with the fact that we're still able to see intact populations of unique bird and mammal species in Peñas.

"The Fogdens contributed greatly to the League's Peñas Blancas Campaign, first by their heartfelt reporting of what was going on in the valley, and later by using their photos in a slideshow that was featured at the Pensíon Quetzal. The slideshow taught visitors about the natural history of the area, and the visitors in turn contributed to the campaign. Patricia put a lot of energy and talent into spreading the word. She spent innumerable evenings presenting the slideshow at local hotels and that way raised a great amount of money for the League. One night she accepted a $100,000 commitment, which is a testament to her persuasive and passionate character."

As fundraising kicked into high gear, the results were increasingly successful. The World Wildlife Fund in Canada ran a well-publicized campaign to "Save the Rainforest" acre by acre. They gave certificates for each $25 donation that stated that the donor had protected one acre of rainforest. In 1986 Bill Haber, the first secretary of the League, negotiated a grant whereby the World Wildlife Fund in the U.S. would match $25,000 raised by the League. The League used this money to purchase properties, beginning in Peñas Blancas.

"The first person to sell his Peñas property for the purpose of protecting the area was my long-time friend Eladio Cruz. He'd worked with the Reserve and believed in conservation. He was hoping to set an example for the other Peñas landowners. Funds were raised by a group of birders led by Mark Smith as part of the Portland Audubon Society, as well as by the Fogdens and Bob Law through the slideshows they were giving to tourists. The funds were handed over to the Tropical Science Center, which bought this first property from Eladio. This was in the beginning when the TSC and the League were working cooperatively, but Eladio's was the only piece in that part of the valley that was bought by the TSC. Then things got complicated between the various parties when the money started rolling in and the League started buying large tracts in Peñas.

"There was an unwritten agreement between the League and the Tropical Science Center that the League would raise the funds and purchase the land in Peñas Blancas. They would then transfer it to the Tropical Science Center, which was to oversee the long-term protection of the area. The TSC wasn't supposed to be involved in the purchasing negotiations as long as the League was raising the funds.

"Once the League got organized and the funds started coming in, the land-purchase campaign really took off. Originally, we targeted about thirty or more squatter claims. The League made arrangements to handle the land transactions here in Monteverde or in Puntarenas, which was a different way of doing things from the time when the Tropical Science Center was purchasing land for the Cloud Forest Reserve and each property owner had to travel to San José to transfer their documents.

"Before we started making purchases, we had Miguel Angel Oviedo come in, who had experience evaluating nontitled forested land. He did a thorough job of going into Peñas and assessing the properties as well as investigating the land values at the bank. His report was the basis for all the purchasing the League did. I had complete confidence that everything was going to go well.

"I was working for the Tropical Science Center in the Cloud Forest Reserve and in 1986 went on the board of the League. After the land purchasing began I started working for the League, on loan from the TSC. From the beginning I insisted that the League handle the money reserved for land purchase. I thought that the people living in Monteverde who made up the League were the ones who should be in charge of the money they were working so hard to raise. However, the TSC kept saying that there was nobody in Monteverde who could manage the processes involved in purchasing land. That ruffled a lot of feathers. In Monteverde, people were saying that the TSC wasn't managing the Reserve very well and that it could be done better by people in the community, and I agreed.

"This all came up in a meeting in San José attended by the League, the TSC and a representative of The Nature Conservancy, which was a major fundraiser. The TSC wanted to receive the funds that were coming in because they'd received monies before and felt they had the experience to do it right. And here was this upstart organization, the Monteverde Conservation League, brand-spanking new, that didn't have the experience or the contacts to be involved in extensive land purchasing. The representative from The Nature Conservancy thought that the TSC was the obvious organization to handle the money as they had a respectable history. But Bill Haber, who was representing the League, said that if the League was going to raise the money, which they'd been doing a great job of, they should administer it.

"As it was, Bill had reason to question the TSC's ability to handle funds properly, which he stated at the meeting. There was history between Bill and the TSC over an error in bookkeeping from an earlier study Bill had worked on. I'd been directly involved so I knew that Bill's questioning was justified. This kind of error had happened with others as well. When the mistakes were proven to be their own, the TSC should've apologized to the individuals they had challenged.

"Following the meeting, the board of the League decided to continue raising funds and making land purchases, working independently of the Tropical Science Center."

The most impressive fundraising campaign was launched in 1987 at Fagerviks School, a primary school in rural Sweden. Visiting American biologist Sharon Kinsman gave a slideshow that highlighted the wonders of the rainforest and the threat of deforestation. The children were so concerned about the future of tropical forests that they decided to collect money to save rainforests by holding fundraisers such as bake sales and school plays. They initially were able to support the purchase of six hectares. But they didn't stop there. They continued raising money and inspired other children throughout Sweden to fundraise as well. The Swedish government then agreed to match the monies raised by the students. In the first year the school children of Sweden raised $100,000. Eha Kern, the teacher at Fagerviks School, and her husband Bernd formed the nonprofit organization Barnens Regnskog (Children's

Rainforest) to receive the donations and transfer them to the Monteverde Conservation League. Between 1988 and 1992, $2,000,000 was sent from Sweden to Monteverde. The funds were used for the League's extended Peñas Blancas Campaign, first for the targeted lands and then for additional pieces.

Organizations began forming in countries around the world to raise funds to help protect rainforests. In 1987 Sharon Kinsmen returned from her inspirational trip to Sweden and formed The Children's Rainforest U.S. A year later Bruce Calhoun began Save the Rainforest, a teacher-student organization based in Wisconsin dedicated to rainforest conservation. In England, Tina Jolliffe founded Children's Tropical Forests U.K., which, before her death from cancer in 1992, raised $160,000. These organizations as well as others in Canada, the United States, Japan and Germany started working together as the International Children's Rainforest Network and have contributed greatly to the protection of tropical forests in Belize, Panama, Ecuador, Thailand and, of course, Costa Rica.

In 1988 Bill Haber arranged for the League to be included in Costa Rica's first debt-for-nature swap. It is a sad fact that developing nations are burdened by spiraling foreign debt. Environmental degradation results when countries, in an attempt to lower their debt, exploit their natural resources. At the same time conservation and protection programs are either nonexistent or lose any financing that had once been available. The debt-for-nature swap allows conservation groups such as The Nature Conservancy and World Wildlife Fund to assume part of the debt of a developing country. They purchase the debt from the creditor bank, which quite often has a low expectation that the debtor will ever repay its loan and is willing to sell it on the secondary-debt market at a discount. The debt is reduced in value and converted into local currency that is held by a commercial bank in the debtor country. According to the agreement, the money is to be used to finance local conservation activities and environmental protection programs. The biological diversity of many countries has benefited from this system since its first appearance in 1984 in Bolivia. The debt-for-nature swap brought more than $200,000 to the Monteverde Conservation League over a five-year period.

Adrian Forsyth is a well-known Canadian biologist and the author of several natural history books, including *Tropical Nature* and *Portraits of the Rainforest* which features the photographs of Patricia and Michael Fogden. In 1978 he received his PhD in tropical ecology from Harvard University, having done his field research in Costa Rica. Dr. Forsyth first visited Monteverde in the 1970s and had a home there for many years. Although he started his career as a scientist and academic interested in studying biology, he has devoted thirty years to working with conservation organizations with an emphasis on protecting rainforests. He was instrumental in getting significant funding through the Canadian International Development Agency and the World Wildlife Fund Canada for reforestation, environmental education and sustainable development projects in Monteverde.

The Monteverde Conservation League used the generous donations that came in from around the world to purchase properties throughout the Peñas Blancas valley. In 1988 the League named this protected area Bosque Eterno de los Niños (BEN), which means the Children's Eternal Rain Forest. This name was given in honor of the 554 hectares of land the Quakers set aside in 1951 and the great contribution made by children worldwide. As funds were received by the League they continued to purchase lands bordering the Cloud Forest Reserve and Arenal Volcano National Park, which was established by the government in 1991. By 1998 BEN encompassed 18,000 hectares, making it the largest private reserve in Central America. It harbors both primary and secondary forest, valleys and mountain ridges, and spring-fed streams that flow into rivers that drain both the Atlantic and Pacific slopes of the Tilarán Mountains. Over fifty percent of the vertebrate species in Costa Rica are found within BEN's borders, including sixty species of amphibians, 100 species of reptiles, over 400 bird species and 120 kinds of mammals. The Children's Eternal Rain Forest is the result of the hard work of thousands of children and adults throughout the world, many who have never had the opportunity to experience its immense biodiversity and natural splendor.

"Thanks to all the incredibly successful fundraising, the League was able to purchase not only land in Peñas Blancas, but properties near Arenal Volcano and as far south as the San Ramón Forest Reserve. The purchase committee, which consisted of Giovanni Bello, Bob Law and me, did our job in our own way, negotiating for the League directly with the landowners. We made the arrangements, took the measurements of the various tracts and conducted the transactions. I knew the value of the work the homesteaders had put into their land, the years of clearing and the labor involved in improving their properties, even though we were no longer considering these things 'improvements.' The fact is that the League paid more for land with clearings and buildings than for forested land, though primary and secondary forest was what we held most valuable and wanted to protect. It worked very well as we knew the people in Peñas Blancas and we offered them some value for their hard work. It was a different story as we moved into purchasing land beyond Peñas Blancas where we didn't know the landowners. We were then dealing with squatters and land speculators who perhaps had a different relationship with the land. They sometimes misrepresented their property lines and could be difficult to deal with.

"Property lines were well established in a few of the claims, but by and large the boundaries were pointed out to us with a wave of the hand. What we needed to do was find the *colindantes,* the people whose property we were purchasing and their neighbors. One of the handicaps we had was that many of the pieces were held by absentee owners who'd abandoned their trails and property lines. In a few cases where we thought we'd bought a piece of land, we had to pay for it twice because properties were overlapping and there would be two owners claiming one piece of land. Some of the mistakes we made were made legitimately, others through carelessness.

"It was a job that took a whole lot of hours in the woods, a whole lot of patience and a whole lot of confidence from the people we were dealing with. It also took having faith in what these people were telling us. When the confidence and faith broke down, that's when problems arose, but at the same time that's all we had to go on. If the landowners hadn't believed in what we were doing and worked cooperatively with us, we never would've purchased what we did. It turned out to be twice as much land as we'd originally anticipated acquiring and it all happened in a very short period of time.

"I couldn't have been involved if I hadn't believed that the people we were dealing with were honest. I worked hard at convincing landowners that the best thing to do was to keep the forest for future generations, that they could take the money for their farm and woods and reinvest it elsewhere for their family's future. We were also fulfilling the government's decree to protect the forest by putting it in the hands of conservation organizations.

"Through the nineties the Tropical Science Center continued putting pressure on the League to transfer the legal ownership of the land purchased during the Peñas Blancas Campaign. This was a significant amount of land. But it didn't work out between the League and the Tropical Science Centre. The League was still negotiating the transfer of land, but we wanted certain conditions of management met. The TSC wasn't willing to accept any conditions so the land transfer never happened.

"In 1998 I was informed by the TSC that they planned to instigate legal action against the League. After the ten years of futile negotiations that had already occurred, their lawsuit would drag on for four more years. I felt trapped in the middle. When they decided to go to court I wrote a letter to both organizations, the TSC and the League, expressing my deep concerns. My Quaker beliefs dictate that conflicts should be resolved through consensus. I didn't believe that suing each other was the way to solve the problem. I realized that we would face a long, hard negotiation – there'd already been many meetings where the two sides had attempted to reach an agreement – but I had to proceed with my faith that the right solution could be found by working together with goodwill, both parties working towards a mutually acceptable solution. I stated that I wouldn't voluntarily give testimony in court. Subsequently, I wasn't asked for my opinion.

"To the credit of everyone involved the conflict was finally resolved in 2001. The TSC withdrew its lawsuit and the League retained ownership of its land purchases in Peñas Blancas. Now the TSC is only responsible for the lands they originally acquired, amounting to 5,180 hectares. The other 5,300 hectares that the League bought in the Peñas Blancas Campaign and that the Reserve managed through the 1990s was returned to the care of the League. The Children's Eternal Rain Forest now encompasses 22,000 hectares. So the League and the Reserve are at each other's back door. These days these same organizations are working to develop a management plan they can carry out together for the future of the protected forests.

"Except for helping with the land purchasing, I wasn't directly involved with the League's program. I did, however, lead many volunteers and visitors on long walks through the tropical tangle where reforestation wasn't necessary. I conducted my own natural history program with anyone who was willing to follow along and share a cup of coffee with me beside the trail.

"I have time alone by the river now and it gives me a chance to reflect on just how much it meant for me to spend time with Bruce Calhoun, our friend in charge of Save the Rainforest. I enjoyed hearing his dreams for saving the tropical rainforest, to bring children here on hikes so they could get to know this forest for themselves. It was a privilege hiking with him and talking about our mutual interest in and appreciation of the rainforest. We had a beautiful day where we really saw it all. It was relaxing to me just to have his fellowship and to share in his enthusiasm.

"The birds are beginning to crank up pretty good, but not like they will in nesting season. By that standard it's really pretty quiet. I can hear a few wrens and a flycatcher, the old standbys. While out walking yesterday one of the men found some fresh tracks, made since the last rain, probably early yesterday morning. A mountain lion had been up and down the trails, following a herd of peccaries that was feeding near the banana patch at Rojas'. In any event, it's nice to know that at least some of my four-legged friends are still here.

"I got to see a snake but it didn't make history because it wasn't poisonous. It was a juvenile black triangle-backed snake, bright and shiny out there on the trail. They look like they've been touched up with a little bit of black shoe polish. It's the only one I've seen on the trail since this morning, though I imagine that two or three of the good kind saw me but I managed to skip by them."

Fermín Arguedas, who grew up in Monteverde and observed with great interest the changes occurring in the area, explains how the local community was affected by the new ideas that were being introduced.

"Bit by bit, people here started to realize what conservation was about, although some people probably still don't get it. I think it was when *La Liga* helped us plant trees that we began as a community to understand what was going on and that the idea of conservation was good. It was a very convincing program. On my farm it's very windy. I have a woodshop and I had to keep the roof tied down by cables so that the wind wouldn't lift it off. I planted many trees. Now that we're much more sheltered, we have a garden and we aren't directly hit by nearly as much wind.

"The trees also protect the spring on my land. In this area there are several rivers that had a lot of water when I was young. Now only the Guacimal River, the one that comes from where the forest hasn't been cut, only this river has water through the dry season. The others dry out. It helped to convince me that saving trees was better than cutting them.

"We soon saw that the tourists came. There were paths through the forest and beautiful mature trees to see along those paths. Thousands of people have come to see the trees. If we'd cut them, we may have had a new house, but we wouldn't have had those trees. You can sell that tree a thousand times as long as you don't cut it down."

On the eastern end of the Peñas Blancas valley, where the river says adios to the Children's Eternal Rain Forest, Laguna Poco Sol was being developed in the early 1980s. It then traded hands and the new owners brought in 100 head of cattle. They cut down trees and built a small, roofed corral that they stacked full of lumber. By the mid-eighties the cutting had stopped and the cattle were gone. Wolf often visited Poco Sol on his treks through Peñas and never stopped dreaming about what a bit of creative thinking and committed work could mean to this jungle oasis that had always enchanted him. In 1989 Wolf entered into an affair over Poco Sol that would test his credibility, his marriage and his reputation.

"My interest in Laguna Poco Sol grew each time I went by. All my life I would've loved one hectare of land for a cottage by a lake such as this. The property was 300 hectares, with the *laguna* and three waterfalls. There were hot sulfur mud pots on the land as well, which we call *volcancillos*.

"One perfect night at Poco Sol I bedded down atop a stack of lumber, the fragrance of *cedro amargo* lulling me to sleep. When I awoke in the morning the uniqueness of the place and the possibilities for its future became crystal clear. I had a dream that Poco Sol could be a small, well-managed site that would be attractive to local people for weekend picnicking.

"I never expected to be involved in the development of Poco Sol, but I kind of started promoting my dream nonetheless. I had the idea that the Corrales family, which had sold its property in Peñas to the League for a substantial amount of money, might be really interested in purchasing the land. The family was generally supportive of protecting the forest. As a result of my persuasion, Carmelo Corrales made a deal with the owners of Poco Sol for the very reasonable price of about U.S. $50,000.

"On the day in 1989 that Carmelo went with the owner to get a purchasing agreement, I went with them. When they made out the document, I said that I'd be a co-signer. A couple of months later I got word that Carmelo was behind in making the first payment. Not wanting to see the whole deal collapse, I borrowed the necessary money and made the payment. From then on I became deeply involved and took the responsibility of seeing that the payments were made.

"Well, everybody who knew about this thought I'd lost it. I could lose my own farm. Yet I still believed in my dream. I didn't want to see the deal fall through, believing that the future held good things. More and more it looked like the San Miguel community was interested in putting a vehicle bridge across the river that would've provided a safer crossing for horses and cows, and the bridge would have also made Poco Sol more accessible and brought more people into the area. That's when Chico Reyes, a land surveyor who was doing work for the League, got involved. He became a partner when he saw what my obligation was and realized that this was an opportunity to make some money out of an investment. Since Carmelo wasn't honoring the purchase agreement, Chico and I worked together to keep the deal alive and keep the owner from foreclosing the contract.

"I just wanted somebody to take over the property, however they might develop it. The Monteverde Conservation League was now purchasing properties near Poco Sol as they were establishing the Children's Eternal Rain Forest in the Peñas valley. My own dream of a small recreational development for Costa Rican families wasn't shared by my partners, who wanted to make money off of the property. Nor was it shared by the League, which started to think about developing a research center there. But I was in well over my head and had few options.

"Jim Crisp, who was the director of the League from 1988 to 1991, knew the mess I was in. He pushed to have the League buy the land. I was a board member and a seller and therefore on both sides of the fence. The value of the property had increased and my partners wanted to get the most they could for it. I tried to stay out of the negotiations but now found myself actually making money on it.

"I get very upset over the whole idea of speculation on property. It goes against the grain of what I was taught and what I believe in concerning land. Land is something that you never own. It's something to be handed down to future generations that should continue to make the best use of it. The idea is, if you don't really 'own' the land, you must be very careful about how you use it. You don't try to make an exaggerated profit when selling to another person. And here I was, making a substantial profit on this land and going against my own beliefs. I was appalled to have been partners with two businessmen who I normally would have been highly critical of and out of agreement with.

"Negotiating the purchase of Laguna Poco Sol made it harder for the League. It was purchasing an adjoining farm and the land prices were being affected. As word got out to the local community, people from Santa Elena publicly objected to the League's involvement in this deal. There was a suggestion that the government investigate what the League was doing with the money. I had to make a special report to the Tropical Science Center, of which I was still an employee. I was in no way supposed to be involved in land dealing.

"In September of 1991 Laguna Poco Sol became part of the League's holdings. I was very happy the day the League bought it, but for many years it was hard for me to go past there without feeling sad that it hadn't become the picnic area that I'd dreamt about.

"Back in 1989 I bought a dugout boat made from Guanacaste wood that I would've liked to see in the *laguna*. Well, it made it to the lake's shores, but by the time it was there the boat was falling apart and hardly usable. After buying the land the League decided that they didn't want any boats there that could be misused. The man who sold me the boat came to my house one day to collect the last payment I owed him but I wasn't there. That was when Lucky found out that not only had I bought the dugout, I'd invested in the Poco Sol property. She had a really hard time with that and never wanted to go to Poco Sol. However, in 1998, along with our son Tonio and his wife Adair, Lucky and I hiked through Peñas to Poco Sol and she finally saw what had inspired my passion and involvement in that risky business.

"In Costa Rica, water is considered public property and legally it must be accessible. The *laguna* should be available for use by the people who live in the area and don't have their own lake or the means to go to a beach. The local people don't have a place like Poco Sol to go to for family weekends, the way it was when I first went there.

"The League built a field station at Poco Sol that's used by local and foreign student groups, albeit not often enough. I still have faith that the League will make this a really attractive place not only for the children of Costa Rica but for children from across the ocean and up-country, that is, in North America. And I wouldn't mind if some day I'm an old person floating around the *laguna* in a little old dugout, telling tales to anyone who will listen. But I don't really need any of that as long as people can stroll through Poco Sol and take a refreshing dip after a long, hot hike and just enjoy the cool water. After all, the lake is there doing 100 percent of its job by providing a wet habitat to help maintain the balance of nature."

To the northwest of Peñas Blancas, in the Caño Negro watershed that drains into Lake Arenal, sat the tiny pioneering community of San Gerardo Arriba. In the 1950s subsistence farmers hoped to make a living there and cleared land to raise crops and livestock. In 1977, with the creation of the Arenal Forest Reserve, the restrictions on cutting down trees and developing homesteads pushed the fledgling community of San Gerardo into conflict with the government. Despite their promises of compensation, the government didn't buy out the landowners or help them develop a road or encourage milk production in the area. In 1991, with the funds from their first debt-for-nature swap, the Monteverde Conservation League bought most of the land, about 1,500 hectares, from the people who wanted to leave, although some families chose to stay. San Gerardo has had its forests protected ever since, but the dream of the original homesteaders to create a sustainable community supported by tourism and student visitors was never realized.

"San Gerardo was another area where the League had a lot of influence. I wasn't involved directly except that this was a time when I was patrolling a lot. When the League started purchasing land in San Gerardo, it bought from the families that really wanted to sell, and for those who wanted to stay the League tried to work out a way they could make a living. The group that had been doing sustainable farming had had several years of the government telling them what they could and couldn't do. So they met with the League to say that they wanted to stay as a community, they wanted to produce a livelihood, and not to sell.

"They had been promised by the government that they would get a better road. There was also a plan to construct three buildings – an interpretive center, a research laboratory and a dormitory and reception area. This was going to be a real attraction for student and tourist groups. But it wasn't until the League stepped in and created a master plan for San Gerardo that things started happening. There were a lot of big *cedro* logs that had already been felled, these being a kind that don't deteriorate quickly and can last many years. They used the logs to build a field station. Then the Swedish International Development Agency provided funds to purchase and install a water-powered electrical generator.

"The beauty of that area is that you look right out at the Arenal Volcano and Lake Arenal. You can walk straight down Rio Caño Negro to the lake. It's also an area with heavier rainfall than on the Pacific slope and this creates a lush rainforest with different species represented. It made sense to put a field station there. They opened the station to groups in 1994. By 1995 only a few of the original homesteaders were left. Their road had never been improved and they were without a school. It was very hard for the people to stay. The field station is the only building that was completed and it receives visitors who are willing to walk in to it. From the parking lot at the Santa Elena Reserve it's an easy hike of about an hour down the old rough road and another half hour on a trail through the woods. Now many student groups use this bunkhouse in the wilderness while doing research in the area. The hopes of a sustainable community have faded, but fortunately people still come to San Gerardo to enjoy the peace of the area, the incredible views and the forest."

The Monteverde Conservation League also purchased properties on the Pacific side of the Continental Divide. There is a twenty-nine-hectare piece nestled on a cliff edge in Monteverde called Bajo del Tigre, which is actually part of BEN. This is a transition zone between premontane wet forest and premontane moist forest. At an elevation that receives less precipitation than other forest reserves in the area, it protects a very different habitat. Much of this type of forest has disappeared, cut for coffee plantations and urban development, but in Bajo del Tigre the trails lead visitors through the remaining woods to vistas of beautiful sunsets over the Pacific.

The League also bought parcels of land that protect forests above and beyond San Luis, the tiny farming community that sits in the valley to the southwest of Monteverde. Since the 1980s the League has worked cooperatively with El Buen Amigo, a community association in San Luis, helping the group to achieve sustainable means of development as the village population increases.

"There's a lot of forest at the headwaters of the San Luis River. The river flows out of the mountain high up near Brilliante and heads towards the Pacific. On its way it tumbles over the cliff edge in a spectacular waterfall. It's real pretty and it's real important to have the whole area protected. Both the Cloud Forest Reserve and the Conservation League protect parts of the forests above San Luis.

"I've always had a positive relationship with our neighbors from below, the Leitóns. I learned a lot about the forest and the animals they hunted as well as the history of the area from Miguel Leitón and his father Rafael. They've been good neighbors, interested in the projects we were promoting and the idea of conservation. They got away from hunting and went to protecting the forest instead. Around 1994 or so they stopped going into the Brilliante area to cut palm trees for *palmito,* and that's well worth remarking on. Sadly, Don Miguel passed away in May of 2006. He will be missed by his family and neighbors but also by his many friends at the Conservation League, including me.

"I've often sat on the hill overlooking San Luis, with one eye on the sunset and the other eye out over the Gulf of Nicoya. The change of land use down in the valley is noticeable by the fact that you see pastures that instead of being grazed off are growing fine even at the height of the dry season. You know they haven't had cattle on it for quite a while. You can still see where people are burning their fields. The farmers do this to eliminate the weeds and clear off the land that they're going to plant. There are burns each year and they often go right up to the borderline of the Reserve. But it's not a good practice to burn off the vegetation that holds the soil in place, and it has an adverse effect on the watershed in the area. There've been lots of landslides here over the years. But even those scars heal over and become green again. For the forest to recoup takes a while and it eventually does, but it will never be the same as the original forest."

In 1991 the Costa Rican government divided the entire country into eleven conservation areas. In this progressive planning scheme all land, be it urban, rural or forested, is afforded some level of environmental protection. The various land uses are integrated in the planning process for each conservation area. The intention is to achieve sustainable development in all sectors with an emphasis on conservation. The Arenal Tilarán Conservation Area, covering over 800,000 hectares, stretches from the town of San Ramón in the southeast to Miramar in the southwest to Tilarán in the northwest. Within its boundaries are the Monteverde Cloud Forest Reserve, the Children's Eternal Rain Forest, the Santa Elena Reserve, Arenal Volcano National Park, Tenorio Volcano National Park and several other private reserves and buffer zones. Over 60,000 hectares of land in the Arenal-Monteverde Protected Zone are now benefiting from a high level of protection.

"One day in 1994 I emerged onto a ridge with a super view of the Arenal Volcano some eight kilometers away, as those with wings travel, or fourteen kilometers, as those without wings travel. The volcano looked its majestic self, but it was those dozens of forested wrinkles between us that impressed me. At that moment the realization hit me that this scene, with all of the forest I could see as I turned full circle, was now owned and managed by public and private organizations that have preservation as their number-one commitment.

"When first the Reserve and then the League got going, it was easy to say, 'let's put these areas, Brilliante, El Valle and now Peñas Blancas, in the bank, and maybe the next generation will really know how to manage it.' If there's a better way of using and developing the land, fine. In the meantime, we'll protect it and see what we come out with. I think most people we dealt with accepted that this was the best way to go. Perhaps the easiest part of securing the long-range protection of the forest was convincing people of the importance of protecting our water supplies, as well as the positive climatic effects that come from leaving the forest uncut.

"Reforestation has been very successful. The League has been very effective at helping small farmers get a better gross income off their land without having to clear more forest. Pastures retain their nutrients when windbreaks are planted, which minimizes wind erosion and moisture loss. The cattle started producing more milk the minute they were protected by shade trees. For many years the League had a *vivero* in Monteverde that provided native tree species that were planted throughout the area. Now there are other organizations doing reforestation.

"The League has done a lot of work at the east end of the Peñas Blancas valley, in San José de La Tigra. It's had an office over there since 1990. Originally, the majority of squatter invasions and poaching violations in the forest came from that side and so teaching environmental education in those communities was very necessary. The League's reforestation program has also been really effective there. In Monteverde, there have always been a lot of conservation-minded people who know about environmental issues, so the challenge has been to explain conservation to the wider community. Though the League has been administered from Monteverde, a lot of its best work has been done over on the San Carlos side.

"Although the big focus was on land purchase in the beginning, it's been clear over the years that our organizations have different philosophies. The main emphasis of the Monteverde Cloud Forest Reserve has been to improve the trails and upgrade the facilities for eco-tourism. The Monteverde Conservation League has always emphasized reforestation and environmental education. It's now harder for both organizations to raise the money they need to support their activities, which take a lot of management. The competition for donated dollars is great worldwide. On a local level, reforestation and environmental education is much more important than another tourist facility. A big part of the joint responsibility of these organizations is to protect the area's natural resources from the rifles and chainsaws. That's been my role in this game since the beginning."

NINE

Lighting the way

"It's good to be patrolling. Sometimes you bump into people who wonder how long it is to the next turnoff or who are looking for that 7/11... my young friend Richard Butgereit and I were thinking of building one here on the Continental Divide. It's good to be able to keep people's morale up by telling them that at least they're still in Costa Rica. Actually, being a forest ranger here is no different from being one anywhere else, you just mix the facts with the fiction and the fiction with the facts and keep people on the trail and moving forward. That's the main thing." *Wolf patrolling the Continental Divide*

The day after I returned home from Costa Rica in May of 1996 my family was struck by dreadful news. My seventy-four year old father, who had always appeared healthy and strong, was told he had metastasized cancer and the prognosis was very poor. Dad decided that he didn't want to suffer for long and so he readied himself for a quick death. After making sure his affairs were in order he stopped eating and within a few days he passed away peacefully with my mother, my sister Maggie and me by his bed. We were at his funeral before we had come to grips with his illness. A simple proud man, Andy Chornook died with the same dignity with which he had lived. Though he could barely talk, he managed to convey through gestures his final wish and so, at his insistence, Maggie tenderly shaved his still handsome face on the morning of what would be his last day on earth.

My father's Ukrainian blood explains my round, olive-skinned appearance, although it was my mother's independent, strong spirit that stoked my personality. There have been many times in my life that I have wondered at the irony that this quiet, conservative, well-groomed man could produce such an outspoken, liberal, somewhat disheveled daughter. As I have aged and seen more of the world around me, I have come to understand the true value of my dad's gentle nature. I grew up in a home festooned with laughter, much of it his. Dad let me speak my mind even when he didn't understand or agree with my ideas. Most importantly, my sister and I had the freedom to choose our own paths, encouraged, not restrained, by our mild-mannered father.

Wolf has been both father and mother to the Cloud Forest Reserve: advisor, defender, caretaker and protector. From the start he assumed the role of forest guard, patrolling the expansive area, watching for signs of the illegal activities such as hunting and tree poaching that threatened the well-being of the woods and its inhabitants. Traditionally, the killing of game was a popular activity that augmented the protein in the diets of local families. Although it is not as commonplace as it was, today's guards still encounter *cazadores*. The Reserve has multiple access points, making it extremely difficult to keep out hunters who are determined to exploit its resources. They know the forest like taxi drivers know city streets, and though they leave signs of their passing, it is hard to catch them.

The harvesting of *palmito* destroys the whole palm tree and is now illegal, but old habits die hard. These days, the hearts of palm bought in grocery stores come from commercial plantations, but some men still cut palm trees as their fathers and grandfathers did before them. Squatters take down trees and set property lines, and if they manage to establish a claim, they must be reimbursed for the "improvements" they have made. Poachers also cut trees to provide lumber for their own buildings or to sell. This activity is now more common along the boundaries of the Reserve where removal of the timber is easier. It is impossible for the guards to control access all around the borders of the protected areas and much easier for poachers to cut and run along the edges of the forest than deep in its depths.

One of the biggest challenges to biological diversity in the country is loss of habitat due to deforestation outside of the protected zones. The protected area then becomes an island, disconnected from other patches of forest by a sea of clear-cut pastures and development. It is increasingly difficult for species to migrate between their isolated habitats in search of nesting sites and food sources.

As Wolf's awareness of these threats grew, so did his commitment to the protection of the area's flora and fauna. For the Reserve's first fifteen years, along with his other responsibilities, Wolf held the position of Head of Vigilance. It was a role he assumed quite naturally since he already spent most of his time in the forest, cutting and following the boundary lines and trails.

"Back in the early 1970s I got myself a government-issued photo ID card that proved I was an honorary forest guard. Anyone could get one, even non-Costa Ricans. The card didn't mean much, but it did give you a little weight as well as free hospitality if you showed it at other guard stations in the country. You didn't need any training to get your card, and it didn't give you any authority, other than being able to file a *denuncia* against people caught breaking forestry or wildlife laws.

"The Tropical Science Centre wasn't interested in giving me formal training as a forest guard, but I realized that I had to learn better methods of dealing with the people who threatened our reserve. Basically I needed to practice good public relations as I often had to reprimand neighbors who were breaking the laws. Many of these people were homesteaders in Peñas Blancas, just like me, and I considered most of them my friends. For the first fifteen years or so, before the forest guards started to receive appropriate training, it was my Quaker upbringing that guided me in my dealings with whatever situation I was confronted with. I always proceeded with the belief that God is in every person, and I approached everyone in a nonviolent manner. I was always certain of how I should act even though I never knew how the other man might react."

Wolf lobbied his bosses at the Tropical Science Center for more forest guards and better training for them. In 1986, following the creation of the Monteverde Conservation League, when a lot more land was added to the overall protected area, there was an increased demand for forest guards. In 1987 Wolf was hired by the League to work on the land-purchase campaign and he continued to patrol the boundary lines that marked the Cloud Forest Reserve as well as the properties that the League was purchasing. The Reserve kept him on the payroll so he could still receive his insurance benefits. As more guards were hired by both organizations, there was often confusion regarding the guards' role and territory. Aware of the importance of what they were doing, Wolf continued to petition for a better system of patrolling.

"In 1987 José Luis Cambronero became the first full-time guard hired by the League. We patrolled together and I enjoyed working with this young man. At around that time Omar Coto was working for the government to coordinate the efforts of the local conservation organizations. He put the push behind getting a proper job description and training program for our guards. By 1990 the League had four other guards besides me patrolling, two out of Santa Elena and two from San José de La Tigra in San Carlos. In July of 1991 Omar became Executive Director of the League as well as Director of Protection. He continued to work towards a better forest guard system. I worked with Omar for years supervising and training the forest guards.

"The League rented a house in Santa Elena as a base for the guards. The house also served as a location where people could apply for tree-cutting permits, eliminating the need to travel several hours to apply directly to the forestry office. This reflected positively on the protection system and aided in building good relations between the guards and the community of Santa Elena.

"I always thought that one organization should be responsible for the protection of the total area and that the organizations benefiting from the guards should share the administration costs and other expenses such as uniforms and equipment. William Aspinall, who was the Reserve's director after 1988, proposed a different system that would divide the patrolling areas and make each organization responsible for their own guards' patrolling schedule and expenses. He designated that the guards hired by the Reserve would be responsible only for the land within the boundaries of the Reserve, and that the guards hired by the League would only patrol in areas purchased by the League. I accepted this system because it was designed to cover the whole area and provided for more guards. As long as the protection was adequate, I was satisfied.

"In 1991 Arenal Volcano National Park was decreed by the government. It was situated on the northern border of the Children's Eternal Rain Forest. There were four guards working within the park. That same year the Arenal Tilarán Conservation Area was created and there were more guards hired by the government. They had an office in Tilarán which gave us more support here in Monteverde. We had a lot of contact with them and they helped us in our own protection work. A government regulation allowed for the sharing of costs between govern-

n't be able to afford any protection facilities other than at the main entrance if it weren't for the agreements made with the government. It allows guards to patrol in the furthest corners of the Reserve."

·   The forest guards have other important roles beyond tracking hunters and poachers. They are constant observers of the environment and have been known to help find and collect plants as well as supply valuable information to scientists and researchers. They also report on the state of the paths and the forest in general, such as providing details about the location of landslides or fallen trees that have obscured the trail. The guard administrator at the League facilitates the paperwork for farmers who require a tree-cutting permit. Before this system was in place the process of getting a permit was difficult and tended to be avoided, meaning that trees were often cut illegally. Through the League it is easier to get a permit and more people adhere to the law when cutting trees on their land.

Most of the guards are from the communities and farms in the area and often the violators they are dealing with are family and friends. Many of the guards were once hunters themselves, as were the majority of local men. Once a local man assumes this new role, his neighbors may resent his anti-hunting attitude as well as the power that comes with his new position. One guard was eventually fired for hunting, an activity that demonstrated his lack of understanding concerning his role as a forest guard. A guard's belief in the protection of the forest must be well-developed and sincere since he will be held to a higher standard, questioned about the validity of the laws and considered responsible for restricting other people's activities.

"A retired nurse once told me that when they had a problem in the hospital, they'd look for the weakest link in the chain. That's where it's going to break. If you want to make a better organization, you look at your administration and at each of your departments and when you find the weakest link you strengthen it. It isn't enough to keep strengthening the strongest links. If the weakest link is in the area of protection, then keep training the guards and supporting them by making sure they have the equipment they need. Another way to support them is by training them in public education. When a guard meets up with somebody who is doing something illegal, he has to focus on good public relations even as he's being firm. The number-one skill for a guard is how to deal with conflict.

"You never know what you might run into while on patrol. The most violent resistance I've ever experienced occurred up near the towers on Cerro Amigos. I was with a new guard and we'd come across some men, brothers from Santa Elena, who had a bag full of palm hearts. I asked them for the palm hearts, which we had the legal obligation to do. One of the brothers drew back to slug the young guard, who dodged his fist by dropping to the ground. Then the aggressor drew his pocketknife. Fortunately, the other brother was a friend of mine and he managed to diffuse the situation. But they had machetes and things could've gotten ugly. We weren't going to be violent ourselves and that's how we managed to avoid a fight. The men left and we picked up the radio and tried to call Omar, who was at the League office. The brothers disconnected the radio at the repeater tower before Omar could answer. We decided not to pursue the men and left. It turned out that Omar did hear our call and came up to deal with the fellows, but by then we weren't around to be witnesses.

"When we confronted hunters, they sometimes said that the meat they were carrying was beef from their own domestic animals. With no witnesses, there was nothing we could do. One time I had word that hunters had gone into Peñas Blancas, so I drove my old Land Rover to block the trail leading from Peñas through the Reserve. The hunters came out on horseback and I was waiting for them. I told them that I was going to confiscate their meat, but I was alone and all I could do was talk to them. They wouldn't let me open their saddlebags, so I drove to Santa Elena and contacted the local policeman and the government forest guard. The guard came with me and we managed to head the hunters off before they got as far as Cerro Plano. We went through the hunters' bags, but of course they'd gotten rid of the meat. At least they knew that we could stop them and had the authority to search them.

"I still have the tusk of a male peccary that was given to me by a famous hunter from Peñas Blancas. He lost his best dog to that peccary along with his enthusiasm to keep hunting. Dogs were worth a lot of money to the hunters. Forest guards could confiscate them and send them to a compound in Heredia. The hunters resented having to go all the way to the city to retrieve their dogs, and they didn't like paying the fine any better. If a guard tried to take away a hunter's dog, it could cause real trouble. This sometimes resulted in the guards being threatened with guns.

"It was a matter of whether the hunters had respect for the guards and the law or not. The hunters knew who I was and where I worked and what laws I was upholding. All in all, I had few serious confrontations. The first reason for that, I think, is that we all tended to know each other. The other reason was that I refused to deal with people when they were drunk or irrational. I'd walk away, knowing I could file a *denuncia* later.

"The guards are also there to help people who are lost or hurt. I've participated in many search parties. In 1994 I spent a whole night looking for a group of twelve that had gone far out into the forest in the daytime and didn't get back before dark. They overestimated their ability to return in good time to the field station. It was a group of Costa Ricans, high school teachers and kids along with some mothers with two small children. They should never have tried to go so far, way past the *refugio* at El Valle. They didn't realize that they couldn't return as fast as they went, tired as the children were. If a mirage in the desert is seeing water where there isn't any, a mirage in the mountains is looking at that ridge across the way and thinking that it's nearer than it is. The closer you get to it, the farther away it looks, and probably is. It's easy to underestimate how far the distance is.

"Well, I went out in the morning and found them at the shelter. Hopefully, we all learned a few tricks from that. As we had more people going further into the forest and staying in the shelters, we wrote a guideline on how to conduct a search. Of course, the next time it'll be something different."

Eladio Cruz, Wolf's friend and partner in his Peñas Blancas adventures, describes Wolf as "the guard dog of the forest." The image is appropriate, though perhaps Wolf is more border collie than pit bull. In the beginning there were few rules of conduct laid out for him to follow. Instead, he was guided by his Quaker beliefs and his ability to listen to and respect the ideas of others even when they differed from his own. It was Wolf's lifelong belief in nonviolence and conflict resolution that set the tone of the forest patrols in the protected zones around Monteverde. Although the Reserve and the League have similar but not identical ideas about the primary role of their guards – at the Reserve the guards are to protect against threats to the land while at the League, which is more involved in education, their job is also to explain forestry and hunting laws and the benefits of conservation – there is one area where they are in complete agreement.

"It was the Tropical Science Center's and the League's joint policy that the guards couldn't carry guns. It was important to minimize confrontations, not increase them. Our only weapon was the ability to file *denuncias* against illegal activities. Our little plastic identification card was all that stood between us and the characters we were confronting.

"I remember a two-day intensive course for Reserve and League guards as well as government forestry guards. A lot of them were from the National Parks system. It was a chance to ask questions and learn more about just how they patrolled and how they dealt with infringements of the law, whether from hunters or squatters or gold miners. It was very valuable information for us. The issues of carrying arms and the use of firearms were really covered. We could ask questions and deal with our feelings about that. There was a lot of support for the idea of not carrying firearms, but we also understood the necessity of having some defense on the occasions that people were violent. A guard has to be firm and react strongly when faced with people who are guilty of breaking the law at a time when they have guns and the guard doesn't. They most always outnumber you. There'd be times when the guards could assert their authority just through the knowledge that they're carrying a firearm. But that's not supported by the Reserve or the League, so our forest guards, if they want to be armed, carry their own gun and their own permit.

"I've had many years of practice dealing with people who were violently against the idea of the Reserve. You have to be very careful in every situation. In the end, it's the conduct and attitude of the guard that's important. A person shouldn't be working as a guard if he isn't truly convinced of the reason for having guards. He needs to be a person who really puts everything into the community, and is honest and uses that honesty to educate adults as well as children.

"I think that my Quaker roots have probably contributed ninety-nine percent to how I approach being a guard. Being a Quaker, in the first place, you aren't spending your weekends in a bar, destroying your rational. Plus, you have faith that the other person probably also has faith in God, and you expect to appeal to that. I want to get across to the person I'm confronting that I recognize him as a person who is equal to me, a person who wants to be fair. If I'd ever gone to war, I would have offered my hand in friendship to the enemy, not raised a gun. In that way you let him know that you're not a threat and that you respect him as a thinking, reasonable man who wants to get out of a tight spot. So that's where you start out from.

"One of the most capable people, barring none including myself, who has been involved in conservation, land purchasing and protection is Gerardo Céspedas. He has a lot of history in the community of La Tigra in San Carlos. He was on the local Red Cross team and is respected in the community for his participation in local organizations. He started working as a forest guard for the League in 1989 and became Director of Protection in 1994. He also ran the League office over in San José de la Tigra for several years. He's a person who worked hard on problems that arose on lands we'd already bought. He also had many contacts when it came to purchasing properties and a good way of negotiating that's been advantageous for the League. Gerardo is also one of the best guards we've had. He's stood up to hunters with guns and confiscated their dogs. He has his detractors yet he still manages to have a lot of support in the community.

"At the League's general assembly in February of 2005, Gerardo presented a video on behalf of the guard patrol. The video had been recorded by some of the guards as they faced hunters armed with guns and tree-cutters armed with chainsaws. It very effectively showed the confrontational aspect of being a forest guard. Gerardo showed it to the League in an attempt to get the board to give permission for the guards to carry guns. Members carried the motion by one vote to allow special units of guards to take arms when expecting a serious situation. It's now in the hands of the board to make the policy and they're still discussing how to proceed. This involves furnishing the guns, stating when they can be carried and providing proper training for their use. I still don't think that's the answer and wouldn't personally carry a gun. But I have immense respect for the guards and if they feel threatened then it must be considered. The question becomes, who is responsible when someone gets shot?

"Here is the tragic irony in this situation. A month after the assembly, on March 8, 2005, there was a hostage-taking and attempted robbery at the local bank in our little town of Santa Elena. An armed man held up to twenty-five people hostage for twenty-nine hours. Most of the people escaped at some point, but six local people and one policeman were killed and the whole community was traumatized. Gerardo Céspedas, who's faced armed adversaries for years in the forest, was shot five times while standing in line to do some banking. Miraculously, he remained alive until he was rescued after about twenty-four hours. His injuries were severe. He lost the sight in one eye and the mobility of his arms was impaired. Gerardo continues to recover but it remains to be seen how he'll be affected in the long-term.

"I feel that the life Gerardo's led, the work he's done and the fact that he survived is proof that he's in the care of a higher power. His first-aid training kept him alive when he could've bled to death. His inner strength saved him from getting a secondary infection. The prayers of his many friends supported his own strong will to live. This terrible incident illustrates completely what guns are for, which is killing and maiming people. It reiterates to me that we must seek alternatives to the use of guns when confronted with violence."

TEN

Footprints

"We have all the early morning calls. It started with the howlers and the crested guans but now the rest of the birds are cranked up, and so it's dawn. We're packed and ready to roll. We've got a good day, you can tell by the buzzing of the horseflies. Got a little view of daylight breaking over the ridge. It'll take about an hour for the sun to get up and over that. From here you can just about see it all. *Pura vida!* It's the kind of a day you should take your cue from the monkeys and climb up on a tree limb, sit back and watch the world go by." *Wolf on a June morning in the Peñas Blancas valley*

I grew up watching my mother's enchantment with the northern cardinals in our backyard. There is no question that this was her favorite bird. A proud and true Canadian, my mom appreciated that this handsome red songster, like her, didn't feel the need to head south in the cold weather. Instead, Mom spent the winter replenishing the birdfeeders, anticipating the sight of the cardinals' scarlet plumage dancing across the white snow, as vibrant as a tropical hibiscus flower adorning a sun-washed beach. She anticipated the cardinals' beautiful singsong – *pretty pretty pretty* – and never failed to smile when she heard it. Standing at the kitchen window, her hands in the dishwater, she watched the pairs of crested birds, captivated by the intimacy of the attentive male gently placing seeds into the open beak of the female.

As with the students who passed through her classroom in a lifetime of teaching, Mom felt hope for the future with the appearance in the spring of each new generation of cardinal fledglings. She lived with that same hope through months of cancer treatments following a mastectomy. She died of breast cancer in May of 1998, at the tender age of 78, exactly two years after my father's death. When friends gathered in our backyard following her funeral, the resident family of cardinals appeared in their own colorful tribute. My mom's spirit lives on in the treetops of southern Ontario, a flash of red and a sweet song marking her presence.

Birdwatchers began flocking to Monteverde in the 1970s, drawn by biologists' reports on the wealth of bird species in the surrounding area. When the idea of eco-tourism exploded on the world scene, Monteverde was one of the premier destinations. Eco-tourism developed as a means of bringing humans into wild spaces to experience firsthand the natural beauty and biodiversity that exists on our planet. The hope is that these tourists, once home, will be compelled to financially support the organizations that care for the wilderness and its inhabitants. Some people argue against bringing tourists into environmentally sensitive areas, that the impact outweighs the benefits. But as long as the visitors have money to spend, there will be parks, reserves, hotels and tour companies to welcome them. And as long as the birds and animals are there, the adventurous and inquisitive will come.

In the 1950s and 1960s, as the Quakers were working tirelessly to establish Monteverde, little thought was given to species extinction. Land was cleared to make pastures for domestic livestock without considering that it also eliminated the nesting and feeding grounds of wild creatures. After all, there was plenty for everyone, or so it seemed. George Powell understood the dangers of limitless development, and when he arrived in the community he introduced a new approach to land stewardship that included concern for the protection of natural habitats.

Along with the establishment of the Monteverde Cloud Forest Reserve came a new understanding of the role wildlife could play in the future of the community. Resplendent quetzals not only attract tourists, they pose for the cameras that record their beauty in photographs that draw in even more visitors. Tapirs laid the groundwork for many of the trails that carry people through the maze of ridges. Even the missing golden toads still manage to arouse the interest of the curious and teach by their very disappearance. On a more basic level, the nonhuman residents of this wilderness neighborhood maintain the cycle of life by pollinating flowers, dispersing seeds, scarifying the ground and taking their place in the food chain.

Many of Wolf's stories of his earliest rainforest wanderings are about hunting and eating animals. As in most places, this was the typical relationship between the people and the beasts of the area. It was acceptable to kill a mountain lion that was after your livestock and to hunt for any form of protein that could feed your family. But as the human population grew and natural habitats were destroyed for farmland, the population of wild species suffered. With the creation of the Reserve hunting was banned and eventually the forest's animals became accustomed to the presence of humans who weren't out to shoot them. Now animals are slowly returning to their old habitats and more sightings are possible. Even so, species such as jaguars and tapirs continue to be furtive and are rarely seen, though their footprints provide proof that they are surviving.

Wolf began as a dairy farmer who understood the necessity of caring for his animals to improve their production. He was also a hunter who experimented with "bagging" many different creatures to ascertain their culinary value. When he finally gave up the gun he became an astute observer who knew that the tracks he followed would lead him and others to a deeper understanding of the value of protecting species and saving habitats. One of the things he saw was the communication that passed between animals – the grunts of the peccaries and the fuss made by the monkeys as they alerted each other or voiced a warning to him. Accompanying a steady stream of biologists who arrived to study in the forest, he learned enough along the way to calculate his own theories about animal conduct. With all the years he has spent on and off the trails, it is reasonable to assume that all the Monteverde fauna know Wolf by scent and sound, if not by name.

"When we first arrived in Monteverde, we were regularly visited at our home site by coatimundis, kinkajous and monkeys. In fact, white-faced monkeys and coatis invaded the cornfields in such numbers that they left us only a sample. During that time we had the need for fresh meat to supplement our starchy diet, and with a curiosity for new dishes we sampled deer, coon, armadillo, agouti and sloth. I even tried howler monkey down in Peñas. On the fowl side were guan, wood quail, pigeon and, only once, a toucanet.

"When I purchased a piece of forested property to homestead on in Peñas in 1954 and started going there, I was assured of seeing or hearing some wild birds and animals, the most common being monkeys and armadillos as well as the guans. I often saw tracks belonging to tapirs, brocket deer, collared peccaries, mountain lions and jaguars that visited those first clearings I made where grass and bananas grew.

"The greatest reward from my energy-consuming hobby of home-steading in Peñas was my friendship with Don Ricardo González. We sometimes shared his dirt-floored *rancho,* which was the only shelter in the area. In the evenings, around a smoke-producing fire, Don Ricardo, with his chew of tobacco, would tell picturesque stories of his tapir-hunting excursions. He told me about one occasion when he and Rafael Vargas followed their dogs that were chasing a tapir up the mountain. The clouds completely closed in on them and they lost the trail of the tapir. The men couldn't see beyond their noses and realized that they were totally lost. They decided that it was very dangerous for them and that it would be wise to climb up into a tree where they would have to spend the night. At first light they came down to the ground and started looking for a way out. It took them all that day, following along the edge of a cliff, to get back home. Finally, they reached a trail they recognized. It was nightfall before they arrived home, soaking wet, miserably cold and very hungry. Don Ricardo laughed as he told me that the big joke was on them when they later realized that the area they'd been in was actually very close to his farm.

"He loved to talk about the danger of meeting *el tigre,* of cures for poisonous snake bites and of encounters with *el dueño de la montaña,* a mythical semi-human creature that frightened frontier people and their cattle at night with its humanlike screams. Sometimes I envision myself as a *dueño de la montaña* and like to startle my neighbors with my howls.

"One evening I was getting close to the shelter where my young hiking companion, Richard Butgereit, was waiting and let out one of my usual arrival calls. It startled Richard. He came to the door and said, 'You shouldn't do that because one of these days you're going to get shot when you surprise the wrong person.' Fortunately, that's never happened. I've developed these calls not only to announce my arrival but also to see if a bird or animal might answer me. And sometimes they do."

One of the tracks Wolf still follows through the rainforest is made by the largest land mammal in Costa Rica, the Baird's tapir, a relative of the horse and rhinoceros. It is one of the world's four species of tapir, all of which are on the endangered species list. Although tapirs appear cumbersome, weighing in the order of 500 pounds, they can run with great agility up and down the steep mountainsides. Their hooves are divided into four toes in the front and three in the back, allowing them easy passage through the muddy areas they frequent. Their thick, reddish-brown hide protects them from thorns and branches as they barrel through the tropical forest, and they are reputed to mow down anything in their path.

Baird's tapirs can be found in the Peñas Blancas valley and other remote areas where there has been little human disturbance. Despite their ability to move quickly when necessary, they spend their days and nights foraging slowly through the forest. Tapirs usually rest in or near freshwater pools, using them as a refuge from predators and insects. It has been observed that captive tapirs defecate while standing in water, and since their scat is usually found floating on water in the wild, biologists believe that they require it to defecate.

Wolf has been following the trails of *la danta* and watching for signs of its existence for decades. In 2005 reported sightings of a tapir roaming the dense forest that covers the cliff edge near the Guindon farm, later confirmed by an old hunter in San Luis, brought a look of pride and satisfaction to Wolf's face. The stories he tells span fifty years, and regardless of the irreverence and humor of his tales, his concern for the animal's survival is as real as its footprint.

"There's nothing more frustrating than seeing where a tapir recently was and hearing it take off in the woods to know I've just missed another tapir. If it had a long tail like a cat, I'm sure that by now I would've seen at least the tail of a tapir because I've been that close to them. I know they're real and I know they're here because they've frequently just left the spot where I'm about to be.

"In Peñas Blancas, I've had lots of experiences seeing the tracks of a tapir where it's come down out of the woods, crossed pastures and followed a stream. When we were trying to make our way back to Monteverde from Arenal through the forest the first time, I guess it was in 1976, the narrow land bridges on the ridges and between the hills were freshly used by tapirs, and this was a source of information about where to cross. We'd watch for those spots, where the trails came together to make one narrow path that crossed the head of a canyon between two hills. We still use those paths. They take you the best way, straight to the river, around the gorge, over the ridge or jumping between hills. If you're following a good old tapir trail, you can count on coming up to the top of a rise at the right place for working your way over and down the other side.

"Tapirs don't prey on human resources. They're herbivores, but they don't bother cornfields that have been developed in farm areas. They're not like jaguars or mountain lions, which are frequently killed because they're preying on cattle or suspected of interfering with a farmer's livelihood. Tapirs have a keen sense of smell and very sharp hearing, but they're very nearsighted. The original hunters said that you'd better get off the trail if a tapir is coming down because he'd come right on over you. He wouldn't dodge or turn off the trail at all.

"I've never even seen the tapir's short tail except at the zoo and once in Honduras in 1974. George Powell had a job to do for a national park in Honduras and invited me, the flunky, to go along. Of course, it was one more time that my poor wife wanted to take his tongue out. The trip depended on us getting back for my son Carlos' high school graduation. You can probably already guess how poorly that part of the plan worked out!

"So we got to Honduras and the deal was to find a guide who could lead us up the high Montaña Celaque. He'd take us to the area we needed to visit and then we'd continue on our own. We had a problem getting anyone to guide us because there was a story about people going up to this area and not coming back. There were marshes further in near a lake where there were supposed to be singing ladies who lured men in. There were fruits that floated down the stream from up there, and people believed that if they ate these fruits, they'd be lost and never return home. So people were generally afraid of going up to that area.

"Of course, George and I wanted to stay all week and see if those gals would really come out. In the meantime, we figured out what happened to the people who got lost up there. It was really cold on that mountain and they likely died of exposure. With nothing to light a fire with and probably no food or suitable clothing, lost souls would've succumbed to hypothermia. We could only hope that those ladies sang for them and then whatever happened maybe didn't hurt so much.

"The guide told us that there were tapirs in the area. He'd seen them himself. He described them as big, monstrous animals that tore through the woods, and he was sure they were quite dangerous. Well, the story goes that we were slightly off the trail, getting a drink from a stream, when the guide's dog flushed out a tapir. It loped by us in a quick flash. So, wow, we saw a tapir! It was a pretty good one to see. Little did I know that that would be the only wild tapir I'd ever have the fortune to see, and I had to go all the way to Honduras to see it.

"Closer to home, tapirs can be found in Chomogo, a swampy area in the Reserve that we call 'the hot spot.' The young are born in little valleys where there are small springs and green growth for their food source. At least, that was true in the one case I've seen where the area was all trampled up and there was evidence of a tapir having spent more than one night there. There's always the hope of seeing a tapir in a certain pool in Chomogo that has a consistent water supply in the dry season. Tapirs used to use that pool to take a dip, but now they seem to have moved out of the area and gone down near the Peñas Blancas River. Still, if we did a little more crisscrossing of the swamp we'd probably bump into at least one spot where they've passed through.

"Miguel Leitón of San Luis told me that in the early days he would go out with his father and other men to the forests now preserved in Brilliante. With their dogs, they'd chase tapirs into Peñas Blancas. When they killed one, somebody would have to go back to the community to get help to carry out the meat while the others would stay and prepare it to be taken out. Tapir was a major source of protein. It could provide a week's worth of valuable meat for a small community if you kept it smoked or salted. It was later that hunters in the backwoods would only take the liver and tongue and some of the nice, soft tenderloin. That's about all they'd take, not the thick hide that was valuable years ago for making straps or twists for the handles of horsewhips.

"Miguel Salazar was one of the main hunters at that time. He told me what it was like when hunters first began coming into the valley, that they'd frequently see as many as three or four tapirs at a time. At first they didn't hunt them very much. It was too hard to take such a large quantity of meat out, and it's a fact that tapir is a tougher brand of horsemeat. Once people got to living in Peñas, they shot them more often.

"Miguel told me that back in El Valle, they used to get a tapir about every week. He thought that in his lifetime he'd been present at the killing of as many as thirty tapirs. The Rojas', who owned property in El Valle, estimated that they'd killed as many as fifteen or more over the period of time they were clearing land out there with a crew of six or seven people. They needed to feed their workers so they definitely would have used the meat.

"A group of dogs hunting a tapir will chase it until it's backed up against a tree or bank for protection. Male tapirs may run away, but the females will plant themselves to protect their young. When they're pregnant, they're naturally not so agile and it's harder for them to get away. Once planted, a tapir will take on anything that comes at it. It can easily kill a dog or at least damage it by biting out chunks of skin and muscle, or it'll put its foot down on the dog to trap it before killing it. You stand a chance of catching a collared peccary with only one dog, but to hunt a tapir you need at least three. The dogs work together to distract the tapir, without actually attacking it and risking being killed, until the hunter can arrive.

"There's a place called *Las Calaveras* in the upper pastures of Monteverde where a trail crosses over the Quebrada Cuecha, a large rocky stream. It's a main animal crossing. There were several skulls left behind by hunters from the days when hunting was a common activity. This was a famous place where the men would take their dogs to flush out the animal they were after. Someone would be stationed at the crossing, waiting to shoot the animal when the dogs would drive it down. The first time I went up there, there were the skulls of peccaries, brocket deer and tapirs. *Las Calaveras* is a historical place on my map of Monteverde.

"It's a sad fact that our tapir population has been greatly reduced partly because of the status people got from killing them. It was a macho thing to do. The tapir is the largest of our mammals in Central and South America, so it was quite the prize to boast about.

"After 1987, once all the families in Peñas Blancas had left the area and taken their dogs and cattle with them, the tapirs moved farther down the valley. They can now range freely as far as the Peñas Blancas River. They've changed their main feeding area, but it's been a real slow change. Once or twice there have been signs that animals belonging to the highland population on the south side of the river have come down to the water. Possibly they crossed to join with the population on the other side. It's important that they do that to keep their bloodlines strong, but it's taken a long time for that to happen.

"The best near-sighting I've had was when we were surveying land in 1988. We were on a hillside to the south of the Peñas Blancas River, working our way downhill to a stream. José Luis Cambronero and I were ahead of the surveyors, hacking out a trail for them to follow. We heard *'DANTA DANTA.'* We threw our machetes down and ran to get back up the hill where the others were. By the time we got there the tapirs had disappeared. We crossed a little stream to where they'd been. The hunters in the crew told me to put my hand down to feel the warm ground where the tapirs had been lying. The odor they left was quite a bit like horse. The other workers had had a great sighting because the tapirs had run across an open landslide area right in front of them. I just missed seeing them by inches. The others wanted to go after the animals, so we stopped following our compass and instead followed the fresh tracks. We probably lost a day of surveying over that.

"The first tapir I nearly met was killed in Peñas Blancas, shot by moonlight on a *playón,* a sandy deposit on the bank of the Peñas Blancas River, by Paco Molino. It was quite a job for people to carry out the meat. I knew a lot of people who went in and brought some back. Miguel Salazar was one of them and that's the way I met that tapir. That was actually pretty good meat, tougher than beef but quite edible. I know that I've eaten tapir at least four times, but not since the land purchase days when I was often a guest of the homesteaders. I suspect that I've probably eaten twice that much, with people not admitting that that's what it was, telling me that we were eating some domestic animal.

"I guess the story about the last time I was served tapir meat, when I had the knowledge it was tapir, is very typical. There was a mentality among some people to keep on killing tapir, even knowing it was illegal, knowing that I was a forest guard and could denounce them for it, and beyond that knowing that there was a small population that needed protection. On this sad occasion I was eating what I'd been told was beef. The man finally admitted that it was tapir being served on the platter and of course went on to explain why he'd shot the animal.

"He'd gone back to the *laguna,* to where he'd been working in an area called Palmital, near Cedral. He and his boys went on a hunting expedition and they were interested in *tepezcuintle* and thought that they had one. But their dogs went off chasing something into another area. It sounded like the animal had planted, so they needed to go to protect the dogs. Sure enough, it was a tapir, which they shot and skinned out and got what meat they could carry, mainly the liver and heart and the softer meat, the *lomo.* They were in the middle of that when out came a young one, very small, still obviously nursing, so they felt sorry for it and shot it too. They gave it to the dogs to eat.

"So there you go, two generations at once. That was quite typical. This is an animal that only reproduces once every two or two and a half years. It's easy to understand how quickly we can reduce the population and how long it can take to recover, especially when starting with a less-than-normal population. Sadly, these hunters couldn't bring out all the meat, and nobody was all that anxious for tapir meat anyway, although I have to admit that it was sure good eating. I almost believed it was veal. So I helped the family understand a little bit more about the life cycle and natural history of tapirs and then they began to consider how important it was to protect them.

"It's going to take a long, long time to get back to having a healthy tapir population. It takes a big area to support tapirs, but we do have a large enough area under protection. Only with environmental education helping people realize the seriousness of killing tapirs will we see a steady increase in the population. The tapirs here are shy, nervous from having been hunted, and though they do come out to clearings, they're real leery. You can take a two- or three-hour walk through the Reserve and never see a tapir, and yet occasionally, with luck, people on two- or three-hour walks have actually seen them.

"It won't bother me a bit to not see the animal as long as I frequently see the tracks of their young. Then I'll know that progress has been made. That's the thing about the old tapir. The challenge is to make sure we have a place where someone will see one someday, and it doesn't have to be me."

One mammal that has survived the hunting in Monteverde is the collared peccary. Active both day and night, these wild, piglike creatures move in herds of up to thirty individuals. Not the prettiest of animals, they are medium-sized, covered with wiry, dark grey bristles, and have a large triangular head and a piggish snout. Although they are generally shy, the fact that they travel in groups and make aggressive sounds – grunts, barks and teeth-clacking – gives them the air of being quite dangerous.

Hunting a herd of peccaries is both difficult and productive – difficult because, when in danger, peccaries circle, plant and defend each other, and productive because many can be shot at once. Yet they have flourished in the protected areas, having proved their ability to adapt to a disturbed habitat. Their cousin, the white-lipped peccary, on the other hand, although considered more aggressive, has been far less successful at adapting and has disappeared from most of its former range. It is now found in significant numbers in Costa Rica only in Corcovado National Park on the Pacific coast. Peccaries are valuable seed-dispersers and, perhaps more importantly, serve as food for larger carnivorous mammals.

"The peccary is one of the mammals I've crossed trails with most frequently. Its scent is a strong musk that lingers on the vegetation, so you know when they've been around. When we were first managing the Reserve, the signs we saw in our forest indicated a small herd, not much more than family size. We'd see the tracks of a very small number of individuals. That's increased now to where guards in the Reserve have counted twenty-five peccaries crossing the trail in a group. Sometimes there are signs that the herds are even larger than that. Instead of just one set of tracks across the trail, there may be as many as three groups of tracks in separate places. The road up to the Reserve and the nearby trails are favorite places where peccaries regularly forage for plants. Now they've crossed to the San Luis side, which is something we never saw in the early years. You see them to a lesser degree back in El Valle and in the swamp of Chomogo.

"Sightings of peccaries are common enough that I don't think of individual sightings so much as of unusual ones. One time, on my way cross-country while patrolling in the early years of the Reserve, I was in the forest and I came across a fallen tree. I vaulted over a log using one hand and my feet landed on the other side, right on a peccary. Fortunately, he didn't respond by attacking but rather was as startled as I was and took off into the bush. In a short time he made a loop back around to see what the heck it was that had poked him so hard. He settled down after that and we both went our separate ways. It could've ended differently if I'd landed on his snorter, or if he'd gotten the idea that I was attacking him.

"One evening I came to an old campsite just off the main trail on the way to Arenal. I thought the first thing I ought to do was go down and get water from the stream before I unpacked and set up the stove or started lighting candles as it was already dark. After finding my containers I was heading down to the stream when I saw a herd of peccaries coming up the trail. I lit a candle and backed up against a tree to let them go by. They saw that there was somebody on their trail and each peccary seemed to have a different idea of what to do. They seemed half scared and half embarrassed, just like I was feeling. The first ones couldn't seem to think of anything else to do except to just keep coming. The bigger ones bristled and went off the trail into the woods. But the nerviest of them came by and seemed to be saying, 'Hey, something's wrong here,' and they really got spunky and started snorting around. It took awhile for them all to go by. I guess I was a bit of a surprise for everybody. Even after the peccaries were gone, as I continued down to the stream to get my water I had my doubts that there wasn't another one lurking around.

"There's nothing more startling and disconcerting than being on the trail at night and having a peccary on the bank give a snort and move around in the underbrush. You have to be aware that this might happen or you'll jump out of your skin. Any time you end up splitting a herd you'll have some excitement. You'll have ones on both sides of the trail that want to get back together. The ones that have been separated seem anxious to reunite with the herd, but the others seem just as anxious to defend them. I've had an individual come out to the trail snorting away, then go back into the undergrowth, then come out again and do that a few times to give the ones that have been separated an opportunity to return to the herd. Sometimes peccaries might be aggressive, but in reality their concern isn't to attack. I've hardly ever heard them clack their teeth. That's another sign that they're really upset and defensive and more apt to be tough.

"Collared peccaries aren't really aggressive. The reason they're noted for not being a good game animal is that when dogs run them, they'll plant and defend themselves and keep their back end protected. As a rule they don't very often run off and go over a cliff. They're more likely to plant. They can take on dogs and if you don't get there in good time they'll very likely have maimed or killed your dog.

"The last time a famous Peñas Blancas hunter, Cornelius Rodríguez, went into the valley to hunt with a really valuable dog, his dog was killed by an old male peccary. That was the end of Señor Rodríguez going into Peñas to hunt. He not only lost one of his best dogs, but that dog was worth a lot of money and couldn't be replaced easily. He decided he wasn't going to lead the hunts for the local people of Peñas anymore, like he'd been doing for many years. The experience showed that wild animals sometimes can defend themselves.

"One time I became the owner of a juvenile peccary that belonged to a friend who lived in Peñas Blancas, practically as far down as Poco Sol. I came by the hunter's house and his wife showed it to me. Like any baby animal, it was cute at the time and would've followed me home. So I said, 'Well, I'd like to buy it.' The idea was to get it over to Eladio's place in Peñas so we could have it as a mascot. I paid for the animal but I didn't want to take it that day as I wasn't going in the right direction. Some months later I was going past the hunter's house again and the man was there and right away began to apologize. Well, Eladio had never come for the peccary and it had started to get more and more bothersome. At milking time it would come around and get into the feed trough and upset the cows, so the man had finally killed it, just that morning, in fact. I guess that was the pig's fate. He offered me some meat to compensate for my great loss. And he gave me my money back! By that time it had grown quite a bit and I wouldn't have wanted to move it anyway and was relieved not to have to deal with it. It was quite a surprise to get both my money back and get a good meal out of the deal.

"I've eaten peccary various times and it's very good. Probably the best I've ever had was the only one we harvested on our farm. We were having trouble one year in a small clearing in our back corner where I wanted to plant grass. First, I put in a crop of *chamol* to take advantage of the fertile soil before the grass went in. Our hired man told me, 'You know, there's peccary eating it up and soon there's not going to be any.' So I went to look and, sure enough, there were only a couple of rows of *chamol* left. Those peccaries had been coming and feeding regularly.

"The next morning I told my son, 'Carlos, if you want to take the rifle and go to that *chamol* patch and see what's cooking, I'll do your chores for you.' He took to that one. I was up milking when Carlos came back and said, 'I shot one and it went down into a little draw off to the side of the patch.' When he went down to retrieve the dead pig, why, a couple of adult peccaries came by and started clacking their teeth. So he shot over their heads, then let off a couple of extra shots for good measure, and they whisked away. He gathered up the peccary he'd shot and started for home.

"In the meantime, our neighbor, George Powell, showed up and he got quite upset with Carlos. George offered to pay for the whole patch of *chamol* if we'd guarantee that we wouldn't shoot another peccary. But it didn't save that pig. We skinned it out and put the meat away in the cooler. That peccary provided us with many great meals. One Sunday night we pulled some frozen meat out when George and Harriett came for dinner and I got a good compliment on those real good pork chops. They didn't have much fat and were real tender without the gamey flavor. Known or unbeknown to George, that was the young peccary that had been shot, and you couldn't have asked for better chops.

"The main thing is to not get into a herd of peccary and make them feel cornered. Or get too close when they have young. It was one thing when we started out seeing numbers of maybe five or something less than ten in a group. Now that we're seeing bigger herds, there are times that you wouldn't want to mess with them. Collared peccary is the one species of the larger mammals that have withstood the pressure of hunting and we can still count on seeing them around. The fact that we have a larger population now increases the food source for the big cats and that's a good thing."

Wild cats are elusive creatures, partly due to their solitary nature, partly due to their scarcity. There are six species in Costa Rica: *el tigre,* the jaguar, which is the largest; *el león,* the light-colored mountain lion or puma; *el breñero,* the weasel-like jaguarundi; *el manigordo,* the ocelot, named for its broad front paws; and the smallest of the cats, *el tigrillo* and *el caucel,* the margay and oncilla, known interchangeably by their Spanish names because they are very similar to each other.

Up until the early 1980s wild cats were hunted extensively for their skins and now all six species are endangered. Regardless of their status, they are still the victims of sport hunters and farmers who are eager to protect their domestic animals. Wild cats are carnivorous and require large areas to hunt in to sustain their population. They will go after just about anything that is available, including amphibians, rodents, small mammals, birds and peccaries. Only occasionally will hungry cats, usually old or injured, attack easy prey such as docile livestock. This happens more often in regions where the cats' natural habitat has been eaten up by farmland.

Although signs exist that in the Monteverde area there is still a significant population of mountain lions it may be too late for the jaguars. Jaguars reproduce infrequently, only one or two cubs every two years, making it difficult for the animal to sustain a healthy population. It is estimated that an isolated population of jaguars needs 400,000 hectares to survive, and despite the success of conservation efforts in and around Monteverde, the total protected area falls far short of this. These disappearing species are sometimes referred to by biologists as "the living dead" since it is almost impossible, with small populations trying to exist in limited habitats, for these species to increase their numbers and survive long-term.

To maintain populations of large cats and many other wildlife species, conservation groups in Costa Rica and elsewhere are now focusing on creating biological corridors between established reserves and protected areas. Studies have shown that with a relatively small amount of land, just enough to allow the animals to move safely from one reserve area to another, a population can survive. To ensure that wild cats continue to roam in their native environment we must not only maintain vast natural wilderness areas, but protect the wildlife corridors that link these sanctuaries.

"In 1952 there was a jaguar here in the Cerro Plano area killing dogs. It was quite a concern as the local hunting dogs were very important for putting protein on the table. At that time only one steer was slaughtered each month for the community. People would share the meat, since it was a problem to store it for any length of time. Beef can be dried, but most people salted it and ate it right away. So people supplemented their protein diet by hunting. To have a couple of hunting dogs killed in a week was really taken seriously.

"I saw that cat one night with a flashlight. We happened to meet at a bend in the trail and for a few seconds we were looking at each other. I think that we were equally surprised and impressed. It was a quick view as she crouched and then melted into the woods. I melted into my boots as I realized that I had just met *la tigra* at five meters.

"She'd been established for some time in the area that we now call Bajo del Tigre, where evidently she had a den and was raising her young. I met up with her on the upper trail, but she'd also come around our tent area and onto the road. She was trying to support her young and was hanging around looking for food.

"After the night that two of Chavarría's dogs were killed, local hunters brought in a dog that was trained to track jaguars and mountain lions. They put the dog on the trail by the cliff edge and in short order it managed to tree the cat. A hunter shot it and later took the skin off, which was quite a trophy. I was in the community when they were taking pictures of her at Arthur Rockwell's, so I had the thrill of placing my hand in her paw and realizing that it more than covered my closed fist. I was fortunate to be able to admire her once again, but I wasn't nearly as impressed as when we'd met on the trail.

"We still occasionally see the tracks of mountain lions and their scat in active dens, and I frequently find territorial markings on the trails in breeding season. It's a population that's been greatly reduced in the forested area, but on the fringes of the Reserve there's still a good number. There's ample food for them as the peccary are there. We often see the signs of other fine meals the cats have enjoyed. A few years ago we came across a spot where a mountain lion had finished off a young sloth that was more fuzz than long hair. The meal was fresh enough that you could see where it was killed and *la leona* had gorged on it, eating most all of it except for a few little bones.

"We see quite a bit more activity as the dry season approaches. That's the breeding season, when there are trails and tracks everywhere. We've seen that animal habits have changed a lot. The animals are certainly getting bolder. One year my hiking companion, Matt Stuckey, and I were followed out of the forest. The next day there were the fresh tracks of two mountain lions, curious about where we were going and what we were doing.

"Early on in Monteverde an ocelot found a chicken hutch that had been left open. Entering the small opening, it knocked down the door prop. The next morning the surprised owners found the ocelot shut in and all the chickens killed. Ocelots and margays are still around, but their tracks aren't as obvious. They eat small animals like *tepezcuintle*, agouti and sloth, and they get into birds' nests. The guides occasionally see margays, which take more to high elevations, up in the cloud forest. But you still see signs of margays in Monteverde, and you see the animal on the rare occasion. In the San Luis valley, you see more of the mountain lion and ocelot.

"Late one afternoon, not so many years ago, I was hiking on the *carril* line into Chomogo. Sitting in a tree were two black guans, big turkey-sized birds, kicking up a fuss, which made me stop to see what was going on. They went higher into the tree, obviously concerned about something, still making a racket. A third guan came and landed

158

nearby on a big spreading branch that was loaded with epiphytes, which hid it from my view. The squawking continued and then, low and behold, a margay came out of the epiphytes and moved along the limb into the canopy to get away from those mad birds. After that things got quiet and the other two guans flew off. I assumed that the margay killed the third guan and would come back to feast once things had calmed down. It was quite the drama that I got to watch, a lot of action in just a few minutes.

"Just an aside about those big birds called black guans. The locals call them 'flying soup.' They're as close to a Thanksgiving turkey as you can get around here. When George Powell was first here, he came up with the idea that we had to have a turkey for our Thanksgiving dinner. He knew there was a guan in the woods where he was working. He felt terrible about doing it, but George shot that bird and we ate it. Then he stuffed it, put glass eyes in it, and had my daughter, Helena, paint blue around the beak. We had it on a shelf at home for a long time, until the feathers all started falling out. It served as a reminder of how we used to do things.

"I had a great sighting by flashlight once. I was in good shape then, steaming uphill at night from Eladio's down by the river. I was pretty well up to the top and was coming to the last stream where there was waist-high vegetation. I saw the movement of an animal and I thought it was probably a small deer. It crouched and I shone my light right in a mountain lion's face. It sprang up and came towards me a little ways, then turned and jumped across the width of the trail and went up the bank, all in beautiful flashlight. What an incredible sight! First I saw his face, the dark markings around his eyes. When he turned and took that graceful leap, I saw his long round tail. The cat went up the bank and disappeared. I watched as it went by, my mouth hanging open. I was real close and got a great view of it.

"I crossed the stream and immediately came across a peccary. I realized that I'd interrupted the mountain lion's game. The strong musk in the area indicated that there were more peccaries nearby. The big cat was obviously stalking peccary, and because of the noise of the nearby stream I'd been able to get that close to the action. I'd messed it up for the mountain lion and no doubt delayed the death of the peccary, which took off in the opposite direction. The peccary is a favorite food of the cats and when they can separate one from the herd they've a better chance of killing it since they can't take on the whole pack.

"We often saw the tracks of peccaries while patrolling, and a cat would be following right along behind, patiently waiting for an easy lunch. It's nice to know that mountain lions are still here and that one time or another we might get a chance to see one. Its print is a bit smaller than a jaguar's, but it's pretty impressive when you think of the machine that made it. I've seen a track made by a cat in the mud, leaving a real nice print that showed how much weight was there. I'd hate to have him on my neck. It's generally more fun to see those tracks by daylight than when you're alone in the forest in the dark. When something is moving around in the underbrush or on a tree limb and doesn't make any other noise except the sound of its movement, it leaves many questions in your mind.

"Whenever there's been evidence of a big cat around pastures or in Peñas Blancas, it's been hunted down and shot. So naturally, we wouldn't see another until one came into the area to establish its territory. One time, when farmers sacrificed a jaguar because it was killing cattle, it didn't even have many teeth. It was probably an old one and couldn't make it in the woods so had headed for easier hunting grounds. Another time a female was shot and left three orphan cubs. They were taken to be raised in captivity. It's always an encouraging thing to come upon a place on the trail where cats have marked their territory by scratching the ground and leaving their musk. It's proof that they're still here despite everything that's working against them.

"In March of 1993 we had an important finding of an ocelot that had been shot over by the Santa Elena Reserve. Its body was left next to the trail by people who wanted to stir up our emotions and show us that they could do illegal things like that. It was a pretty big blow for those of us who had been working a long time at educating people on the laws protecting our wild cats.

"There was a report in more recent years of a couple of steer killed in Ojo de Agua near Cedral. There were definitely jaguars in that area at the time. We're always trying to figure out a way to deal with farmers who lose domestic animals. We ask them to be rational and to realize that it's something we all have to cope with together. Our goal is to gain the support of the area farmers who are going to lose animals occasionally.

"The law states that only government guards are allowed to destroy a wild cat, and only after they've decided the cat is a problem. It also states that the government will reimburse farmers for any loss of livestock they can prove was due to a wild animal. Unfortunately, the government has never paid the indemnity despite our efforts to support the area farmers by getting the necessary proof. Yet only occasionally do we have real evidence of killings by jaguars in farm areas. We feel we've been successful when people contact us to say that they suspect a wild cat has killed a domestic animal on their farm rather than go out and track it down themselves. When we're informed we can take responsibility for seeing that the cat returns to the forest. We maintain a presence around the carcass until the cat comes back to eat and then we prevent the cat from getting at the kill. It eventually will give up and head for the forest. If we can save a wild cat from being shot, I think that's a major victory.

"Just because you can kill them doesn't mean that you have to. It all goes hand in hand with the idea that they're a part of what we're saving. We need a big chunk of protected forest not just because of our demand for natural resources, but because we want all of these fellas in there too."

In the treetops around Monteverde reside three of the four species of monkey found in Costa Rica: the Central American spider monkey, or *mono colorado;* the mantled howler monkey, or *congo;* and the white-throated capuchin, also known as the white-faced monkey, or *mono carablanca.* There are distinctions in the eating habits of these species that allow them to co-exist. While they all eat fruit, the spider monkey relies on it much more heavily than the others. Spider monkeys are quite active throughout the day, only resting about one-fifth of the time. Although a typical community of spider monkeys may number between twenty and forty, they travel in subgroups to exploit fruiting trees, which are scattered, more efficiently.

Howler monkeys feed extensively on a variety of leaves, preferring the tasty new ones. They can often be seen sprawled about the upper branches of trees, soaking up the sun, which heats their bodies to speed up the fermentation of their cellulose-heavy diet. Howlers are most famous for the roar of the adult males, a sound that travels for miles, heralding both dawn and dusk as well as announcing the troop's position sporadically throughout the day.

Like the others, white-faced monkeys eat fruit, but they are the only ones that rely heavily on insects. They swing through the forest searching for their favorite foods, which can also include lizards, frogs, birds and small mammals. Animals such as peccaries and coatis can be found following below on the ground, picking up the food that the monkeys drop. White-faced monkeys are important seed-dispersers and excellent tree pruners. By eating a tree's new growth they encourage the tree to branch out and in some species to produce more fruit.

The biggest threat to the survival of these primates is from their most abusive cousin, *Homo sapiens*. In the past monkeys were hunted for their meat and also captured for research or to be used as pets. In the 1950s an estimated 200,000 monkeys were exported to the United States each year. In that same decade a yellow fever epidemic amongst humans decimated the monkey populations in Monteverde. When hunting in some areas greatly reduced the numbers of some of their principal predators, such as the puma and harpy eagle, they thrived once again. But as habitat loss and fragmentation occurs, the diversity of their food sources diminishes and the movement of troops is hampered, which can result in inbreeding and diminished genetic diversity. Only by protecting their natural habitat will we continue to see monkeys playing in the forest instead of languishing in cages at the zoo.

"At various times I've seen all three species of monkeys in the woods here. I suppose you might say that loss of habitat has influenced every animal that didn't want to get down on the ground and eat the grass. Spider monkeys had other big handicaps. People shot at them to capture their young to sell or tame as pets, and they ate the adult monkeys whether or not they had young. So there was a loss of population with that species that came from more than just habitat loss. But there are still a lot of woods in the area and the other two species, the white-faced and howler monkeys, maintain a healthy population.

"In the Peñas Blancas valley there were several troops of spider monkeys right from early on. At that time it was common to hear or see them. Later the population was diminished, mainly by hunting. There was also the yellow fever epidemic in the 1950s that infected the population of all species of monkeys and many were lost. The epidemic might've been more fatal to some species of monkeys. Either way, the spider monkeys were severely reduced in population to where at one time the only significant troop I knew of was past El Valle, up above the Peñas Blancas valley.

"I frequently observed small troops of spider monkeys on my patrols, especially around the base of Cerro Amigos, on the backside toward Rio Negro. In the last few years I've seen adults with two young, so I think that spider monkeys are on the comeback in Peñas, where they're now on both sides of the river. They've also been seen in San Luis, and I've often met up with them on my trail to the volcano at Arenal by the Aguas Gatas River and on the ridges there, around the perimeter of the Children's Eternal Rain Forest. They're also common down around the Observatory Lodge at Arenal and in Arenal Volcano National Park.

"Howler monkeys are still the most frequently seen and heard. The perimeter areas of the clearings in Monteverde, Cerro Plano and San Luis sustain a good population. In fact, I think the troops' numbers have been maintained. Howler monkeys seem to have learned early on about what we humans were up to. They were mainly stirred up by the noise the chainsaws made as we were tree clearing, but they were also vocal as we cleared trails with machetes. You'd never get directly under one before the big guys would be howling. And they do like to poop and urinate on you. It only took one time for me to learn that. Years ago a lady came to the Reserve reception and she was quite perturbed as her camera was all covered with monkey poop. She scolded us soundly for not warning her that she shouldn't get underneath them. If you want to photograph or admire them in any way you'd better not get underneath them. May this be your warning!

"In our first year here I decided it would be great to be the first Monteverdian to have a tamed monkey. One day I was going up through our woods and there was a spider monkey with a young one on her back. I shot the mother but didn't know that unless a monkey is out on a limb where it can fall to the ground, it does exactly what this monkey did, which was fall right into the crotch of the tree. There was a cry from the mother I'd shot and then one from the baby too. Then other monkeys came and passed right above me, and one picked up the baby and carried it off. There was no way I could climb up to get the mother I'd shot, so I had to leave her hung up in the tree. I really felt bad and learned that killing a mother for her baby wasn't a very good practice. Whether you were after monkeys for food, for their young or for what is rumored to be the medicinal benefits of their lard and glands, obviously you had to be smarter than I was.

"We never intended to be caught raising monkeys. The ones we had were brought to us when they were orphaned and there wasn't any chance of them surviving on their own. It was quite a thing to try and raise them, to get them to adapt to captivity and later, hopefully, to get them orientated to being in the wild. That was something we were never successful with.

"Yet we ended up raising three. One of these was brought to us by a visiting short-term student when it was just a few weeks old. We were supposed to take care of it for two weeks as the student finished her term of study. She was going back to the States and wanted to take the spider monkey with her. So she worked to get the papers to do that, but it never happened because she couldn't get the permits. We kept it and raised it, trying to think of somewhere it could be taken. As the monkey got older it became more problematic. We had to keep it on a chain, but it would get loose and jump up on the hummingbird feeder, its favorite thing being getting into their food. The last time this happened Lucky had come outside and responded instinctively by grabbing it. Luck got very seriously bit. So that was the end of having it around here.

"We'd heard that the Curú Biological Reserve on the Nicoya Peninsula was advertising that they were rehabilitating spider monkeys. They had an area where they could release the monkeys and then supervise them until they joined with a troop. So our son Benito took our monkey down to Curú. They weren't very pleased to have it because by that time their experiment hadn't been very successful. It took a lot of time and work to get the monkeys reintroduced into the forest. But they did take our monkey. It never really went anywhere with the troop nor did it come around the buildings, but the monkey did survive.

"We had two howler monkeys as well. The first we'd had for little more than a year when it got the flu, a virus that our family had, and died. With the second one we were more careful and tried not to expose it to our germs. It lasted a couple of years, staying out in the barn at night. It adapted to living outside on its own. However, eventually it too got the flu. We started treating it immediately with antibiotics that we used on our domestic animals, but it didn't survive either. That was their big weakness. They'd easily pick up diseases, just as their earlier relatives had succumbed to the yellow fever.

"We learned a lot about monkeys from raising our orphans. Whenever anybody came to the house and excited or upset them, the howler monkeys would automatically have diarrhea. It was something you had to be prepared for, part of their nature. Just like our kids, the howler monkeys disliked being bathed and would make a big fuss about it and object loudly. The spider monkeys, however, would dabble their hand in the warm water, walk around and fuss about, then climb right in and enjoy the bath. There was quite a difference in their natural responses.

"One story local people tell about howlers is that they call to welcome the rain. But having raised little ones and observed them closely, I think that they're objecting to the rain and the idea of getting wet. When the rain clouds move in, they start to complain. The howlers are also great talkers early in the morning. At first sun on the treetops they'll be calling back and forth, sometimes between two or three different troops. In Peñas Blancas, in my rainforest, I call the howler monkey my *gallo*, the rooster of the morning. They're a pretty dependable alarm clock."

There are two deer species in the Monteverde area, the commonly seen *cabro de monte*, or red brocket deer, and the seldom-seen *venado*, or white-tailed deer. Their habitats are different, with the smaller brocket deer favoring dense woods while the white-tailed deer inhabits open areas where unfortunately it is more at risk from hunters. Monteverde is the upper limit of the range of this deer, which is often found in small groups foraging for leaves, fruit, seeds, twigs and bark. In the past white-tailed deer were an important game animal, but the passing of hunting laws, the establishment of protected areas and the disappearance of many of its main predators – the big cats – have allowed its populations to recover.

Brocket deer are solitary animals that feed on fruits and seeds they find along the trails or in the open areas at the edge of the forest. They move with their heads held low, and the males have short, unbranched, backward-pointing antlers that enable them to push through heavy vegetation and evade threats by escaping into thick bush.

"The *cabro de monte* has always been seen here. It's been great, all the years of traveling around, seeing them around old clearings, on the trail and at night. Going into Peñas Blancas, occasionally I've flushed one out that was bedded down right on the trail. In the past I had plenty of meals of brocket deer down in Peñas. One day, years ago, I was heading through Peñas to Poco Sol. The first home I came to, the family had just got a *tepezcuintle* dressed out and was frying it. That was a fine morning meal. Then I went on down and by evening got to a house where they'd just cooked up a brocket deer. So I had a little venison. Today I'd expect to see such animals alive rather than on the table.

"I remember the time when I went down in the valley one morning to visit a homesteader. He was out hunting. You could hear the dogs running in the woods, so I waited at the cabin with his wife and daughter. A brocket deer came up the stream to the forks and doubled back on the other branch of the stream, being careful to stay in the water to throw the dogs off its scent. It wasn't worried about us sitting there because its business was to worry about those dogs. The main thing I remember was the wife's comment. She said, 'Well, you know, that's the first time I've ever seen one of those alive. I didn't realize how graceful, how beautiful an animal it is.'"

A bird-lover's paradise: that is Costa Rica. The Monteverde area has more than 400 species. Many of these are plain little brown birds whose songs grace the air from morning to night. Flashy tanagers, busy flycatchers and nest-robbing jays are all present and accounted for on the bird-watching lists. Of course, it is the unique and colorful birds that bring in the tourists, lured by photographs they have seen of famous local species such as the mythical resplendent quetzal, the gregarious keel-billed toucan, the friendly paddle-tailed, blue-crowned motmot and the shimmering violet sabrewing. You don't have to be a life-list bird-watcher to appreciate their winged beauty.

With good planning and a pair of decent binoculars, it is possible to observe the nesting behavior and marvel at the mating displays of many of Costa Rica's birds. Monteverde provides a wide range of habitats for observers to indulge their passion, from the wet cloud forest to the drier montane deciduous forest. Within these wooded habitats is one of the most diverse families of trees in Monteverde, the *Lauraceae* or avocado family. There are seventy species of avocados found here, supplying the main food for the resplendent quetzal and the three-wattled bellbird. These birds, like migrant fruit pickers, follow the harvest. It brings them to the cloud forest in the dry season, with the quetzals arriving in January and the bellbirds, around March. They breed and then pursue the ripening avocados back down the hill to the lowlands.

Quetzals appear to be quite vain, with good reason. At times they almost insist on presenting themselves, bobbing through the air above the heads of hikers, their long tails trailing like ribbons behind a glittering gift package of iridescent green and blue. At other times they can be found by following their plaintive cries through the forest until a flash of their blood-red breast or vivid jade plumage shining in the sunlight gives away their presence. It isn't hard to imagine why the Mayans considered them as precious as gold.

"When I first came here the only quetzal I knew of was the one printed on the Guatemalan money. The first quetzal I actually saw alive had a nest in a snag near our barn. It was a beautiful bird, a male with a long metallic green tail. It's always nice to see one, but until I got involved with the Reserve it really didn't mean anything spectacular. My first ten, fifteen, twenty years running around back here I didn't know that it was something that would be attractive to so many people. A note about quetzals: it seems that if you see twenty females, you say, well, I didn't really see a quetzal at all. It only counts when you see the male.

"In the late nineties my son Benito raised one. A nestling was found over near Rio Negro by forest guards, in a nest that had been broken up, raided by other animals, we think. When he got that young bird, it wasn't ready to go completely on its own. The deal was that Benito took an interest, like he always does, and looked into what he should feed it, getting that information from a report that the Fogdens had written from observing them. So Benito worked away at mothering that bird.

"It was almost big enough to take fruit. Benito started collecting fruits for the bird, and then taught it how to pick fruit. Benito would pin the fruit to the cage in a way that would force the young quetzal to pick it off the stem, which it learned to do. So it stayed alive and matured. The good fortune was that when it was time for it to fledge, there were quetzals feeding in a tree near our house. Benito would take the fledgling there to the tree. At first it was strange for it, but after a few days the bird began to be comfortable in the tree and you could see it picking fruit. It would fly from one branch to another and eventually come down to return to the house with Benito. One day he waited and waited for it, but the quetzal had finally flown away.

"Over the years the Reserve has been a center for quetzals during its pre-breeding and nesting season. George Powell's work of putting transmitters on quetzals and studying their natural history has provided us with lots of information. He showed that some quetzals stay around all year, although others migrate to the lower-elevation forests for a couple of months. I can certainly understand why they like to get off this cold, windy, wet mountaintop.

"There are always a few back in the actual primary forest, but to a greater degree they live on the fringes of the clearings. On a good day you can hear the quetzals calling nearby. One really good day I heard pairs courting in five different locations. The ideal time for birdwatchers is when the quetzals are working at nesting, ordinarily between February and June. There isn't any question that the quetzal has been the *gancho,* the hook, for the Monteverde Cloud Forest Reserve."

The three-wattled bellbird is the latest flag species of the conservation movement in the Monteverde area. Studies by George Powell and others found that this large brown bird, distinguishable by its white head and what appears to be three worms dangling from its beak, migrates over a large region from southern Nicaragua to the Pacific coast of Costa Rica to the highlands of Monteverde and then back down the Pacific slope. Now, with heavy deforestation throughout the country (the north-central part of Costa Rica has become one big banana plantation) bellbirds have to fly greater distances to find the forests that furnish them with their food. They are important dispersers of avocado seeds, carrying them from fruiting trees to exposed snags where the birds perch and sing out, their loud sharp *BRONK* audible at least a kilometer away.

"The three-wattled bellbirds are another altitudinal migrant. The males are white and brown with three distinctive dangling wattles. We always hear their unmistakable *BRONK* when they're in our area during their nesting season. I never shot a quetzal, but I shot a bellbird to get it down here to see what was dangling from its beak. That's what we sacrificed its life for, because it was *BRONKing* away and shaking its wattles.

I really didn't know what kind of bird could make that sound. The bell-birds are also endangered due to the fact that their migratory corridors have been deforested. The Costa Rican Conservation Foundation, amongst others, is working to raise funds to buy lands that will protect this corridor."

Scarlet macaws and great green macaws are large, raucous members of the parrot family whose numbers have been so greatly diminished that they are now amongst the most endangered birds in Costa Rica. Their primary habitat is the wet lowland forest, which has been swallowed up by agricultural development. The vibrantly colored macaws are well loved in the pet trade, but the sight of these magnificent birds stuffed in a cage pales significantly once you have seen a pair of macaws, their elegant bodies entwined, perched high on the branch of a tropical hardwood tree.

"In the good old days we could count on seeing species that we don't see now. In the case of the great green macaw, we miss hearing its loud screeching in Peñas Blancas, as well as seeing pairs of these beautiful greenish-blue birds flying through the valley. They would come up from the coastal regions, usually in December and January, to feed on the fruits of the *peine de mico* trees in Peñas. You could hear them squawking from quite a ways away. George Powell later put transmitters on these birds and furnished us with knowledge about them. His monitoring showed that people kill and eat great green macaws. One time he followed a signal right to the dinner table where people were feasting on a macaw, having put the curious little transmitter off to the side before digging in.

"Due to deforestation in the macaw's nesting area in the lowlands, the population was greatly reduced and several years went by without any sightings being reported in our area. So it was a big surprise when a report came in around 1997 from Laguna Poco Sol. My old friend Miguel Salazar and his companions were working on a trail and saw five or six pairs of great green macaws fly over. It was really impressive, as probably six years had gone by since the last time anybody had reported seeing them in the valley. We're always happy with a good sighting like that."

One of my most memorable birding experiences took place in Peñas Blancas. In May of 1995 I accompanied Wolf down to the German's and we spent the night on the cabin's plank beds. Our alarm was set for 3:30 a.m., when we dragged ourselves out of our beds and quickly got dressed. In the pitch-dark of the river valley we headed up the trail through the damp forest, flashlights in hand, to a spot where bare-necked umbrellabirds were known to be mating. We arrived and settled onto a log just as the light was delicately lacing the sky above the treetops. At what must have been a genetically programmed moment for these big black birds, a male quietly flew in and perched on a branch nearby. The silhouette of his umbrella-like crested head was revealed as the day seeped in around us. As the tension mounted, the male puffed his large red throat sac up to twice its size and started to call in his lover. It was as if he were blowing across a bottle – *HOOOOOM*. The steady bass voice continued until we could first sense, then hear, and finally see three smaller black females approach from the surrounding trees. The mating ceremony seemed to take place in slow motion in the muted tones of a fading photograph, and then ended abruptly just as the last of the night was replaced by day.

"The umbrellabirds live down in the rainforest where it's really tropical. That's where you see and hear them, the males doing their display, puffing out their red throat sacs and making their mating calls. We first saw them when we started going further down into the Peñas valley, developing clearings and maintaining property lines. Many years ago I shot one of them. I was looking at this big bird and thinking, 'Look at that little wild turkey.' So I bagged it. When I got my hands on it and saw what it was, I realized it definitely wasn't a wild turkey. I skinned it and brought the skin home and took it to Harriett Powell to find out what it might be. Well, she hit the ceiling. She said that we'd better keep the skin until George came back from whatever trip he was on. He hadn't seen an umbrellabird and wanted to know where they might be. That was the beginning of being taught to be more concerned about the special birds I was shooting.

"The umbrellabird has always been a big attraction to birders. There's a lot of good birding down around the Audubon Centre, near Eladio's in Peñas. I've always thought that we should develop that area as the birder's paradise that it is."

Another bird found in Peñas, wading along the shores of streams but difficult to spot, are sunbitterns. These are solitary birds that when threatened raise their feathers in an intricate display. The pattern, which features a large eye-like design meant to frighten their adversaries, mainly large snakes, mimics the sun-flecked forest they live in.

"Sunbitterns are also called *pava de agua,* or water turkeys. I never bagged one of them, though I tried to kill both a sunbittern and me one time. There was a nice one sitting on a rock in the river and I shot at it, but the bullet hit the rock and ricocheted. *Piiinnnggg,* it went by. I decided that I wouldn't take another shot at one of those again. How quick and fatal that could've been, and it was just as well that I didn't kill one of those birds.

"In 1986 Michael and Patricia Fogden made the sunbittern famous when, together with Bruce Lyons, they photographed a nest on the Peñas River, near Eladio's. The nesting ecology of the sunbittern had never been recorded, so the Fogdens set up a blind and watched the birds every day until the young fledged. They made detailed records of their daily activities. One thing they noticed was that the adults picked food, such as frogs, tadpoles and lizards, from the streams for their nestlings.

"These birds make an impressive display when threatened, turning their wings out to show the flashy, eye-like design of their feathers. It was observed that the fledgling sunbitterns had to be taught to do their display before leaving the nest. Even if a butterfly flew by, they would raise their wings. The adults would do it to teach their young. Biologists had thought that sunbitterns were similar to other species that had a short time to develop before fledgling. Evidently, sunbitterns need more time to become agile with their display before they can leave the nest."

When the songs of the frogs and toads fade from the sensory landscape, we notice the loss. We don't miss the song of the snake, and yet snake and lizard populations have also shown declines as their chief food source – frogs and toads – disappear. Climatic changes may also be negatively affecting the country's reptilian populations.

There are roughly 100 species of reptiles in the Monteverde region. We tend to think of serpents as solitary creatures, but many people don't wish to see even one snake. A nest of slithering, venomous snakes may be the subject of nightmares, but their continued presence within a healthy ecosystem is part of the dream for our collective future.

Gary Diller tells a great Wolf story concerning snakes. Back in the 1980s, in his second year of guiding, Gary was returning along the path to the entrance of the Reserve with two tourists in tow. He greeted Wolf, who was in his customary position at a picnic table, barefoot, legs crossed, coffee cup in hand, having just returned from Peñas Blancas. Gary looked down and there, lying across the trail, was a two-meter-long fer-de-lance, quite dead but still an imposing sight, its large mouth wide open. It was obvious that Wolf had brought it back from the lowlands. Gary beckoned the tourists closer and, bending down on his knees, proceeded to explain the features of the beautiful specimen to his clients.

"The *terciopelo*, what we call the fer-de-lance, is the most dangerous snake of Central and South America, and causes more human deaths than any other American reptile," Gary explained. Putting his hand into the mouth of the snake, he continued, "Notice the incredible fangs...", but before he could finish his sentence the snake's mouth clamped down in a final reflexive action and caught his hand. He pulled it away, staring in horror at the small mark on his index finger. He looked up and said, "My God, Wolf, what will I do now?"

Without missing a beat, Wolf replied, "Well, I guess you're going to die, big guy!" He then started laughing so hard that he had to take his false teeth out and throw them on the picnic table before he choked on them. Gary saw that the snake had barely grazed his skin and realized that, once again, he had been set up by the master, and soon they were all laughing. The tourists were most likely as intrigued by the Wolf-sighting as they were by the snake.

"I've seen many *terciopelos*. I thought maybe I'd seen a dozen, but one time I started counting and when I got to twenty, I quit. So maybe I've seen more than I thought. Something the old timers say is that if you kill one then you know there's a mate within twenty meters as they're usually in pairs. Those folks have said many things that aren't necessarily true, but I think that one might be.

"The first time I saw one of those big snakes, I practically put my foot in its mouth. Eladio and I were working where a tree had fallen on a corner of my property in Peñas. We'd decided to plant some grass. We came to an opening in the brush from the tree fall and started planting.

I stepped up on a log, walked across it, and jumped off the end of it. I tossed the hook stick, which we use with the machete when clearing brush, back to Eladio. A moment later I heard him say, 'Hey, come and see where you put that stick for me.' There was this big ol' fer-de-lance right beside the log that I'd walked on, sleeping there calm as anything. We had to kill that one before we could keep planting grass amongst the fallen branches.

"Another time we had a new hand, Carlos Suarez, working for the Reserve down in Peñas Blancas. There were three of us set to go clear on down to Camp Three. Before we headed off the father of this new helper said, 'You know, I don't approve of my son working down there. There are two dangers that worry me. One is the snakes, the other is the river.' But Carlos came with us to see for himself.

"I went off to clear a trail, and when I caught up to the other two, they'd killed two fer-de-lance. Looking pretty pale, they explained what they'd done. They'd got to the cabin and there was a snake curled up in front of the doorway. So they killed it. Then they went to put their backpacks on the wooden bench inside, and Carlos turned and right under the counter was another snake. You could see from the boy's tracks in the soft dirt floor how he'd jumped right over to the other door. So that was his introduction to Peñas. We skinned those snakes out. One of them had sixteen or so little ones inside, but they were too young to survive. I don't know if Carlos saw any more snakes while he worked with us, but I do remember that later on he had trouble with the river too, and Eladio had to fish him out. Fortunately, young Carlos survived it all.

"I was coming out of the forest one night, when the snakes are more active, and I stopped at the side of a pool for a minute. I was looking around with my flashlight and realized that what looked like a lump of dirt was a fer-de-lance staring me in the eye. I'd been told that bright light aggravates them and that they won't be so aggressive if you don't have the light. So I turned mine off and pressed against the bank away from him. Then I turned the light back on to watch which way he'd go so I wouldn't head in the same direction. I was happy to see that he had completely disappeared. You sure have to be in an experimental mood to turn that light off.

"The biggest story about killing snakes comes from the crew that worked with the surveyors in Peñas in the 1980s. They returned to camp one day all excited about killing twenty-six *terciopelos*. They were clearing out a treetop that had fallen down into the middle of the river. Snakes like little islands of protected brush like that. They can swim and it's probably a good place to hunt for toads and lizards. As the men were hacking away, they met up with a pregnant snake, a real inner tube of a gal. They killed the snake and opened it up. Inside were twenty-five snakelings, big enough to crawl and jump around. So when they were finished with those, they had twenty-six to their credit. That seems to be a record.

"Another time I was with the surveying crew and there were several hunters in the group who knew the best way to get around in Peñas. One day they led us down into a place called Rancho Escondido, a little clearing with a shack. We got there by dark and had a place to bed down for the night. They built a fire to cook on and it warmed up the cabin and then smoked up the roof. The next thing we knew there were snakes dropping down in one place and another. They were the kind we call chunk-headed and had obviously been living in the roof, which stays warm from the sunshine. It kept everyone on edge and before it was over we had seven snakes drop down on us.

"Naturally, you'll see snakes if you go fooling around in the lowlands. In Peñas Blancas, around the old clearings and especially in the secondary forest, there are lots of rats and toads. Those are the two main food staples of many snakes. Fortunately, they don't take on tapirs or me. In all the years of doing development in the valley, from 1964 to 1990, I only knew of two people in Peñas who got bit by poisonous snakes. One of them was a man hunting *tepezcuintle* at night. He'd had a dog go in to get the animal in its den. The dog scared up a snake, came out yelping and wouldn't go back in. He got another dog to go in but it came running back out too. So the fellow thought he'd jab his machete in the den and get the animal, not knowing a snake was in there. It was a fer-de-lance. That was the third strike. The first dog died, the second dog survived, and the man was the last strike. He survived because the two dogs had taken most of the venom, but he still had to go to the hospital in Puntarenas for three weeks of treatments.

"I think that snakes only came up the mountain from the lowlands when the farmers were burning their pastures. We never had any fer-de-lance in Monteverde, but they killed one once in Santa Elena. There are coral snakes, which are poisonous, in Monteverde. Two people have been bit by coral snakes that I know of, one while on his way home from the dairy plant. The clinic had advertised that they didn't have a good supply of anti-venom, and they were always trying to get people to bring in coral snakes to increase the supply. So this fellow, heading home after work, saw a coral snake and thought he'd pick it up and leave it at the clinic, which was nearby. He got bit and ended up going all the way to the hospital in San José because, as advertised, the clinic was low on anti-venom. He had a very serious reaction to that bite, bad enough that he needed more help than he could receive here.

"We used to have snake-bite kits at the shelters in Peñas. The serum would expire and if you ever needed them, they'd be useless. Nowadays they have a powder you can mix with distilled water before injecting it. That way the anti-venom serum lasts longer. But before taking it you're supposed to do a test to see if you're allergic. You have to wait three to five minutes to see if you're going to have a reaction. It isn't very practical. Now the advice is to get to a hospital as soon as possible where they can treat you.

"The first thing that happens when you're bit is you feel a pain that nobody can describe. It's more a burning sensation than the pain of being cut. Then you're going to bleed out of any body opening, because your blood won't clot. You bruise from the blood rushing to your skin. Don't cut it out. That's the worst thing you can do as it causes the blood to rush to the area and absorb the venom. You should just sit down and relax, that's the best thing to do. Right. I sure don't picture myself doing that. They say to do everything you can to slow down the absorption. If you smoke, have a cigarette. Relax. The bad thing about alcohol is that you can use it to relax and think that you've done something good, but it actually speeds up your absorption. So this is when you just sit on the bank and meditate and stay calm. Don't run, don't walk fast, but do proceed to the doctor's. You need to be there in two hour's time. Mostly, hope that the snake ate a meal before he bit you so there'll be less venom. That would be what they call a 'dry strike.' That's what I would call a lucky strike.

"One thing I do think those snakes contribute to the area is that they keep a lot of people from coming to the forest who might otherwise rush right in here and overuse our facilities and eliminate animal habitats that we want to keep."

There are obviously vast differences between the wildlife of Costa Rica and the wildlife of Canada, however, there are species that we share. As many as 100 of our northern birds are actually tropical birds that have migrated north to breed. We are all at risk of losing species if their migratory paths remain unprotected, and if a species loses its habitat in one region, it must adapt or it will be missed in other regions.

In both countries, in the struggle between man and beast, more often than not the beast loses. When a black bear steps out of the northern bush into a campsite or community, she always loses in the ensuing contest of wits and strength. She will be shot. Just like the jaguar in Costa Rica that gets too close to livestock. All wildlife will ultimately lose unless there are programs in place to ensure their survival.

The one time it does feel like the beast might be winning is when we talk about bugs. In Costa Rica there is an incredible diversity of insects, from beetles to weevils to butterflies, many of which are beneficial and beautiful. They all play a crucial role in pollinating plants or as part of the food chain. There are also many insects that are harmful to agriculture or to human health. Although Costa Rica hosts more species than Canada does, our northern insects are easily as virile. In the tropics, mosquitoes spread malaria, while in the north, West Nile virus is a new and serious threat. But in our attempts to control bugs with chemicals, we end up poisoning ourselves and our environment, and in the natural world, even hostile bugs have their healthy functions. It is a difficult relationship with nature that we share the world over.

"I don't kill much of anything anymore, except bugs. Like horseflies. I'm sure I've killed over a million horseflies. I often imagine what it would be like now if I hadn't killed a million of them! You'd have to wear protective space suits when you went outside. But I don't notice them so much anymore even though I see that other people are still being bothered by them.

"Sometimes there are a few mosquitoes around, but they have their rights too. If you really believe in everybody having their fair ecological share, and no one wiping out any species, then you have to be willing to sacrifice a little blood here and there along the trail. We have our own part to play in the food chain.

"I think that most of us don't get close enough to realize how it's all tied together with the intricacies of the flora and fauna in the forest, including our own future. We have to be more careful about how we treat it. This has become more obvious since the days when my great-grandfather, then my grandfather, then my father, and then myself were harvesting the forest. There was a lot left then and we weren't thinking too much about how it might need protecting.

"How are we going to protect the forest's creatures? This is the challenge. We have to continue to put more money into protection, but part of the money could be for education of both the tourists and the locals. When money became tight at the League, it was the educational programs in the surrounding communities that suffered. The consequence of not teaching people about endangered species and the benefits of conservation is evident in the continuing presence of hunters in our forests and in the negative attitude towards our guards. I think that this is our weakest link.

"One program could be to invite families from the fringe communities into the protected areas, perhaps on a Sunday afternoon, so they could walk with a guide and ask questions. This could help local people understand the need to conserve wild spaces. Hopefully, they would feel that this is their forest and that they have the right to enjoy it as well as the responsibility to protect it.

"It's also good when hiring forest guards to employ people from the local communities who are respected and will be listened to. There's a program in some areas where people are invited to go on a walk with the guards on *Semana Santa*. They learn about the forest and the role of the guards, and they act as witnesses if they come across violators cutting palm trees or hunting. These programs could be more effective if used throughout the whole area on other weekends, not just during Holy Week.

"Not long ago a fellow was fixing the waterline in the forest above Monteverde and saw from the tracks that some tapir had come through and broken the line. That's an area of Bosqueterno where we've not had any tapir for several years. It's more proof that they'll utilize their old trails, even close to civilization, as long as they're protected and feel safe. I'd say that as long as we're seeing the tapirs' footprints, it's a sign that we're doing something right."

ELEVEN

Following a lucky star

"It's 3 a.m. and all's well. I wake up when nature takes its course. I was thinking it was cloudy, but it's just the Milky Way up there. All the stars are out tonight for there's nowhere for them to hide.

"I really don't know what my wife thinks at this time of the night. I know she does wonder about me and that means a lot. That knowledge keeps me from being careless along the trail. I appreciate that we have each other. On my part, I say out loud, 'Sweetheart, I love you,' and hope that gets through. And I'm sure it does because I believe in the power of thought, otherwise, I wouldn't take the trouble to think things through." *Wolf in his hammock near Eladio's in Peñas*

"It's at night, when I'm lying in bed, that I start thinking and wondering why he's not back yet. Every little sound seems like the motor of his pickup coming. So many times I've wondered, when he hasn't come home on time, 'When, when should I start worrying?' Through everything, I've become more and more convinced that Wolf has a very good Guardian Angel. There are so many stories about his shortcuts that take much longer than the original trail and take him who knows where. So I always have to figure that his Guardian Angel is taking care of him and at least he knows where Wolf is." *Lucky at the Guindon farm*

In 1998, following the deaths of my father and mother and the impending sale of our family home, I was feeling set adrift. My parents had provided an emotional base from which my gypsy soul wandered with ease, secure in the knowledge that no matter where I lived and what befell me, I always had a home. Now only my sister Maggie and her husband Tom were left in my immediate family and they lived thousands of kilometers away in the mountains of Washington State. While searching for a renewed sense of stability, I surrounded myself with the most restorative salves I know: music, laughter and love.

For me, music has always been an instrument for healing. When I was very ill with cancer and could barely walk up a set of stairs, I could still dance all night, oblivious to my shortness of breath and diminishing strength. My parents had both loved music, and in our house there was always some tune playing on the radio or the record player. They encouraged my sister and me to play the piano and sing in the choir, but we both preferred to get up on our feet and boogie. When I first went to Costa Rica, I quickly discovered that there would be many opportunities to do just that, be it twirling to salsa in a local restaurant or country dancing in the meeting house. For anyone whose spirit is lifted by song, Monteverde is a panacea.

The community indulges itself frequently with the power of music. Though the Quakers meet in silence, they also gather to sing, put on musical theatre and square dance. From early on the *Ticos* came to the dances and joined in with their guitars as well as entertained the crowd with their own tunes. Over the years educational programs in the area taught both young and old to play a wide variety of instruments, and the appreciation of music flourished. In the 1990s the community began supporting the annual Monteverde Music Festival, which had been gathering together top talent from the rich cultural garden of Central America since 1992. Classical, jazz, calypso, *nueva canción* and a variety of Latin rhythms were all represented.

Because of this welcoming atmosphere, international musicians on vacation in the area would offer to perform just for the delight of playing in one of the stunning concert venues on the mountaintop. I became intimate with the music of Costa Rica through the nineties, particularly in 1998 and 1999, when as a volunteer I managed the house the musicians stayed in during the festival. Being part of this celebration widened my musical horizon, introduced my hips to a whole new kind of movement, and restored my spirit despite the losses I had recently experienced.

The Guindon family also understands the value of music and laughter and employs both liberally, not only as curatives during hard times but as a means of sharing. They recognize that through melody, tempo,

Young Wilford in 1943 (personal archives)

Guindon family with Sam the horse in 1957 (personal archives).

(from left) The Guindons in 1969: Alberto, Tomás, Helena, Carlos, Benito, Ricardo, Antonio, Melody & Wolf (personal archives)

(from left) The Guindons in 1994: Lucky, Alberto, Tomás, Helena, Carlos, Benito, Ricardo, Antonio, Melody, granddaughter Naomi Solano, Wolf and guest spider monkey (personal archives)

Maryjka Mychajlowycz, Wolf & Kay with papayas and hibiscus celebrating Valentine's Day 1990 in the Peñas Blancas valley (Art Pedersen)

Art Pedersen, Wolf & Maryjka Mychajlowycz near Poco Sol in February 1990

The view west from Monteverde over the deforested foothills and the Gulf of Nicoya

The beauty of the uncut forest in the Peñas Blancas valley

Lucky & Wolf in 1992 (personal archives)

Wolf and Miguel Leitón in 2005

Laguna Poco Sol

The shelter known as the German's in 1990

View from Eladio's cabin across the Peñas Blancas River valley in 1990

George Powell, Eladio Cruz, Wolf Guindon in 2002 (Wagner Lopez)

Wolf and the Grandfather Oak (Brett Cole, Wild Northwest Photography)

laughter and tears we can build bridges with people even when we don't speak the same language. Although Wolf has always had a unique and somewhat garbled way of speaking Spanish (and English for that matter), he has never had difficulty engaging with people, his charismatic smile an uncomplicated tool that is universally understood. Laughing is not only a manifestation of personal well-being, but can collectively move us towards world peace and, at a minimum, brighten our day.

As for love, well, shortly after my mother's death I became involved with a very interesting and talented man. However, as I was falling in love with him, I slowly became aware that he was living his own struggle with mental illness. Much of the time I couldn't fathom what was going on inside his head. Though he was highly entertaining and brought me great joy, I soon became caught up in his dysfunction. It is a hard, illogical road that one follows when living with a lack of serotonin, and it leads to a lifetime of misunderstandings and complicated relationships. I have great respect for people who face their demons and get help, and a profound empathy for their families and partners who try to keep up with them on this rollercoaster ride through life. I learned many things while traveling on this bumpy road, particularly how much love can endure and the therapeutic nature of laughter.

When I met Wolf in 1990 he had been taking lithium for his bipolar disorder for about six years. He sometimes got sidetracked while on long overnight hikes, with irregular eating and sleeping throwing him off his lithium schedule. On that first trip through Peñas, I can remember him moving restlessly, like a large mouse, about the Poco Sol cabin at night, kindly going outside when he felt the need to bay at the moon. Art, Maryjka and I were all so tired that we barely registered his howls, but the mumbling, coffee-making and shuffling of feet as he found his way in the darkened cabin were hard to completely ignore. At dawn we missed the opportunity to observe a seven-foot fer-de-lance eating an agouti, but we couldn't rouse ourselves quickly enough when we heard Wolf's shouts to get down the road, where he had gone for an early morning visit with the neighbor. Wolf returned to the cabin as we were getting dressed, scolded us for our tardiness, and started boiling water for our morning nectar.

We were enjoying the freshly washed beauty of the humid green landscape along with cups of delicious coffee when the change in Wolf became apparent. After his active night he was much less animated. One moment he was laughing as he expressed his love for Poco Sol and his dreams for its future, the next he was curled up on the floor in a fetal position, bemoaning his past mistakes. There was an eccentricity to Wolf's personality that was both comical and disturbing. It was impossible not to be drawn to his charismatic energy, but his entertaining storytelling was often punctuated with sudden flashes of anger or sadness. It was hard to keep up with his changing emotions.

I didn't know about manic depression at the time, but since then I have encountered it frequently. Chemical imbalances and personality disorders are everywhere in society. Fortunately, those among us who suffer from depression, schizophrenia, obsessive/compulsive behavior or manic episodes no longer need to be locked away, as Wolf's mother was. They now have a multitude of drugs and treatments at their disposal. The first step on this long, rough road is recognizing behavior as irrational or delusional or self-abusive. Beyond that first difficult insight, along with the appropriate treatment, it is the support of family and community that provides the secure environment from which the person affected can deal with these psychological obstacles. Even with that, you are ultimately alone with your struggle, and the strength to endure must come from within.

Wolf lived apart from his mother for most of his life. The love and stability he received came from his father, his Aunt Mary and the Quaker community. He didn't really understand his mother's condition, but he carried the weight of uncertainty throughout his life, afraid that he would be afflicted with similar episodes. The signs of his own manic depression didn't show up until mid-life, and his truly irrational behavior occurred through the 1970s and early 1980s, when he was caught up in the protection of the forest and the administration of the Cloud Forest Reserve.

An incredible amount of energy accompanies bipolar disorder. Wolf likes to move and keep moving. He isn't good at finishing projects. Typically, knowing that he won't get things completed, he delays starting, and thus his house remains unfinished to this day. Trail work – constantly going forward, productive and worthwhile, with no end in sight – is perfect for him. Looking back at his actions before his diagnosis, he claims that it was harder on those around him than on himself. When I asked what helped him through the difficult times, thinking it would be his faith, his family or his work, he replied simply, "lithium."

"During those times I let a lot of water roll off my back. I carried on like I'd always carried on, and it wasn't me being bothered so much as my family. I didn't care what anybody else was thinking about what I did. It was just me, right or wrong. That was when I thought I could tell clever stories when they weren't really acceptable. My perspective of what was humorous was obviously skewed. I was talking too much, inappropriately at times, and not sleeping really well.

"But I was never violent. There's a story about me threatening a man with a machete over a disagreement while working on the road to Peñas Blancas. It's not true! What is true is that I cut the ropes on an oxcart full of posts that were being taken out of a property adjoining the Reserve. Even though this was the neighbor's private property, I was feeling protective of the Reserve. The driver of the oxcart felt that I was threatening him. I would never have done something like that seriously with bad intent. To me, it was just showing off.

"In the late seventies I was having a problem with the Tropical Science Center. They kept telling me that the TSC wasn't making any money and that community members should be putting more into the Reserve. They wanted me to get more participation from within the Monteverde community. TSC employees worked very hard and were very underpaid. I was super-geared up as the administrator, but I wasn't making decisions easily. It got that I couldn't handle much else from Dr. Tosi, my boss, who was demanding more of me than I could deliver.

"At the same time Lucky was having serious health problems of her own and really needed my support and attention. But I was having a real hard time just handling what I was doing. I always seemed to feel that I'd done something that I shouldn't have done, or worse, that I hadn't done something that I should've. With Luck, I felt that I should've taken her to the doctor, but I didn't. One time, while in San José, our son Berto took her to the hospital when she needed treatment. I should've done that but I just wasn't capable of making the decision. I guess I was depressed, although I never thought that I was. I was always taught that it was all right to cry. And I cry easy enough, although during that period I didn't know whether to cry or what to do next.

"By 1982 I couldn't handle the Reserve. Small problems would get blown out of proportion in my head. Eventually, my kids took control of things. One morning when I returned from the Reserve they were waiting for me. They told me that I had to get help. They said that I wasn't rational and needed to get medical aid as my behavior was affecting Lucky too much. I don't remember all they said, but I remember their concern. I said, 'Fine, well, I'll go to San José.'

"So the TSC had to get somebody else. Dr. Tosi said, 'Go and get whatever help you need. Don't worry about it.' That was a great relief to me. After feeling worried and guilty about not being able to meet my commitments to the Reserve or my family, knowing that I would still be paid while seeking treatment was very important to my peace of mind. In 1983 my son, Benito, who worked with biologists from time to time, took over some of my responsibilities at the Reserve. Then the Tropical Science Center hired Vicente Watson to replace me and he stayed for most of a year. It wasn't that long of a period, but it seemed like forever before I felt normal again and went back to work.

"I went looking for medical attention and right away I was improperly diagnosed by a private doctor. He gave me something that made it nearly impossible for me to relax and fall asleep, and then he gave me a sleeping pill to counter that. The medication was wrong and I had a real bad reaction to it. I got this fear. We were in San José at Berto's and my daughter Helena wanted me to go out for a walk, but I couldn't go past the gate. I felt that if I went outside the gate something terrible would happen and I would never come back.

"When Lucky was in the hospital I didn't want to go see her at all. I couldn't go in a car, even to visit her. But one day they put me in the car and we went. When we were in the hospital I thought that we'd never get out. I felt sure that Berto would never get us out of that building. It was just fear. All these imagined things. I know now that it was because the medication was wrong.

"They never put me in the hospital to monitor the dose and that probably led to the reactions I had to that first treatment. The medicine was really expensive and we couldn't afford it anyway. Fortunately, we found a psychiatrist at the Calderón Guardia Hospital who helped me get straightened out. Since that doctor was part of the social security system all the costs of the visits and the medication were covered by my insurance. By the end of 1983 I was taking lithium and back at work.

This time they monitored my dosage and luckily I was never hospitalized, which I was resisting anyway. I've been very fortunate because I've never had to increase the dose by any amount and the results continue to be great. By 1984 I was working at the Reserve again as co-director alongside Giovanni Bello."

Wolf's wife Lucky is a remarkable woman, although she would probably scoff at the compliment. Young and naïve, with a strength she hadn't yet discovered, she followed her new husband to Costa Rica, up the green mountain and onto their remote piece of land. She started raising children in a canvas tent, learned a new language and adapted to a pioneering way of life. Beyond developing their farm, her restless husband took on work that kept him moving across the countryside. Lucky created a home, nurtured her family, bonded with the other Monteverde women and grew accustomed to waiting for Wolf.

Lucky had her own share of illnesses, beginning with uterine cysts that caused pain during her menstrual cycle. In the sixth month of her fifth pregnancy, she had an emergency operation to remove a cyst that weighed twenty pounds and held three liters of fluid. The doctor was worried that she wouldn't be able to carry the child to term. A healthy baby, Carlos, was born three months later at home in Monteverde, as were seven of her eight children. Even the doctor knew that heavenly intervention, more than his skill as a surgeon, saved that baby.

In the early 1980s, when Wolf's illness was reaching a climax, Lucky was suffering from fibrosis in her uterus. She was hemorrhaging every month and getting weaker and weaker. During this period Wolf was on the wrong medication and couldn't help her. The difficult challenges she faced in those years, often without the support of her husband, added to Lucky's resentment of Wolf's love affair with the forest.

"He loved the woods right from the beginning, and when the first people started going into Peñas Blancas he was right behind them. We used to joke about the Peñas Blancas widows. It was hard because the men would go off for six or seven days and we'd be on our own. Wolf didn't just go into Peñas, he also trucked pigs to market in Alajuela. I had my hands full with babies and little kids so I was kept busy and just had to get used to him being gone.

"Back when Wolf was clearing the woods for our pastures with a chainsaw, I could hear the saw going and the trees falling. I'd hear the whir of the chainsaw, followed by the crash of the tree, and then it would go quiet. My heart would stop until I heard the chainsaw going again. He always talked about the times a tree got hung up or the chainsaw got pinched or a branch just missed him. So those were the images I had in my head. I'd think about what I would do if something happened to him. I never learned to milk the cows or had anything to do with the dairy. There are a lot of things that I think I should've learned how to take care of, that I should've paid more attention to. It's in the quiet of night when I start thinking about it all. Fortunately, I'm now more relaxed than I used to be.

"When George got the idea for the Reserve, he and Wolf were out all the time hiking around, trying to figure out the boundaries. George was a young man, no kids, full of energy, and here was Wolf, also full of energy. Well, the two of them were unstoppable. When they got back from their work they'd just keep on talking together and the family was kept out of it. The boys were left with the milking. I never heard the boys say that they resented it and I never asked. It was the early 1970s and most of our kids were older by that time. Tonio and Melody were the youngest, around nine and six years old, and they didn't get his attention. Wolf had always been a good father, dropping his work to do things with his kids, so it was a loss to the youngest ones when he started at the Reserve and was never home. They didn't see him and missed out on a lot of good times with their father.

"As far as I was concerned Wolf sacrificed his family for the Reserve. It became his sole obsession. He poured his energies into it and also our money. He bought supplies, equipment and tools for the Reserve. If they needed items at the shelter, he bought them. The same with tools. He 'loaned' them and they almost never came back. Wolf was responsible for so much, but he didn't get paid a decent salary. Not only were we losing a husband, caretaker and father, there wasn't enough money coming in to compensate for it. And the decent salary never came. Other people, including the biologists, complained to the TSC on Wolf's behalf. Nothing. It was something that really hurt him and it hurt me.

"Many years later the salary was better and more regulated and there were compensations and honors given. And there was leniency when he needed to get medical attention and to make extended trips out of the country. I had to change my attitude and accept the fact that Wolf was doing what he enjoyed. That was what was important.

"It took me many years to realize that this jealousy I had of the Reserve wasn't a healthy thing. It was ruining my life. I couldn't change him. Wolf was always someone who was very community-minded, putting his energies into a lot of community things. But when he started with the Reserve, he wasn't there for the family and he wasn't there for the community or for the meeting. He was off in the woods and his energies were all taken up in that. Being totally unfair to him, I was still trying to hang on to this other part of him. I had to learn to be more independent rather than dependent. So I started to be the one doing things in the community.

"It was really hard when Wolf was going through his manic-depressive state, especially before we realized just what it was. He'd have a spell about once a year in the beginning, but we didn't recognize it as such. Looking back, we saw that he'd get hyperactive about the same time every year. He became very upset whenever anybody crossed him in any way about the Reserve.

"Wolf got to the point that he wasn't capable of managing himself, let alone the Reserve. I was in such an emotional place that I was ready to break down myself. I recognized that the Reserve needed him. The TSC was considering getting someone to stay at the Reserve, so I considered moving up there if that would help Wolf's stress and calm his mental state. We didn't yet understand just what was going on. I'm glad that we never did move up there for it wouldn't have solved the problem and in the end, would've been very difficult.

"The first doctor's prescription made things much worse. Seeing Wolf was worse, I'd urge him to take more pills, and they would make him even more irrational. He didn't want to take lithium. When he was sick he didn't want to recognize that he was sick. Taking the pills would have been an admission that he was ill. Wolf didn't want to admit to having something wrong as he feared that he'd spend the rest of his life in a mental hospital as his mother had. So it wasn't until we went through six months of pure hell that Wolf was finally ready to try lithium. Immediately, he started doing better.

"His crisis and my own health crisis came at the same time. Our daughter Helena and her husband Tim were here and provided strength and support. The last time I hemorrhaged was up in Monteverde. I went into shock and just about didn't make it to the hospital that time, but Wolf was on the right medication and was better by then. He got me to the hospital in Puntarenas where I was told that I needed a hysterectomy. A doctor checking on patients came by and warned me that having a hysterectomy would mean that I couldn't have any more children. I told him that I was fifty-two years old and had eight children. To the amusement of the other patients in the ward, the doctor was taken aback and left without saying anything more. Those were real rough years, the seventies and early eighties. Fortunately, the family came together to be the strong unit that carried us through."

Lucky is a vibrant, creative member of the Monteverde community. She is a storyteller like her husband, and her entertaining tales have been published in the Monteverde Family Albums for all to enjoy. In 1972 she started taking art classes when two artists from the U.S., Ron Tomlinson and Bill Kucha, came to teach art at the school as well as to the wider community. Lucky became known for her finely detailed pen and ink images of the forest. She held her first solo show in 1988. On view in many buildings in Monteverde, Lucky's drawings are eagerly sought out by visitors. These days she spends her personal time, as much as possible, patiently capturing the delicate beauty of her surroundings, at peace with her life.

Lucky and Wolf need only look to their children to gauge the success of their lives. Barely adults themselves when they started their family away from the support of relatives left behind in the United States, they relied on each other and the community to help them through those hard-working, child-rearing years. They raised eight children who are each energetic, community-minded and highly creative individuals. Like their father and mother, they have an ever-present sense of humor that erupts into a story, a jig or a roar of laughter with little provocation. The Guindon clan is one of the most enjoyable and respected families in Monteverde. Wolf is proud of each of his children, a fact that is apparent whenever he speaks of them.

"Alberto, or Berto, as we called him, was our first child, born on my birthday in 1951 in the United States. He was named after my father. He's spent most of his life in Costa Rica, and married a Costa Rican woman, Norma Chévez. Berto received his Bachelor of Fine Arts at the University of Costa Rica in San José, and then went on to get his Masters in Fine Arts, specializing in bronze sculpture. He worked for several years at La Nación, the national daily newspaper, doing layout and artwork. He got into doing art with computer programs and later making maps as well. Berto returned to live in Monteverde in the late 1990s. He worked with a local biologist, Bruce Young, and also used his computer skills at the Monteverde Institute. He's always remained a member of our Quaker meeting. Alberto and his wife divorced in 2004. He moved temporarily to the U.S. and married a close friend from his youth, Angelina Nidia Gätjens, who's also *Tica*. I know that he'd like to return to Monteverde and is planning to, but beyond that only the Lord knows and He hasn't told me yet."

Alberto looks forward to returning to his roots and the community he loves. With Angelina, he plans to build their home on the family farm in 2008. He wants to dedicate himself to his sculpture and painting as well as working with Lucky and his siblings to create a Guindon family art gallery in Monteverde. When talking about Wolf, Alberto shakes his head as he recalls his father's notorious sense of humor.

"We children learned very early on that Papa was the softy when it came to discipline or to get permission for anything. If we did something wrong and knew that we were in for a reprimand, we would go to him to confess our misdoing rather than to Mama. Because both of them had to give us permission to go somewhere, say to a friend's house to play, we would go to Papa first. Then we could say to Mama, 'Papa already said it's okay!' He got in his own trouble with her because his humor was so often over the top.

"You never knew what he would do for a laugh. One Sunday afternoon, while playing baseball in Howard Rockwell's cow pasture with members of the community, Papa was in the outfield attempting to catch anything that came his way. A beautiful fly ball was hit high in the air. As it was coming down directly to him, he pulled out both plates of his false teeth and held them up, opened wide, to receive the ball. It was a perfect catch and quite a memorable mouthful.

"Saturday night was usually square-dancing night in Monteverde. We all grew up knowing how to dosado and dip and dive. We'd dance at the schoolhouse with live musicians or scratchy old records providing the music. Papa was often the caller but otherwise was on his feet, dancing. One night he came prancing around the square, ending up with Mama as his partner. He kicked off his shoes and trotted along with her, jumping up on the benches along the side, all the while promenading her. He finished by whisking her off her feet in a grand swing that brought the house down. It was antics like this that made Mama's face turn red!"

Tomás was the first Guindon son born in Monteverde, in 1953. He followed Wolf into the forest and is very similar to his father, with the same restless spirit and a terrific amount of energy. He married Lindi Maxson in 1975 and they developed their own dairy farm, having bought the property from Wolf's Aunt Mary and Uncle Walter. Although Tomás went to business school in San José, his childhood love for the woods has continued. He tells his own story, as each of the Guindons are apt to do.

"I grew up in the woods. My brothers Carlos and Antonio and I spent most of our time in the forest, going there as much as we could between doing chores on the farm. We were always building little houses and camping out, climbing strangler figs and swinging on vines. We wandered the dirt roads freely. I pretty much grew up barefoot and didn't start wearing shoes until I was about ten years old or so. Something I particularly enjoyed was the time we spent with Papa and Mama. We'd go hiking or cutting down trees and clearing pastures with Papa. We'd play baseball or volleyball and they'd both play with us.

"I was a different kind of birdwatcher in those days. We'd sometimes carry our slingshots. Our favorite bird to shoot at was the emerald toucanet. We felt justified killing them as they were nest-robbers and we were defending the other birds. We also liked making necklaces out of their beaks. But in those days there were big groups, sixty or seventy toucanets in a group. Now you don't see more than fifteen at once, usually a lot fewer.

"I was about eighteen when the Reserve started. I worked with George, Papa and Eladio clearing the trails and helping with the ground surveying. At first the work was enjoyable because it meant being in the woods all the time. But as far as conservation, I hadn't thought too much about it. It seemed odd to me to be setting aside what seemed like good farming land.

"I only worked for the Reserve for about a year and then I got tired of it. It meant being away all the time, trying to make fires with wet wood, one thing or another. Then Antonio and I started working on our homestead in Peñas Blancas, which we bought from Papa and Marcos Vargas. That was where all my free time was spent. There were about ten families trying to make a living in there and Lindi and I were thinking of setting up a school. At that time, if anything, I was disillusioned with the idea of the Reserve as the administration was putting pressure on to close the roadway to Peñas. We'd invested money in the road and now we were being told that we couldn't use it.

"In the eighties Peñas Blancas became protected as well and we eventually sold our property to the Reserve. My understanding about the need for conservation finally came in the late 1980s when I was working with the Monteverde Institute. That's when I became aware of the loss of species that was happening globally.

"I believe we should live with nature as part of the whole picture, although typically we haven't and that's the problem. I consider how things have changed in my own life. As a kid we cleared land to make more pastures. When I first started buying land, one of the things I liked was that it included quite a bit of forest. I thought that once I got the cleared land producing, well, I could start cutting down the woods and expand. Now I think that one of the biggest values of the farm is the woods in its natural state. The old pastures are regenerating, and instead of seeing them as a waste of all the labor that cleared them, I actually appreciate the diversity that's returning. It's been a slow and gradual change to a different kind of thinking.

"Our family has really gotten into the whole conservation picture, studying nature in one way or another. In what each of my brothers and sisters is doing, there's art or there's the woods. The art comes right from nature, from feeling the forest around you. There's the human need for peace and tranquility, for a spiritual calm that you only get when you're surrounded by nature."

As a child Tomás was afraid of the dark, but he overcame his fear by spending time in the nocturnal forest. As an adult he created guided night walks to help other people become comfortable in the darkened forest, where there is always something amazing to see, even without a flashlight. These walks have become a regular part of a visit to Monteverde. In 1980 Tomás and Lindi had a son, LeRoy, the first of what are presently sixteen grandchildren in the Guindon clan. Wolf's hope is that his grandchildren will appreciate his life's work and perhaps carry it on.

"Tomás and Lindi have three children, LeRoy, Keila and Ari. When LeRoy was born I thought, here's our chance for our first great-grand-child. It took until 2007, but finally one of our grandchildren, Keila, is pregnant. Tomás and Lindi's marriage didn't hold up, perhaps because life in Monteverde, as in many small communities, has its pressures and can be quite difficult. Tomás remarried in 2003. He's now living in California with his second wife, Gretchen Schultz, and in 2006 they had a baby boy, Julian. Tomás is very much a *Tico* at heart, and I think that one day he'll return to live out his life in Monteverde.

"Our first daughter, Helena, was born in 1954. She has her mother's sensitivity to spiritual things as well as Lucky's natural artistic talent. Helena went to the University of Boston but left before receiving her Bachelor of Fine Arts. In 1984 she married Tim Curtis, a man from the U.S. whom she met in Monteverde while he was teaching at the Friends School. They have their own home on our farm where they've lived for several years with their two sons, Silvio and Tulio. Both Helena and Tim are very involved in the Friends School, the meeting and the community. Through her beautiful artwork, Helena has shared the stunning vista we have from our farm of the Gulf of Nicoya."

Being the first girl on the farm with only brothers to play with was a challenge for Helena. She had a respect and affinity for nature that was at odds with the destructive activities that amused the boys, who were happy shooting birds and cutting down trees. As a girl she was expected to keep her mother company and work in the house, but she always preferred being outside. Helena is a deeply introspective person who speaks passionately, laughs readily and expresses her love of the forest with her paintbrush. In 1974 she went to study in the United States, and when she returned to Monteverde three years later she was surprised at the changes that had taken place in her absence.

"In our family, the difference between the older group of children and the younger group is big, almost like having two different families. Those of us who are older had a dad who was present. Sure, he was moving all the time except when he stopped to have a conversation with someone, but he was there. He was the one who took care of things. If he got mad about something he would have a fit, but he could always turn things into a joke. Although all Papa really had was debts, kids and cows, we didn't feel particularly poor because of the way we lived. He didn't mind spending a little extra and enjoying life.

"When I was growing up, I don't remember anybody ever really saying 'be careful.' Considering how many risks there were, what with the frequent use of machetes and such, I don't know how any of us actually grew up in one piece. We played outside, with the trees, logs and many plants as our toys. One of the most fun things we did was play in our grass houses. When a tree was uprooted, grass would grow in the mass of roots and dirt that rose out of the ground and that was our castle, on all the new soft grass. You could climb up high and hang onto the roots and be on top of the world. The hollow that was left where the roots came out of the ground would also fill in with grass and be the moat. The long tree trunk lying in the sun provided a place where every kind of plant would grow and that was our garden. We made up names for all the plants and many of them are the only names I still know. We ate anything that was edible. We did everything outside and that was the best thing in the world for me.

"I always identified with nature, and everything outdoors was my friend. I had one girlfriend who lived nearby but I mostly depended on my mother and brothers for company. But my brothers liked to shoot things and that really bothered me. I kept quiet about it as I was the different one. Just before I went off to university Papa became involved with George and interested in preserving the woods. My brothers became interested in studying the birds and animals instead of hunting them. It was quite a turnabout. Even though Papa was still cutting things down with his machete, he now did it with a different purpose.

"Papa is basically an idealistic person. He had this community and his family and had great ideals about these things. But the farm work didn't offer that – it was just about survival. He always loved being in the woods and the whole idea of preserving forests for future generations gave him what he needed to run on, the big picture that meant something to him. When he made that step from the farm to the Reserve, he didn't step, he jumped. He didn't say anything to anyone else, he didn't plan who was going to take care of the cows, the way most people would have gone about handling a big change. But it wasn't like he wasn't dedicated to our family. We got him to go to the doctor when he was sick, when he would rather have run away into the woods. He listened to us because ultimately he is dedicated to the family.

"When I was a young child everything done in Monteverde seemed quite bubbly and perfect, new and exciting, decisions were being made communally and people seemed to get along. As I became a teenager, in the late 1960s, divisions were starting to surface. I would go to community meetings that would become quite emotionally charged. Even though I didn't understand all the issues, I could feel the negativity. When the tension in the room would be about as tight as it could get, Papa would stand up, say something right to the point that included everyone, that wasn't one-sided, and that would make everyone laugh. It would break the tension and bring unity back to the room. It helped but didn't totally succeed in bringing unity to the community. Papa and Mama had the ability to not take sides, but always tried to find a balance to help center the discussion. I truly feel that their ability to do this was a key factor in the continuation of the community even though several families decided to leave. Papa's talent for coming up with humor in tense situations probably also helped him in his work as a forest guard, when he was communicating in a second language with people from a different culture, using laughter as a healing tool."

Wolf and Lucky's third son, Carlos, was born in 1956. Carlos has spent much of his life pursuing his education in the United States and has the distinction of being the first graduate of the Monteverde Friends School to earn a PhD, which he received from the School of Forestry and Environmental Studies at Yale University in 1997. He married Lidieth Wallace, who comes from another of Monteverde's original families, and they have two sons, Marcelo and Sergio. They live in New Hampshire, where Carlos periodically teaches field courses in biology and tropical ecology as Resident Professor at the Organization for Tropical Studies. This position brings him back to Costa Rica with student groups and allows him to share his wealth of scientific knowledge on tropical ecology with budding biologists.

Carlos recognizes that his Quaker background, particularly the Monteverde meeting, has deeply influenced his work as a biologist and teacher and is responsible for the strong association he feels between his spirituality and the forest. Carlos teaches students to understand the intrinsic links between humans and the natural world. He also works with local conservation organizations to create links between forest fragments, establishing protected migratory corridors that connect nature reserves with habitats on private property.

"George and Harriett Powell were big influences on me when I was in high school. Harriett taught me biology at the Friends School and George would come and tell stories about buying land to protect it. I was beginning to relate biology, which I enjoyed, with the idea that we should work towards protecting natural habitats. I loved to hike, and we would go down into Peñas where we would camp and work on our property down there. When Papa started running around the woods with George and began to see the value of saving the forest, well, the pieces started to fall into place for me.

"I enjoyed school, but I had to work hard and be very disciplined about studying as learning didn't come easily to me. Probably the hardest learning experience I remember happened with George. He and Papa had already established the Reserve and I had come home from Earlham College in the U.S. and was working on our family farm for the summer. We started having problems with peccaries eating *chamol* from a small patch at the back of our property. I knew that peccaries were protected in the Reserve, but they were having an impact on the farm, so I thought it would be okay to harvest one of them in return for what they had eaten, and it would get them out of our *chamol* patch.

"So I took the .22 and went out and by chance found the peccaries right at the edge of the woods. I picked one, shot it, and it rolled down over the cliff edge. I was on my way down to get it when some of the other ones came chasing me, snapping their teeth. I shot in their general direction to scare them off. They turned right around and came back at me. I shot at the one in front, hit it, though I don't think I killed it, and they finally ran off. I went down, bled the peccary, put it on my shoulders and hauled it up the cliff edge. I was proudly bringing it home when I met George coming down from the house.

"He said several things that let me know that he wasn't happy with what I had done. After that he didn't speak to me for a long time. He and Harriett would come for dinner on Sunday nights and one night, months later, George commented on how good the stew was that we were eating. We didn't have the nerve to tell him that it had peccary meat in it.

"That was the last time I took a gun and did any hunting. The connection had been made. I learned that animals needed to migrate down the slope on the Pacific side, and maybe what I was doing was harvesting the same peccaries that were protected in the Reserve the other part of the year. I could see that the same learning process was happening with Papa. We went from being farmers, using slingshots, BB guns and then .22 rifles, killing anything we could eat basically, to using binoculars and a camera and having a whole different way of looking at things. Now I teach others to make these same connections.

"If I couldn't go into the forest to be rejuvenated and re-inspired, I would suffer and become more and more isolated from the spiritual component of my work. I think a lot of people who come here are getting reacquainted with the forest, and that has a value that you have to weigh against the idea of not allowing tourists in so that the land can be completely protected. Some areas are too fragile or unique and shouldn't be used by people for the most part. But if you don't let people into the forest, you lose the secondary benefits that come from them feeling part of nature and willing to protect it for future generations."

When Wolf began working with George in the forest in the early 1970s he left the responsibility of the family dairy farm to his sons along with Digno Arce, the hired man. For a good many years Wolf's salary at the Reserve wasn't enough to cover much more than his work-related costs and it was the farm that continued to pay the bills and feed the family. His fourth son, Benito, became the dairy farmer.

"Our Christmas present in 1958 was our son Benito. He was born between doing chores and participating in the community gift exchange. Little did I realize that he'd be the one to keep the dairy farm going. He reflects his mother's diversity and many talents, whether it's singing in the community choir, weaving baskets, doing pine needle art or creating his well-known line of jams, dried bananas, goat cheese and frozen yoghurt. He has the endurance of a migratory bird in flight, having ridden his bicycle across the continental U.S. and participated in several bicycle rallies around Lake Arenal here in Costa Rica. Perhaps his greatest claim to fame is completing, more than once, the annual twelve-kilometer Monteverde walkathon on stilts!"

Benito always had an affinity with animals and considered studying to be a veterinarian. After graduating from high school he went to Tennessee for a year to work at a veterinary clinic, but decided that it wasn't for him and returned to the farm. Although farming ties a person down and Benito felt restless at times, he gracefully accepted his lot. He says he didn't feel resentful and claims that he had an easier go of it than many young people. He never had to decide what he was going to do with his life or where he was going to do it as long as he stayed on the farm.

Then in 2003 Benito announced that he was quitting the dairy business and selling the cows. It was a difficult decision but one made after much reflection. While perusing his personal diary that he had kept since he was young, Benito realized he was doing the same things, almost daily, at forty-five that he had been doing at fifteen. He needed to step back from farming and his responsibilities in the community so that he could leave home on occasion and have new experiences. Benito has used his freedom from chores to travel to the United States, Mexico, Peru and elsewhere, but he has slowly refilled the barnyard with goats, rabbits and, at last count, a pet tayra. He continues to try to find a balance between his love of the farm and his other yearnings. Wolf can empathize with his son's restlessness, and greatly appreciates the hard work Benito has put in to maintaining the farm.

"Benito is a man with many interests. He has worked for several of the biologists in the area and has become somewhat of an expert on the natural history of the region. He's taken in and nursed a quetzal, a margay, a paca, sloths, monkeys and several other wild creatures. After a lifetime of caring for his animals as well as our dairy, he's easing himself out of farming to be free to move on if and when the desire arises. His physical strength and wide variety of skills won't be wasted, whatever he decides to do.

"Our next son, Ricardo, was born in 1961. He went to the Friends School and then to Earlham College in the U.S. He spent a few years studying modern dance and voice before returning to Costa Rica. Ricky is married to a local Costa Rican, Maritza Badilla, and they have three children, Hazel, David and Francis. Like his brothers, he's spent most of his adult life in the forest, assisting biologists and working as a very enthusiastic and focused nature guide. He studied ornithology under Bill Buskirk at Earlham and is a local expert on birds.

"Ricky and his family are active members of the Church of God in Santa Elena, and he was ordained a minister in that congregation. He'd say that Quakerism doesn't have enough emphasis on guidance and scripture and that as an adult he was drawn to the teachings of a different church. I'd say that he's kept many of the values he learned from his Quaker upbringing such as honesty and respect for others."

Ricardo began working as a nature guide in 1987 after putting up a sign offering his services in Monteverde's two *pensions*. During this same time the silent worship of the Friends meeting was becoming a frustration for Ricardo. As a result he became involved with an evangelical church in Santa Elena where he could orally express his spiritual beliefs. Now he is the musical director there, a position that merges his love of singing with his devotion to God.

It was a long road that brought him to his present life. His personal quest sent him first to Virginia, then to Portugal and finally, Vermont. Eventually, he returned to Costa Rica – to his family, his home and the forest. Along the way he found his voice.

"Growing up in Costa Rica, I always felt, outside of here in Monteverde, like a foreigner. I was light-skinned, spoke English as a first language and adopted certain North American hobbies such as birdwatching, which is something a Costa Rican wouldn't do in those days. I didn't play soccer like some of my brothers did, which led to them having strong relationships with *Ticos*. So I always felt a little strange amongst the Costa Ricans and a little ashamed of my accent.

"As I was deciding what to do with my life, it came down to two things, staying on the farm and being a dairy farmer, or being a biologist. I received my first pair of binoculars and started identifying birds, and decided I would like ornithology. That led me to Earlham College in

Iowa and studying under Bill Buskirk. That was the main thing that led me to the U.S., but it was also my curiosity, wondering if I would feel better living in an American setting.

"I often remark to people that one of the best things I learned from the experience was just how Latin I am at heart. I always felt like a foreigner in the U.S. too, and had a strong identification with anyone who was definitely Latino with dark hair, dark eyes and dark skin. I would immediately feel, 'that's my brother, that's my family, those are my people.' I realized just how Costa Rican I am.

"While in the U.S. an emotional crisis led me to giving my life over to Jesus. It was a major transformation and a spiritual healing, and because I feel I inherited my spiritual calling from my parents, I wanted to come back and share it with them. I didn't have any money and called home to ask if they could help me. I don't know where they came up with the money, but my dad bought the plane ticket for me. In the meantime, I'd returned to where my spiritual mother was living and was convinced that I should stay in the U.S. So I wrote my parents and told them I wasn't coming home. Luckily, Benito was in the States and was able to use the ticket, otherwise it would have been wasted. And my parents didn't have that kind of money to be throwing it away. I felt very ashamed and knew I'd let them down.

"When I finally decided to come back to Costa Rica I didn't let my parents know I was coming until I was in San José. I was so embarrassed about what I'd done the last time. In those days there was only one bus from San José to Puntarenas, and then one from there to Monteverde. I went by bus to Puntarenas and when I arrived I immediately saw my father who had come down off the mountain to meet me. Even though I'd gone astray in the U.S. and no doubt disappointed them, Papa took the time to come to receive me and welcome me home. It was only in recent years that I realized how special it was, that Papa was living out the Christian principle of forgiveness and acceptance, and I was able to sincerely thank him.

"It was always an honor for me to work for the organization that my father founded. For five years I was a fellow employee at the Reserve and then for many years I've been a guide there as well. It's an honor to share with other people the forest that he's worked so hard to protect. I have the chance to go on walks with Papa and now I can actually keep up, and sometimes I can even get ahead of him!"

Wolf and Lucky's youngest two children, Antonio and Melody, experienced life on the farm differently than their older brothers and sister did. The dairy was well established, and by the time they were teenagers their father was working full-time at the Reserve. They both loved Monteverde and planned on staying there, but life had something else in store for Antonio.

"Our son Antonio, who was born in 1963, has become a fine carpenter and cabinetmaker. When he was a teenager, he emphatically told me that he'd never go to live in the United States like so many of his brothers and his sister Helena had done. He couldn't see why they'd ever do that. Then, in 1987, he married Alison Dorsey, a young American volunteer at the Friends School. They went to live in New Hampshire where Antonio apprenticed with a friend who was a house-builder and cabinetmaker. Tonio bought tools and upon returning to Monteverde built a well-equipped woodworking shop on our farm. Their marriage lasted a few years, long enough to produce our beautiful granddaughter, Oriana. When the marriage broke up he continued to share in the raising of his daughter and lived in the United States part of the time. A few years later, when he was once again living in Monteverde, he met a biologist from the U.S., Adair Mali, and eventually they married and returned to the U.S. to be with her terminally ill mother. They now have a lively set of twins, Skye and Sam, and live in Connecticut where he again set up a woodworking shop. They maintain a home here on our farm and spend time here when they can.

"Our youngest, my chichi, Melody, was born in 1966. She's remained true to her roots and close to home. She married Rodrigo Solano, who was a very attentive student of hers when she was teaching English one year. He happens to be the son of one of my earliest farmhands. They have two lovely daughters, Noelia and Naomi. Melody's been the pre-school and kindergarten teacher at the Friends School since her own graduation from there in 1983. She got her Montessori Teacher's Certificate through a correspondence course. Although she teaches at the Quaker school, she's a practicing Seventh Day Adventist. Like the rest of our family, she has art in her soul and the love of nature and sports running through her veins."

Melody describes her childhood as idyllic, which is why she never left Monteverde. She has a full appreciation of growing up with a supportive family in this special community surrounded by forest. Like her father, she loves hiking and believes in conservation, but she has always been leery of animals, tracing her nervousness to the menagerie of critters that she lived with as a child.

"I was always scared of the cows, the dogs, the horses. Unless it was a horse I knew, I'd cross under fences to get away from them. It wasn't like I didn't handle animals, I was around them all my life. But Beni always kept wild creatures in our bathroom and when you had to go in there, well, sometimes there would be a snake, another time a bird. I was pretty young when one of our dogs got rabies. I was with Mama when she met the dog, which was foaming at the mouth, and she had to tie it up. I don't know how she didn't get bit herself. Another time George and Harriett had a *pizote* that had been injured. It had the habit of biting your heels. One bad experience after another made it hard for me to feel comfortable.

"Yet I've always loved being on the farm, being outdoors and hiking. When I was very young I had all kinds of fun times and opportunities to tag along with my father. He always enjoyed having me jump up and ride on the tractor with him. After the Reserve started he wasn't as accessible for me. But I saw how he was socially, happy and talkative and generous, and people seemed drawn to him even if they didn't understand half of what he was saying. When I was young I did very little hiking with Papa. Any time I went into the Reserve it was with my brothers. Now that I'm older, I'd like to go hiking more often with my dad. I've gone on his Tapir Trail to Arenal a couple of times with him. The first time was when he was inaugurating the trail. He was doing this incredibly hard hike at age seventy and I was only in my thirties and struggling along. And that was the third time in a month that he was walking that trail! I have great respect for him.

"One of the fun things about growing up and having Papa working in the Reserve was that we never knew when he might show up after one of his trips in the woods. We'd hear him whooping and hollering as he was coming through the bullpen on his way home. And I have always loved the fresh, earthy smell of the woods on him.

"Being the youngest and probably having the least notion of anyone in the family of what really was going on, I was able to grow up so relaxed. My mother hid her nervousness very well. Even during the worst days, when my dad wasn't well, Mama always gave this impression that she had everything under control. We didn't have to worry about anything. There was a time when she went through a near-death experience, she was hemorrhaging and didn't know if she was going to make it. She called Tonio and me into her room to let us know that she was very ill but everything was going to be okay. People found someone to take her to Puntarenas and of course she survived.

"It means so much to me that even with all the ups and downs, my parents gave me this sense of peace. I'm so happy that they came to Costa Rica and raised us here in Monteverde. Now I hope my own two daughters have that same appreciation of living here.

"Monteverde has grown and changed over the years, but the core hasn't changed. The core is very much Quaker. Especially the respect for others and for our differences, to me, that's at the core of Quaker beliefs. The other thing is that we live what we believe, and that's what I've seen with my parents. It isn't something they do Wednesday and Sunday at meeting, it's the way they live. For this I have great respect for both Mama and Papa, who live what they believe day in and day out. That's been such a great example to me and influenced the way I live my life. The biggest change in me is my relationship with Christ, which, moment by moment, is what makes me the person I am. I've been Seventh Day Adventist for many years, but the foundation of who I am and what I believe is Quaker.

"I've always liked the way my dad sees conservation. I agree with him 100 percent. We're all a part of nature and though we may have conflicting ideas, if we proceed with respect we can keep everyone happy. I bet Papa has had more fulfilling meetings with God out in the woods than anywhere else. I understand this because nature speaks to me so clearly of God. To me it's His creation, and to be part of it is really such a privilege."

The blend of rural *Tico* simplicity and Quaker sensibility provided a gentle and thoughtful approach to life, which was fortunate, because the realities of living in a developing country required imagination, flexibility and patience. As in every other aspect of living in Monteverde, raising children had special demands. In areas such as medical care, sports, culture and education, the pioneers' children were products of their remote environment.

"One of the most memorable things about raising our children was the annual trip we had to make to San José to have their teeth attended to. That was quite an item by the time we got through all eight kids. Usually we took four at a time, sometimes six. We worked it pretty smooth most of the time. One year, the whole family went down to Boca Barranca, near Puntarenas, and stayed at Chase Conover's, a Quaker who'd spent time in Monteverde. Chase had a cabin near the beach and invited people to stop there overnight on their way to or from San José.

"While Luck would stay with the others at the beach, I'd take a couple of the kids on the train to the dentist. There was an electric-powered train that went from Puntarenas to San José, and on a good day it took about four hours. The usual response when we called for a reservation would be, 'Yes, I guess we can make room for you.' We'd be up to catch the 4 a.m. train and we'd come back the same day. We sat on wooden benches amidst the rest of the freight. So we worked it out that way, taking up two children one day and another two the next.

"Before I got involved with the Reserve we were always doing things with the kids. I'd try to find activities to do together that would be enjoyable and educational. We used to visit different areas such as the farming community in San Luis. At that time it was just a trail over the cliff edge that took us down there. We shared many ideas and experiences with the people of San Luis, particularly with the Leitón and Cruz families. Our kids grew up speaking Spanish mostly due to spending much of their time with Costa Rican neighbors who also taught our boys to play soccer. There were teams in San Luis that they were a part of, especially Tomás and Carlos and later Antonio. That was a really good experience that evolved into continuing to 'kick in the grass' with the Santa Elena soccer teams.

"I took all my kids into Peñas when they were old enough. All of them, at one time or another, went down at least to where we had our clearing. Eston's son, Bernie, and my son, Tomás, came for the adventure, but they also liked to hunt. They and the younger ones, Carlos and Tonio, worked for me clearing and planting pasture. It was entertainment to go in and camp and sometimes head down to the pool in the Peñas Blancas River and take a dip.

"I think it's probably true that Helena was the first female to walk through to the other side of Peñas. It's about thirty kilometers to La Tigra! She'd certainly have been the youngest as she was only seventeen at the time. We went to visit a family over on the San Carlos side, the Castros. The three Castro daughters, who I called the *palomas,* the doves, all wanted to make the trek through to Monteverde. They kept bothering their father to allow them to go, but he felt that it was way too far and much too dangerous and wouldn't let them, but when young Helena arrived with me, all the way from Monteverde, they really gave him a hard time. They could've done that strenuous hike because they worked with their father planting grass, milking cows and basically doing the same manual work that he did. They were physically able to go through. After we stirred things up in that household, we carried on to La Tigra. We hitchhiked our way home, getting a ride on the highway from San Ramón to Esparza on the back of a lumber truck. We couldn't take a public bus because they wouldn't let us on with our backpacks since there wasn't any storage underneath. That shows you how much things have changed in this country.

"Later, when the kids were older, we took trips to the Pacific beaches. We used to camp out at Tamarindo and other Guanacaste beaches before they were developed. We'd go once a year at vacation time. These trips were important for getting acquainted with the Costa Ricans and other areas of the country. Part of our idea was for the kids to know how to swim, to be comfortable in deep water, and to be familiar with the ocean.

"Here in Monteverde, the kids would go to Stuckey's pond, which was cold as ice, where Jean Stuckey taught swimming. One warm afternoon, many years ago, there were a lot of kids there and everyone was having a great time. Many could swim but many could only dog paddle. There was a young boy sitting on the bank, as he'd do most Sundays, come and just sit since he didn't know how to swim. But this day, he jumped in unobserved. Nobody missed him until they were getting ready to go and they saw his clothes on the bank. He'd peeled them off and gone in the water. He must've just gone down, boom, to the bottom. It would've been mucky and impossible for him to orient himself.

It was a terrible tragedy for everyone and reinforced the importance of our kids knowing how to handle the water.

"We got acquainted with Santa Rosa after it became a national park. We'd pack our children in the old Land Rover and haul a trailer behind with our camping supplies. When we hit the long rough dirt road through the park to the beach, the more adventurous of the boys would sit on the hood, hanging on. The kids got to see turtles coming onto the beach at night to lay their eggs. One morning we saw the newly hatched turtles pushing their way out of the nest and heading back to the sea. That was the last beach we went to as a family. By then our children were getting older and starting to go on their own adventures.

"Luck and I put in a lot of volunteer work at the Friends School, many, many hours, to make it possible for the children in the community to have an adequate education. It's a private school and is very expensive for the families who send their kids there. The community helped us pay for our children's schooling. The truth of the matter is, those of our children who went anywhere in school did it with very, very, very little financial help. They all got their send-off from raising calves. At the appropriate age, I'd let them choose a calf that would become their responsibility, and when they finished high school and needed money for their future, that cow was theirs to sell. Either I'd buy it or somebody else would. At one point they found out that the neighbors' kids were receiving some money for the milk their cow was giving. I didn't give our kids that milk money. They began to question why they weren't getting paid for their cow's milk and why they would have to sell their cow before they got any money. They figured that there was something fishy in that deal for them.

"Helena and Ricky were probably the only two who made a bit of cash from their cows, but it wasn't enough to go very far. Mostly, the ones who wanted to further their studies found their own financial help through getting scholarships. In the case of Carlos, he was an exceptional student and wanted to keep learning, so he managed to get scholarships all the way through his university education, including one year of graduate school. He got into Yale through a program especially designed to help Latin American students. At the time it was a new thing to go into environmental studies. Carlos benefited from the fact that he was from a tropical country and wanted to study tropical field biology. There were programs that aided foreign students, but our kids are also

American citizens and so could register either as Costa Ricans or Americans.

"In the 1970s, after having been in Costa Rica for over twenty years, Lucky and I made the big decision to give up our American citizenship. At that time we couldn't have both. We already had our Costa Rican citizenship and we'd no plans to ever go back to the U.S. to live permanently. Most of our children, however, managed to have dual citizenship according to the laws of the time. They've made use of that privilege for traveling, higher education and working in the United States.

"I never went beyond a twelfth-grade education in a formal way. I had the good fortune of learning farming know-how from my father and many skills such as repairing machinery. I learned a lot from Costa Ricans while developing the local forest into farmland and later while clearing boundary lines and building shelters in the larger protected area. I then had the privilege of working with and learning from the many biologists who have done their research here. It's brought me great satisfaction to have several of our kids attend college. Carlos is the only one who's gone on to a doctorate and Alberto has the equivalent of his masters. I suppose the only thing I could have a degree in is life in general and staying out of trouble, and that's quite an accomplishment in itself, I think."

The Guindon children were encouraged by their Quaker schooling to be curious, open-minded and involved in community. They each chose their own paths in religion as well as in secondary education, embracing a variety of religious followings. The original Monteverdians were Quakers and the Costa Ricans mostly Catholic, but the wider community now includes Seventh Day Adventists, Baptists, Evangelicals and Jehovah's Witnesses. The Quaker influence remains in community planning and social interaction.

There are Quaker communities throughout Central and South America, many of which at times have been supported and funded by Friends meetings in the U.S. There is a branch of Quakerism that is evangelical, spreading the Quaker word globally. Other meetings, such as Monteverde's, are silent and follow more closely the original traditions of George Fox's Quakerism. There are international committees that link meetings throughout the Americas and the world, and as the Guindon children grew up and left home, this gave Wolf and Lucky the opportunity to travel. They attended many conferences as members of the American Section of the Friends World Committee, sharing the Monteverde experience globally.

"Lucky and I got involved with the Friends of Latin America after being invited as representatives of our meeting to a conference in Wichita, Kansas, in 1977. In Wichita there's a university that's governed by Friends who believe in having a pastor and doing missionary work. Quakers have done a lot of evangelical work, especially in Africa and Central and South America. At this conference they brought together those of us in Latin America from the silent type of worship, who were also somewhat bilingual, with the Friends in Mexico, Guatemala, Bolivia and Peru. This gathering was important in that it opened the way for the Friends of Latin America to later be included in the larger American section of the Friends World Committee.

"Following Wichita there were annual gatherings. I was eventually on the executive of the American section, always representing the Monteverde meeting at these assemblies. Immediately, the difficulty of language had to be met. It took the expertise of bilingual members and the initiative of one woman in particular to incorporate translation into the gatherings over the following years. She insisted on getting the necessary equipment and training people to interpret. This made it possible for everyone who was participating to understand each other.

"Later, the issue of being conscripted into the army arose in Nicaragua, Peru and Bolivia. Members of Quaker meetings in these countries sought support from us in finding alternative services for their children and keeping them out of the army. Our committee was able to help them raise the issue of pacifism with their governments and we supported them through the process.

"In the early eighties I became a representative of the American Section of the Friends World Committee for Consultation. I was able to visit Kenya, Canada, Holland, Germany and Japan, and I attended numerous meetings throughout the United States. The FWCC's mission statement is to facilitate communication and understanding between the various branches and ways of worship.

"I was on the committee for six years. My first meeting was in Toronto, Canada, but being new, I didn't understand the rules of the game. On the morning of the orientation a person contacted me from the Toronto Metro Zoo. He'd been to the Cloud Forest Reserve and offered to take me to the zoo. He was a staff member on a project that was raising frogs in captivity to be reintroduced into the wild. He wanted to show me their facility, as they were interested in getting golden toad specimens for their project. When I should have been orientating I was visiting with the animals, so I started on that committee with a bit of a strain on the relationship. I soon realized the importance of every hour of our agenda and after that first meeting took my position very seriously. Every conference I went to, I met up with old friends and made many new ones. My involvement furnished me with opportunities to be in unique places. It was a privilege to be involved with the World Friends and to represent our own Monteverde meeting.

"During the eighties and nineties Monteverde was deeply involved with helping refugees from the Nicaraguan and Salvadorian civil wars. Two of our older members, Molly and Miguel Figuerola, visited these countries, taking medical supplies and school materials. They also set up a variety of projects that helped churches function and people raise money. They helped hundreds of orphans in Guatemala, raising donations both here and internationally, and taking the money there themselves. Molly and Miguel represented our meeting in this work for several years. They had a unique way of working with individuals, including the authorities, and accomplished a lot by blending into many dangerous situations. Molly was from a Dutch background and was a language teacher for many years. She had a great proficiency in at least five languages. Miguel was from Spain and had suffered political persecution himself so he could relate to people living under oppressive regimes. Nobody else at our meeting would've been as effective as they were and we truly appreciated their contribution.

"In our Monteverde meeting we've had our differences. We're an independent meeting and decide by consensus what we're going to do. For instance, together we decided we'd enjoy singing before worship, to accept teachers who are homosexual, and to collectively volunteer and schedule our time to help community projects. The school is run by a committee of the meeting. Decisions on any topic may be influenced by residents and visitors who don't come to meeting regularly but are part of the community. I think it's that kind of openness that has allowed us to survive and grow spiritually. I don't think we'd have done as well if we'd been closed to non-Quakers or new neighbors joining in our meeting's activities. We've had to discuss, analyze and reach consensus on many, many issues, and not everyone has always felt comfortable with the changes.

"A lot of people have sympathy with our principles. I think that here in Costa Rica people are generally pacifists, though they might fight any minute at the bar or on the way home, perhaps less up here in Monteverde than elsewhere in the country. It's our philosophy to accept visitors at our meetings and in our activities whether they're Quakers or not. Although we haven't had many converts, we've certainly had many people share in our meetings and send their children to our school. We've had over ninety children attend the Friends school for several years."

At any community event in Monteverde there will be a Guindon. They can be found milling about the baked goods table at concerts, leading the square dances at the meeting house, performing in local plays and coffee houses at the school, and on the side of the road, binoculars in hand, pointing out a bird to a visitor. Their artwork beautifies most buildings and their laughter rings out at any gathering.

On most Friday afternoons Lucky can be found at the co-operative Scrabble game, a weekly feature in Monteverde since the 1950s. It was held for years at Dorothy Rockwell's, but is now held in other homes since Dorothy's death in 2004. When Lucky isn't sitting in on a committee meeting, volunteering for a fundraising event or welcoming family and friends in her home, you can find her sitting in the forest, pen in hand, sketchbook at the ready.

"I always thought of myself as a mother, that this was my role. I put my energies into my kids. But in the seventies, as Wolf got more involved with the Reserve and my kids were busy with their own lives, I started getting into art. That was the beginning of a new life for me. I think this was a real relief for Wolf too, that I'd found something I could use my energies for. Now we both head off into the woods but for different reasons. He goes off to hike and I go off just to sit and be a part of the woods. I enjoy that. Now we live a much calmer life."

His family and the community have given Wolf the support to pursue his dreams and to contribute his energies to the protection of the surrounding forest. His thoughts encompass all of Monteverde, but with the passing years, keep him closer to home.

"I'm thinking that there's a lot more to life than just tramping in the woods and mumbling to myself and telling tales. Raising a family has been the most important thing I've ever been involved in. Of all that Lucky and I have done, seeing our children with their husbands and wives and our grandchildren brings the greatest satisfaction.

"All our children are working on various interesting projects, many of them taking place in this area. It shows that the schooling our children had and the influence of our close community encouraged them to take on their life's work that, in turn, is valuable and beneficial to the larger community. Having selected certain values and concerns, the children have grown to realize that they have options, and if they put their energies into it they can have a really satisfactory life.

"The shell of our house is the family center, but our children have their own homes here on our farm or close by. Even those in the U.S. have houses here in Monteverde. Thankfully, they all manage to come back often. They continue to contribute to the activities of the community, such as the school, and to the welfare of our own family.

"My pride dictated that I make a home place for us that would produce enough income to be able to hire someone to help. And so I've always had an extra hand in the barn. I wanted Lucky to have the kind of help that I had, someone to clean the house or do the wash or whatever else she might want done. But she preferred to do it herself. The kids, of course, did a lot as they grew up. But having six boys and only two girls wasn't much help in the house. Lucky might've done better with six girls and two boys. I benefited from my boys taking over the dairy when I went to the Reserve. But Lucky did all the rest, everything.

"My biggest regret is that I never finished up the house. Lucky's sewing room never got done. Miraculously, I have finally properly completed the shower. But there are so many different unfinished projects. I think about these things and I talk about them at home. I think about them when I'm walking around in San José. I'm out walking on my trails in the woods and thinking about what I should be doing at home. I don't need to be up at the Reserve as much anymore, yet I'm still thinking about the trails when I know that I should be putting my energy into the house. While I've been hiking, the termites have been eating away at the wood of the house and that fact gives me another excuse not to get started. Now I'll just wait until they're done and that won't be long.

"All you have to do is see Luck's art to appreciate her perfectionism. This unfinished house is the only thing that I've ever seen her cry about, out of pure frustration. I can see it in the crossword puzzles. Lucky started doing crossword puzzles way back when I was having trouble. She's quite frank about saying that it's what's kept her mind sane, to relax doing something that has nothing to do with the rest of the world.

"Lucky's always said that if you're going to do something, do it well. You're the one who must direct your actions to the best of your abilities. It isn't true to say that somebody else made you do something that you didn't want to do. We're responsible for our own deeds. So I accept that I'm responsible for my own regrets. I also believe that God never sleeps. I guess He must have heard all my excuses by now.

"In our family, we've all been different – Baptists, Adventists and silent Quakers – but we're community people, all of us. That's the Guindons, from way back. Laughter is a big part of us. We laugh so that we're ready for any surprises. My father had a great sense of humor. He taught me so much by example and by understanding. I don't think that I've done quite as well as a father, but I did learn some things. I learned that you have to be very careful when your children are young. You have to watch what you say and do because if they find out you told them a lie you're in big trouble. It's very hard to rebuild their confidence.

"I also think that it's kind of nice that we don't all think alike and do alike. It's a good thing that Lucky has her own interests and a strong creative personality. It's nice to have someone who puts the brakes on or I'd be running back into the woods, spending all my time thinking about reserves, protection and how to better manage it all. Without Lucky's ideas and influence, I would've seen less of what's around me and understood less about myself.

"I'm proud of our family. I'm proud of every one of them. I don't take much credit for the community's success but I do credit Lucky with surviving all the ups and downs of these fifty-seven years together. And I'm grateful that my lucky star is still shining."

TWELVE

Shortcuts

"People talk about taking shortcuts. Well, that's what I've been taking in these woods for as long as I can remember, 'short' meaning the most challenging way of getting there. One of the things I learned in geometry and took very seriously was that the shortest distance between two points was a straight line. That's obviously true when you look on a map. However, time-wise, the shortcut frequently takes longer. But you need to enjoy the woods in between the roads and trails that most normal people are on. Even getting lost pays off, just to have it all to myself once in awhile." *Wolf wandering through Caño Negro*

By the age of ten I knew that I didn't want to live my life in the city where I was growing up, or in any city for that matter. In fact, once I left the area in my late teens, I swore I would never live in densely populated southern Ontario again, preferring the boreal forests, rocky outcrops and deep-water lakes of the Canadian north. So it is with the refrain of "never say never" in the back of my mind that I admit to writing this book from my home in Hamilton, a red-brick industrial city in the congested heart of south-central Ontario. Hamilton couldn't be more different from Monteverde, but even here in the urban jungle, if you wander off the concrete paths you will find Mother Nature's green eyes shining through the smoggy haze.

When I started transcribing these stories in 1990, the thought that Wolf and I would one day turn this collection of memories into a book was an ambitious idea we often joked about. We are like two butterflies flitting through a garden, passing close enough to feel the other's breeze on our wings but seldom settling on the same leaf for long. To think that we could be disciplined enough to produce a memoir together was, well, fanciful. Even though we laughed about it, just the possibility gave my mother an explanation for her friends when asked what I was up to annually in Costa Rica, and her belief in my ability to actually complete this book was both encouraging and daunting.

Over the years the Guindon clan grew accustomed to me following Wolf around. However, at the beginning of our project, there was definitely a period of adjustment. I arrived one afternoon at the Guindon house in search of Wolf, who had just returned from another of his business trips into the woods. He was getting used to talking into the black box, and I was trying to impress upon him not to sit beside a waterfall while recording for the sake of the poor transcriber who could barely hear his voice above the cacophony of the cascading water.

I walked into the house and greeted Lucky and Benito. They looked at me with expressions that lay somewhere between exasperation and fatigue. I asked what they thought of Wolf's and my project. Their eyes turned to the dinner table. I curiously followed their gaze and saw, in the middle of the table, our precious little tape recorder, waiting like an old radio in the parlor for the family to gather around and listen to the war news.

Benito shook his head and, turning back to me, replied, "It isn't enough that when Papa's here, we listen to him talk all day long. But now he goes off into the forest with the recorder you got him and talks to himself. Then he brings it back to us and says, 'Hey, you should hear this.' Now we listen to his ramblings on tape as well. Kay, I think you may have unleashed a monster."

Before I could respond, wondering if I should apologize or defend the process, Lucky and Benito broke into that contagious Guindon laughter, a sound I equate with Monteverde as much as I do the mournful cry of the quetzal and the distant roar of the howler monkey. Wolf's family has always been welcoming and patient with my intrusion into their lives, perhaps believing, as Wolf and I did, that we would never really get around to finishing the book and exposing their lives.

As the years went by and the pile of transcribed pages grew, I began to truly understand that it was my duty to follow through with this project. When I noticed a slight downward shift in Wolf's health and spirit in the first years of the new millennium, I really felt the clock ticking. But I was afraid to get started, overwhelmed by the enormity of the task and unsure of my ability to do justice to Wolf's life story. By 2002, when Wolf's knees were giving him trouble, making walking painful, and he was noticeably depressed, the persistent voice in my head couldn't be quieted any longer and so I got serious. I knew that I had better begin turning the Wolfspeak into something readable while we were both able, no longer one to take my own future, or his, for granted. When Wolf officially retired in 2003 we had more time to work together during the months I was in Monteverde. Despite the detours that have temporarily derailed us over the years, we actually found the time to follow through with our project. Something I have learned in the process is that there are no shortcuts when writing a book. Only with day-to-day persever-ance did the story get on the page, word by word unveiling the essence of this man I am fortunate to call my friend.

This book is not a tale of heroics or celebrity, triumphs or failures, saintliness or morality; instead, it is the record of a man whose life has been characterized by conviction and contradiction. Most of Wolf's adult years were spent doing menial work and hard physical labor. His stories come from the hours, days, weeks and years he toiled on the land, often by himself, occasionally side by side with other tough men and women, uncomfortable, soaking wet and cold, but just as likely too hot.

Wolf doesn't view his work as extraordinary, though his natural humility is tempered by his passionate belief in what he is doing. When you sit across from him at a Monteverde Friends meeting on a Sunday morning, he appears to be exactly what he is, a simple man of modest means. He is the freshly scrubbed farmer in a pastel-colored *guayabera* shirt, eyes shut in private thought or crinkling at the corners in a friend-ly greeting to his neighbors. But the vigorous labor he performed deep in the forest is a big part of the Wolf legend. Driven by a strong spiri-tual intuition towards a philanthropic goal, Wolf always put his legs where his heart was.

From the first days of the Reserve in the 1970s when he was estab-lishing boundary lines in the forest, to the land purchasing and survey-ing in the late 1980s for the Conservation League, through the years of increased tourism and trail use in the 1990s, Wolf was the leader of the machete gang. He would never leave home without his trusty blade, a skilled swordsman always prepared to keep the forces of uncontrollable vegetative growth at bay. He was tireless and unconcerned about being uncomfortable or getting lost, so happily would lead the way, chopping a route for others to follow. Very serious about his work but quick to erupt with laughter when things went awry, Wolf was a natural enthusiast when it came to cutting paths through the wet, dense wilderness.

There are a few hardy souls who have worked extensively with Wolf, spending hundreds of hours on the endless trails: Eladio Cruz, José Luis Cambronero, Alexander Molina, Lucas Ramírez and Wolf's son Tomás, among others. Wolf has worn out many pairs of rubber boots and lost or broken more than his share of machetes and flashlights as well as a number of tape recorders. Over the many years and many miles he has hiked, he has been accompanied by old and new friends, volunteers and dignitaries from around the world, and an overworked Guardian Angel. Until a few years ago he could out-walk all of them, except, perhaps, the Angel. It is only worn-out knees and the inevitable process of aging that have slowed him down. Now likely to be found from time to time taking a breather on a stump at the edge of the trail, Wolf can look back with pride at his many projects.

"Manufacturing *carril* lines was a task you didn't get much credit for, but I consider it something of an art. The goal on a terrain that is very broken is always to select the best place to make the division between properties. This land is hilly and irregular with streams winding through it. The jungle is dense and you can't see very far ahead of you, so you keep cutting your way through and often make false starts when you run into an obstacle. Cliffs and treefalls stop your progress. Of course, it was in the interests of the donors who trusted our work as well as the people who came behind surveying the lines that you did the very best you could. So those of us clearing boundaries and trails were always challenged to keep the lines as straight as possible, which, really, was impossible.

"In 1973 or so George, Eladio, Tomás and I did our own survey of the first tracts of land that were purchased for the Cloud Forest Reserve. In the years between the beginning of the Reserve and before the first official survey by the Tropical Science Center in 1983, there were no mapped boundary lines. From the beginning, purchases were made according to the *carta de venta,* a document that each owner had that roughly stated the size of the piece. This was the only information we had to go on as we worked at cutting the boundaries. We would head out into the forest with our equipment and, when we figured we were in the right spot according to the *carta de venta,* we would choose a logical place to start measuring and start in. We would often be out for most of a week, coming home finally to dry out before heading back into the forest. It was one big job and it wasn't easy to do because of the complex terrain. It was hit and miss, with the information on the document seldom matching what we were looking at standing in the wet forest.

"In 1983 the Tropical Science Center did a major survey to define the outside boundaries of the Reserve and determine its actual size. This included new parcels that had been bought in the upper parts of Peñas Blancas as well as the lands already established in Brilliante and El Valle. The Bosqueterno S.A., those 554 hectares the community set aside in our first year, also had to be officially measured for the first time.

"Before the survey team came in, Giovanni Bello, Eliezar Mejías and I went through a new section of the area that was to be surveyed. This was on the south side of the Peñas Blancas River and was an area that nobody, not hunters, I would say not even God, knew just where it was nor cared too much about. We were constantly circling around, retracing our steps as we tried to avoid the most difficult terrain, which was almost impossible to get through. No boundary lines had ever been established through this broken, rough piece of national forest that bordered the Reserve to the south. As we cut the boundary lines, we called them 'rubber boundaries' as we were stretching them whenever we could to include government forest where no owners had taken possession.

No claims had been made on these steep hillsides but they still needed to be included in the survey. The idea was that this land was undesirable, almost inaccessible, and if the Reserve bought the land around it and connected the properties that were established, we could protect all of it. The forest, in turn, would protect the headwaters of the Peñas Blancas River. Unbelievably, eventually two claims were made in this no man's land! Finally, the people who were making the claims withdrew them as it was too hard for them to clear the pieces and establish the legal claim.

"I got involved in this not long after my sick leave. I knew the work was going to be extremely difficult and I'd sincerely hoped it would be done before I returned to the Reserve. That was the plan, but I was already back when the surveyors came. I knew that cutting lines in this large area would be very slow and that the surveyors would be following us, breathing down our necks as we tried to sort out where to go.

"The survey team was a group of at least ten men and sometimes a couple more. They were assisted by the Reserve's maintenance crew, mainly me and Eliezar. The survey took place in November and, being a wet and often windy month, it's a silly time to be attempting to do this work in the blustery forest. Eliezar and I had the job of hacking our way through the vegetation in an attempt to define a route through a deep gorge for the surveying crew. The surveyors wanted to do the hardest part first, even though we told them that we didn't have the scouting work done nor the lines cut and we just weren't ready for them there. But they got their way and we started out in the Peñas Blancas valley heading south. We crossed the river and went up into those hills that were so difficult to get through. There was a big canyon and we kept following tapir trails thinking that one of them would lead us to the right place to cross the canyon. However, the trails would drop off into thin air.

"When it came to measuring, the engineers wanted the straightest line possible. In one place they had to make a sighting across a canyon that was about a kilometer wide, with a beautiful high waterfall cascading down one of the walls. To get a clear sighting there had to be no clouds and no rain, so we had to wait two days to get the right conditions. This kind of work maybe went unnoticed, but that's what we spent a lot of time and effort over, as well as a few nights out in the forest that I don't even care to remember.

"It was an impossible situation for Eliezar and me, trying to keep ahead of the surveyors. At night we'd usually walk the two or three hours home while the surveyors would stay in the closest shelter. They'd begin the day's work near whatever cabin they were in. We'd return in the morning with fresh bread and meat and other supplies. The rest of the food was organized by Giovanni, who brought it in as far as he could by horseback. In just over a week that large crew of surveyors used fifty pounds of beans and almost 100 pounds of rice. Supplying food was no little thing on that survey.

"In some places we were held up by clouds, in other places, by a lack of clear lines. After a few days of following our zigzagging lines the surveyors were getting tired and confused. On about the fourth day Eliezar and I thought we were doing pretty well until around three o'clock in the afternoon when the surveyors caught up with us and said that they weren't surveying anymore. They told us, 'You guys are heading east and sometimes west and sometimes south and we aren't going to survey those lines.' We replied, 'Give us time and we'll tell you which lines to survey.' But they decided to move to easier land up on top in Brilliante, where there were pastures and clean trails and the outside boundary was already defined.

"I was in charge of the compass, an instrument that Eliezar didn't believe in. About ten days into the survey we were trying to work blind in the clouds and it was impossible to determine the best route. We worked our way down to a stream and crossed over on some boulders. We headed up to the top on the other side just to find the nice fresh trail we'd made the day before. We'd misjudged that one and we lost that day. At this point Eliezar just grunted to me, but later he told Giovanni, 'That's the last time I'm following Wolf and his compass.'

"A couple of days after that I got a new partner, Mario Méndez, who'd been working with the surveyors. He came with me and we scouted around until we found what we'd been looking for all this time, a tapir trail that would take us from Brilliante down off the ridge and link us back up with the work we had abandoned in Peñas near the Aranjuez River. We were finally able to finish a line that the surveyors could follow.

"We were quite pleased with ourselves. After completing the line we headed back to the shelter to let the surveyors know that we'd found the crossing. Well, when we got to the shelter all that was there was a note. Between the wind and the rain the surveyors had been having a hard time working, even on the long, straight, well-cut lines. The crew had given up, having done all they could do in that bad weather. They'd gone home, happy to leave the cloudy forest behind, expecting to return in a more favorable season.

"So, after about three weeks in the wet forest, the surveyors left. There would be no more on-the-ground work, which was the exacting way to conduct a survey. A decision was made in San José by the surveyors that the survey would be completed by establishing three points on a topographical map and drawing straight lines to connect them. These would become the boundary lines on the official property map.

"As they were finalizing the survey map the engineers realized that there was one piece of about 250 hectares in the area that they'd abandoned that needed an owner to complete the total purchase of the larger tract of forest. I volunteered that Eliezar and I had known this tract for at least ten years and we could be called the owners and would be willing to transfer it to the TSC. So the lawyer for the TSC drew up a *carta de venta* for the piece in my name. It was the only piece of land I ever donated to the TSC. I felt very generous about it, and it was the solution to a big problem that the engineers were having finishing off the map.

"Once the Conservation League started buying up land during the Peñas Blancas Campaign in 1988, I was the one who dealt with people in the Peñas valley. By this point the TSC had a map of their holdings. As the League bought land they insisted on having maps drawn up for each property, hoping to avoid the problems the TSC had had in the previous years. But we frequently came up against the same situation. No piece ever had a cleared boundary on all four sides. It might have three sides, it might have a stream or a ridge as a boundary, or it might be up and across the hilltop. So I did the very same thing we'd done from the beginning, I looked to get the best route I could, wherever I could, to get the neighbors to agree on a common boundary. The League also hired a surveyor who was to survey the lines as we bought land.

"We were extending our land purchasing further east down the Peñas valley. The League conducted a survey in 1990 to define the outside boundary of the land they'd purchased beyond the Reserve. It would include all the small pieces that had been bought previously. This was basically the beginning of the Children's Eternal Rain Forest. This piece of land was later part of the conflict between the TSC and the League over who was going to administer it. The survey took about fourteen days. Once again we were in areas where nothing could ever be developed because of gorges or ridges. But then we'd run into a claimed piece and need to define what the claimant considered his land. It was a difficult thing to find out who the person with the claim was and where to find him, since he'd seldom be living on it. As we continued to purchase land it took more than a year to complete the surveying by the League. I imagine that the next round of land purchasing, if anyone can get the millions of dollars together, will be done in a more professional way.

"To me this was a lot of hard work but it was also a great adventure. We didn't have the Global Positioning System then, but even if we had, we'd probably still be out there fooling around, trying to figure out exactly where to go! And sometimes it's better not to know. This was all part of the conservation exercise that probably took years off my life, but they were great years anyway.

"Since the early 1970s, when we started buying the clearings and homesteads that had been carved out of the forest by the squatters, an expanding tropical forest puzzle has been fitted together piece by piece in the name of conservation. For me, each piece commemorates the person or family that, out of a sense of adventure or speculation, or in the hopes of developing a homestead, staked a claim to a parcel of tropical wilderness. Although many properties that were purchased were re-designated to the donors' name, we shouldn't forget those rugged people with names from Arguedas to Zamora who handmade the trails and shared with me and other travelers through Peñas Blancas their hospitality, coffee and dreams."

The area Wolf wandered endlessly through is divided by the Peñas Blancas River. In the dry season, when the water is lower, there are safe places to cross on boulders and in pools with shallow currents, but for much of the year fording the river is a challenge. As more tourists and student groups came to the valley there was a greater need for a safe way to cross year-round. Walking from Monteverde, the main destinations on the other side of the river are Eladio's cabin and the Portland Audubon Center. For many years there was a poorly designed pulley-and-cable system partway between the German's and Eladio's that could transport one person, and eventually two, across the often raging water. In 1990 plans were put into motion to build a suspension bridge, *la hamaca,* to replace the unsafe cable car, a year-long event that Wolf spent many hours laboring over.

"It's the beginning of April in 1990 and I want to make one last comment about the cable car, what we call the finger trimmer. The cable car wasn't well designed. The metal cage, which replaced the original wooden cage, moves on a pulley-and-cable system and the rider controls his passage by pulling a rope. You climb up from the riverbank to a wooden platform and then step into the cage while holding the rope to keep the cage in position. You release yourself and the car will coast down to the lowest point on the cable. Then you have to pull the rope to get the cage to move up to the platform on the far side of the river, reaching up with your hands above your head. It's very easy to pinch your fingers between the pulley and the cable, so the rope should be further from the overhead pulley. And until you're ready to really launch out, there should be a proper brake control that holds the cage in place. I can picture someone between the platform and the car dangling by one arm over the river and that person might be me. A really necessary thing to have would be a big label: Handle with Care!

"Anyway, that's only one person's opinion. But this thing has done more damage to humans than any snake in Peñas Blancas I know of. The new option we're getting is sure going to be used, so that makes it worth the effort. Once we get *la hamaca,* fingers will be saved.

"For me, the need for the cable bridge became personal one day when I was attempting to cross the river by myself. Back in the mid-eighties José Luis Cambronero, Eliezar Mejías and I were exploring the area beyond Camp Three. Early that morning, on the trek home, I suggested that they go on ahead as I wanted to make a loop to check out a squatter's claim in the Quebrada Portal area. I planned on catching up with them later.

"When I arrived at the river, which was real wet, I decided to stay dry and cross with the cable car since it had been conveniently left on my side of the river. Back then the cable car was a wooden cage. I climbed aboard and coasted out to the middle. I took the rope and started to pull myself across to the other platform. At that moment, midway to the other side and about thirty feet above the water, I crashed down on a huge rock. BOOM! The wooden frame of the car broke into pieces and the loose cables came down around me. With the initial impact my first focus was on the natural beauty downstream and I found myself thinking, 'I always expected that heaven would look just like Peñas Blancas.'

"It took me a few minutes to decide that I was still alive. I was in shock, though I didn't realize it. I could actually walk and miraculously nothing was broken. So I decided that I should take my pack and go on to the nearest shelter, which was the German's. Once I got there I didn't really know what to do, whether to stay or go home. After a while of circling around, dazed and confused, I decided that I should definitely head for home. What I discovered was that I couldn't take normal-sized steps. Evidently, I'd damaged a tendon in my leg in some way. It took me over three hours to walk what would normally have taken just over an hour. As I was making my slow way up the hill, it got dark.

"Meanwhile, José Luis, who was boarding with us at the time, had arrived at our home hours before and expected me to get in well before nightfall. When I didn't come he prepared to go back to look for me. I finally got home and of course everyone was curious as to what had happened. I told them a vague story of the cables coming loose and landing on the rock. At first they laughed, but Lucky quickly realized that I was in shock and that, truthfully, anything could have happened. I took the whole event quite seriously and decided then and there that nobody else should have the opportunity to go through what obviously could have killed me."

Wolf thought his involvement in building the suspension bridge would be to cut the trail to the site and perhaps help carry materials in. However, his boss, William Aspinall, decided that Wolf should be in charge of the project. He ended up being responsible for calculating the materials that were needed, getting them the twelve kilometers or so to their destination, and overseeing the construction. Eladio Cruz and Wolf studied the site and figured out where to mount the cable anchors, or 'dead men' as Wolf called them. He had high hopes that the bridge would be done by the end of the year, and it did get done, more or less, on schedule.

"Well, we've made it all the way to November of 1990. We know the weather is going to change soon. The mountains above 1,500 meters have been in the clouds all week and I guess it shouldn't be any surprise just how much water that adds up to down here. In any event, if we had *la hamaca,* you could sure bet that it would get used by this hiker! Not that many people come this far down the river to cross, but I think they will once they have the bridge. Anybody who's used the cable car more than once uses it a second time only because they have to. I tend to wade across the river if at all possible.

"I have to say, it's been real neat to have a great volunteer, Victoria Rich, out here with me. She's a really good hiker to work with out on the trail and to be good buddies with. It's been a very easy three days as far as having somebody right there in my footprints. That's why I call her The Shadow. She's always pitching in to get our meal together and to keep up morale. If I can always get volunteers like Victoria, then we're home safe. On this one, I've really done well.

"The old twenty-seventh of November was quite a day. We were coming down the Catarata Trail from El Valle. We spent about an hour trying to figure out where the trail had gone since it had been blocked by a treefall. That hour cost us a late arrival at the river crossing. The river was high and we tried to cross where I usually do but it was just too swift. So we finally sorted out a place that Victoria had noticed upstream. I got all the way across the main river except for the last two meters or so. It was the last little bit before the other bank. I could taste it. There was a pretty deep chute in the river with quite a bit of current. I stepped in and got caught in between two big boulders so I couldn't step forward or back. When I lifted my leg the current took my foot right on around behind me.

"I was tired, it was almost dark and I couldn't fight it anymore, so I did the next best thing. I made a lunge across the current, seeing that I was going to get carried down and land up against a tree limb hanging out from the bank. When I reached the limb I was pretty much soaked, having played roly-poly in the river. I'd taken in a bit of water and a whole lot of what the current wanted to do with me. Anyway, I caught hold of the limb and pulled myself out and was safe.

"I went on up to Eladio's cabin and went back with a rope to help Victoria across. It was really deep and if it hadn't been for the rope, she'd never have kept right side up while crossing. That was a long day. I felt so darned stupid for my first mistake, which was getting us here to the crossing much too late in the day, and so tired and wet from the second one, having stepped into the water with both feet before testing the current or depth, that I didn't care much about anything after that.

"That was my first and only time getting dunked by the river. You get the feeling that only the Lord's going to pull you out because when that current hits you, you know that you're going to bounce around off those rocks. It's not just anybody who would follow me around for that many days and still be standing. Victoria should have known better and maybe she does. To have a day like that and take it with a smile is what it's all about. The mixture of trail and river doesn't get any tougher, and I should know because I've been running around here for quite awhile.

"When you're following this old wanderer, why, it's one of those chances you take and too often you get caught and come up late. It's a whole new ballgame after dark. I've put in a thousand hours alone and I don't always do things logically, like plan things the way the book says they should be planned. Probably the book's right, but it's kind of fun sometimes to do it on your own. Anyway, it proves my theory that the new *hamaca* across the river will have happy customers and I'll be the first one.

"Now we're back on the Peñas Blancas side of life. It's supposed to be the sunny side at this time of day, six a.m., but she looks a little misty and there's quite a bit of wind. I've got another load and a half of materials for *la hamaca* and I think I won't have any problem getting it down there.

"I relayed my first load from the German's to the construction site in the old backpack. Quite a load: two gallons of gook and two plastic Coke bottles full of nails and a lot of other stuff to go with it. Now I have to run back and pick up the rod. Because of the difficulty of traveling on this abandoned trail I'm using, it might take an hour and a half hauling that little bit of steel, half an inch around and about four meters long. I'll try to carry half of it between my pack and my head and shoulders. The rest can drag. The rain's here just a drip at a time, nothing to get excited about, but the sun seems to be completely wiped out. The old river looks pretty calm today and I'm looking forward to going down and taking just a minute to dip, even though the weather is cool and blowing and misting.

"The fellows got all the cables down yesterday clear to the *hamaca* site. We were able to take the boards to the far shore by sliding a light rope over a heavier rope strung across the river. They've got things pretty well figured out and can start building the bridge on the other side. I predict that before Christmas we'll have that thing functioning. Of course, predictions are something that you do every day and naturally the prediction isn't the thing that gets the job done. It's so muddy that anything with any brains is just sitting in its den waiting for the weather to change. So we'll see what we can do on Monday to get this thing finished before I grow old and really lose my enthusiasm.

"December 21, 1990. You know, it's funny. We were talking about this being the shortest day of the year. I find out its got twenty-four hours just like any other day, so I'm not scared about it anymore because it's just as long as the long days. It's just a matter of whether you have a good flashlight or not. I got the community Christmas barbeque done, then drank about six cups of coffee and had just a little bit of steak to keep me alive until I get down to the Guindon ranch in Peñas Blancas.

"It was really a good day and I got a little more work done on that thing called *la hamaca*. We got there at almost noon to put the penetrating grease on the new cable, so we're making progress. I actually got to ride across the river in a ten-gallon bucket hanging from the cable. That's what I've been waiting to do for a long time, cross the river without getting wet. Well, I did a beautiful job of it on the downhill slide, but of course, pulling yourself up, you're kind of a dead weight, so it's not really recommended yet to go across uphill. But it was great.

"I'm really pleased with the structure that we poured. That was worth the whole trip, to see that done and to see what a good job the fellows are doing. But what the Head of Protection is doing supervising the construction of a cable bridge, I don't know. Of course, once a guard walks across it, it becomes part of protection. At this point, the engineering and building of it by someone with no experience, along with a crew that has no experience, is beyond my thinking. Soon there'll be new trails on both sides of it designed for guard patrols. Now, trail design, that's talking down my alley. I think that'll be something I'll be doing over the next year and I look forward to it."

There is an art to trail-making. A well-designed trail system brings people close to spectacular views and keeps them away from sensitive nesting sites. Switchbacks, where the path zigzags up steep inclines, not only save wear and tear on a hiker's knees, they prevent erosion by limiting the vertical flow of rainwater that can easily wash away a hillside. If a path is too narrow, hikers will naturally widen it, a footstep at a time. If a route is poorly marked, they will create their own path or quite likely get lost. If the goal is to limit the impact of traffic on the wilderness, it is necessary to keep the hikers happy on the trails that are provided.

Over the years, as the number of visitors to the Reserve has increased, the trail system has evolved. Most visitors are content to follow the paths in the Triangle, where they can walk for hours without straying too far from the Reserve's entrance. Initially, only energetic wanderers like Wolf or dedicated hunters and biologists would venture into the forest's depths. With the increased popularity of eco-tourism bringing less experienced hikers determined to explore deeper into the forest, better trails were needed to keep them safe and provide them with a variety of sights and degrees of difficulty in terrain. Proper steps made of blocks and stepping-stones called "cookies" made of log slices help to prevent people from widening the trail around muddy spots. In recent years small-gauge chicken wire was laid over the cookies to prevent slipping.

Since 2005 the Reserve has utilized a wood substitute made of recycled plastic on the trails in the Triangle for steps, edging and platforms as well as for information signs. This material, which should last between twenty and twenty-five years and is impervious to mold and the constant moisture of the forest, keeps the trails smooth and less prone to erosion. Although it is a costly alternative, after the initial installation much less maintenance is needed. Using this recycled product also provides a solution to the growing problem of garbage in our "disposable" culture, which Costa Rica is very much a part of.

Although Wolf has been involved in the development of most of the trails in the area, his own preference is to save time by following an animal trail straight up a hillside or by heading in a direct line, cross-country as the macaw flies, using a distant tree as a marker. Of course, saving time isn't always what happens. Wolf's curiosity has just about killed him at times, something a string of hiking partners can attest to. But he has always had the energy and will to keep going, and more importantly, the strength of mind not to panic, even after realizing he has walked for hours only to hit the same spot he departed from.

In the 1970s Wolf began working on a trail that would link the Cloud Forest Reserve with the Arenal Volcano. Looking for the best route through the jungle and across the steep ridges, he followed tapir trails and the existing boundary lines of the Arenal National Forest, in the process making several false starts. Plugging away year after year, accompanied by anyone he could entice into making the trip, Wolf finally succeeded in creating a footpath between these two spectacular regions of Costa Rica. It is at least a two-day hike, even for the heartiest traveler, with the option of staying in a rustic camp in a couple of spots along the way.

"My interest in going to Arenal started back in the early 1970s when they were building the dam. The first three times I hiked over there, I accompanied groups of visiting North American students who were on an international exchange program. At that time we could walk from Monteverde through Santa Elena, along the road through upper San Gerardo, then down into the valley, ending up on land that would later

227

be flooded and become Lake Arenal. Before the lake was there, we would walk through forest and pastures until we arrived at the village of Caño Negro, which was eventually relocated. We would walk all the way to the original village of Arenal and then catch a bus to Tilarán and home.

"Once the dam was completed but before the water gates were closed, in about 1976, Eladio Cruz, a couple of volunteers and I decided to go over to see the finished structure. We walked there by the usual route through upper San Gerardo, but planned on returning the more tempting way through the forest. This meant putting our faith in a topographical map and a compass and heading out from the volcano in a southwestern direction towards El Valle and the northern boundary of the Reserve.

"We got over to the construction camp near the dam beyond the base of the volcano in one day and camped out there. After breakfast the next morning we started searching for the proper route that would get us to the ridge that we figured would be our starting point into the forest. We assumed that we'd still find homesteaders living in the area who could point us in the right direction. We not only found no people, but all of the houses except one were also gone. They had been destroyed in preparation for the flooding that would follow the closing of the waterway and lead to the creation of Lake Arenal.

"Fortunately, by mid-afternoon we found a little building that was above the flood line. A family lived there and the man told us that we were headed in the right direction and that we were about an hour's walk from a shelter where we could spend the night. We were told that the following morning we should cross a swampy pasture and climb a ridge. On that ridge we'd find a boundary line and we were to follow that line to the end. He said that we should then look for the highest hill and head for that. He'd never been beyond that point himself but he'd been told that that's where hunters came through from Castillo, a local village. Of course, there were many details he didn't tell us.

"One of the things he didn't tell us was that it was going to rain for twenty-four hours and that we'd be soaking wet after our first night. Another thing he didn't say was that there were two hills that were very similar in height and it was hard to tell which was the highest. The third thing he didn't mention was that tapir trails were always the best way around the canyons, something we soon became aware of and profited by learning.

"On the next night, just when we were thinking we were going to have to set up camp soaking wet again, we came across a log that had been cut by a chainsaw, so we knew we were probably near someone's camp. We abandoned our compass and followed a manmade trail to a shelter that was a wonderful place to spend the night. It had thick mattresses and a fire to dry us out and *naranjillas* to make juice. It was paradise. But we'd deviated from our topographical map. The next morning we should've returned to our original route but decided we didn't want to go back that far and took a new bearing on the compass. For once I looked seriously at the map and told the others that if we found ourselves going downhill and south, we had to stop as that would mean we were going wrong. Round about lunchtime I realized that we were doing exactly what we shouldn't be doing. So we stopped, backtracked to a good place to have lunch, and reoriented ourselves. We could tell by looking at the surrounding ridges that we were nearing the high ridge where we would find the *carril* line of the Reserve. On the third day we made it all the way through and by 4:30 p.m. arrived at the El Valle shelter.

"So now I knew that we could walk through the great unknown forest to the volcano. The San Gerardo route was basically a horse trail that passed through cleared pastures. Who wanted to follow a horse trail to get to Arenal? Certainly not me! This first hike convinced me that one day I could make a trail that people could take from Monteverde to Arenal through these beautiful woods. The error I made was not permanently marking the spot on the *carril* line where we'd come out. This turned out to be the key to entering the maze of ridges that would deliver you to Arenal.

"In 1978 an Englishman, Leonard Bird, came to Monteverde. He was a Quaker as well as the ex-mayor of a town in England. In his younger years he'd been a long-distance runner and had gone to the Olympic Games as a judge. The other angle was that he was very interested, as a Quaker, in the fact that Costa Rica had abolished its military. So he came to Costa Rica and eventually wrote a booklet called *Costa Rica, A Country Without an Army*.

"Every time Len came he wanted to go hiking. He especially wanted to go to the Arenal Volcano. In two attempts we didn't come anywhere near the volcano. The first time we spent three days trying to make it all the way through, then turned around and came back. The original *piquete* was lost and we couldn't find our way. We never got to the right ridge. It was late in March and should've been dry but instead we were hiking in the clouds and we had three days of being soaking wet with no visibility. So we didn't make it.

"By the next time we attempted the trip, in February of 1981, I thought I had a good idea of where we should be heading. We started out once again in bad weather, along with another companion. We had a miserable night and got soaked. We didn't carry tents, only hammocks, so we made shelters by cutting palm trees and using the stalks as a support. We used the palm fronds and heliconia leaves to make loosely thatched roofs, hoping that it wouldn't rain. That was when I was having a problem being rational. I'd look at a map and couldn't make head or tail of it, so we didn't get through then either.

"An Italian volcanologist, Andre Borgia, who was working with the University of Costa Rica, came to Monteverde for the first time in August of 1981. He also wanted to go to Arenal. Andre wanted to take samples of all the different strata of eruptions from around the volcano. So I said that I'd take him and his hiking friend to the place on the *carril* line where the Arenal trail began and I'd point him in the right direction. He and his partner came back a couple of days later and said that they were doing fine right until they ended up in the Caño Negro River gorge. They cleared trail as they went until they realized that they were in the wrong place. So they would have to leave it till another time.

"I went with Andre on a second attempt and we extended the trail they'd started cutting, but we still didn't make it to the volcano. Our third trip together, along with Frank Joyce, was the first time we made it all the way through. That was in 1982, and that was the beginning of my trail to Volcán Arenal.

"A couple of years later Leonard Bird came again. Since I'd recently been scouting through the area and I now knew where to go, we finally made it through to the volcano. We were rewarded on our last night when we camped in a pasture and watched the volcano's fireworks and listened to its thunder all night long.

"It was many years before I got the chance to work on that trail again. In the mid-1990s I finally completed the trail to my satisfaction, about thirty kilometers in all, with a camp midway. Eventually a second camp was added a few kilometers further and even more rustic than the first, to give another option for those people wanting to walk slower and stay longer in the forest. I've now hiked on this trail either by myself or with a variety of hiking partners as many as thirty times. I named it the Tapir Trail because following the conspicuous, worn-down tracks of those animals often guided me through the rough places and across the heads of steep ravines.

"In recent years I've had a few memorable hikes on my trail to Arenal. It's real encouraging to see tapir tracks around again. On one trip the tracks were on my trail coming up out of Peñas and returning through the Laguna Escondida area back down to the river. It's great to see them still crossing back and forth between the Peñas Blancas purchases and Caño Negro. So everything is under control there. I've seen white-faced monkeys and howlers and I also happened to see spider monkeys down near the Observatory Lodge in the area by the volcano. That's a beautiful chunk of rainforest.

"I'm real proud to have had a species of frog observed near this trail that hadn't been seen in Costa Rica since 1987. In August of 2002 local biologists Bill Haber, Willow Zuchowski and Mark Wainwright came on the Tapir Trail along with Eladio Cruz, Lucas Ramírez, my son Ricky and me. Near a section of the trail that's in the Children's Rain Forest they found one adult green-eyed frog, *Rana vibicaria,* and thousands of tadpoles. I felt real pleased that these serious biologists had taken the time and energy to go out on a real hiking trail, two good days of walking to the volcano.

"On May 1, 2003 I led a group that included members of my family, Reserve employees and even an ex-director of the Reserve, Francisco Chamberlain, on what I promoted as the inaugural trek of my Tapir Trail. We hiked on the trail from Monteverde to the Observatory Lodge at Arenal in two days. We then returned by chartered bus to Monteverde. Although this is a fast way of doing this trip, allowing you to sleep in your own bed on the second night, the disadvantage is that you miss all the extras, the hot springs, the local town of La Fortuna, and a whole lot more that you can only experience when you do it the old-fashioned way, by foot and public transport.

"The Tapir Trail is there and it looks like it has a future. That's good, because it goes the right way, that is, my way. Just go along the ridge and look for those land bridges that the animals use to get from one set of hills to the next. Before you know it you'll be at the foot of the volcano, so long as you don't wander off the trail and onto the wrong ridge."

Eladio Cruz, who sits on the board of the Conservation League, adds the official view of Wolf's Tapir Trail.

"I've worked on the trail that Wilford constructed that goes to the volcano. The League and others are now considering it a priority to maintain it, so even when Wolf is no longer able to walk, that trail will be kept up. He always had the idea that we should get groups of back-packers using it, and we've now had several groups do so. It's a better path now. Wilford also wants the people of the community to walk on his trail. He hopes that everyone who does will then tell others how unique and valuable it is."

Richard Butgereit was a wiry youth of eighteen when he first went to Monteverde. His father, Roy, had been one of the original settlers of the community but after a few years had returned to Fairhope, Alabama, married Elsie Arnold, who was a childhood friend of Wolf's, and remained in the United States. In 1990 Richard traveled with his parents to see this place he had heard about all his life. In a local restaurant, over milkshakes, Wolf asked him if he would like to live with the Guindons and work with him in the forest. Struggling with his education plans at the time, he eagerly accepted this opportunity for adventure, little know-ing what "working with Wolf" truly meant.

For seven months Richard followed Wolf through the Reserve and lived on the Guindon farm, learning as much about farm life from Lucky and Benito as he did from Wolf about the woods. Influenced by his experiences in Monteverde, he returned to the U.S. and enrolled in biology at New College in Sarasota, Florida, eventually receiving his bachelor's degree. This led to work as a field biologist and eventually to a specialization in the application of Geographic Information Systems for the Florida Department of Environmental Protection.

"At that young age I had the opportunity to become 'numbered among the victims,' which is a way of saying blessed beyond belief with the opportunity to walk in the woods with Wolf. There are many stories from our trips, but one stands out in particular as The Trip.

"It was a simple proposition, to head out through the Reserve to the cabin at El Valle, then down the trail to the Peñas Blancas River. We were to make our way along a trail that supposedly once existed but was now lost and meet up with the trail that followed the river to Eladio's. We would head out after lunch from the *casona* and take an easy three-hour hike to El Valle, spend the night and then continue on the trail the next day.

"We got started late and whatever the reason was, it's been totally lost, as we soon were. But I'm sure, like all of the other reasons we ever had, it was a good one. Needless to say, even though darkness was approaching, we carried on right past the shelter and comfort of El Valle and headed down towards the river on the Catarata Trail. It was just about dark when the well-marked part of the trail disappeared. We then scouted from tree to tree, looking for telltale signs of machete cuts, trodden earth or broken limbs to show us the way. It would have been a few hours walk back to El Valle over the trail we had now cleared, but the decision was made to go forward. Our bellies were full, the water was plentiful, the machetes were sharp, the headlamps were on, so forget about daylight, down the ridge we went.

"It was only an hour or so past dark when we made our mistake. The trail hit a large flat area with drop-offs on either side. There was evidence to suggest that the path continued in a couple of directions so we had choices. Unfortunately, we chose poorly.

"The first thing to go was any semblance of a trail. The second thing was my flashlight battery. Now I was following Wolf as close as I dared since his machete was swinging wildly, but he had the flashlight and I didn't want to take a fatal misstep. The third thing to go was his machete, springing from his hand, turning lazy flips off into the darkness, deeper and deeper into space. Wolf dropped down a bank and dug around until, miraculously, he retrieved it. It may have been better if we'd left it there for not once but twice within the next few hours in the all-consuming darkness, I got too close, or Wolf pulled back too far, and the edge of his machete lightly kissed my forehead. It was so delicate a touch that we hardly noticed, but in fact we were aware that, wow, that was close. After the second time I considered death by falling versus death by split skull, and opting for the former, moved back and maintained a good few steps from Wolf.

233

"We changed our plan. Because we were going downhill, the terrain in front of us frequently simply quit, falling off in a sheer cliff. We'd follow a stream down, hear some noise, and then find that the next dark step was over a 100-foot waterfall. So the new plan was to work our way up by following a stream to its headwater on a ridge, and hopefully follow the ridge down to the big river. It was now past 4 a.m., we'd been on the trail for over twelve hours, the first three easy, the rest hard and in the dark. Our joints were aching, our senses were dulling like the edge of Wolf's machete, and our outlook was dimming like his flashlight.

"We encountered a small waterfall. I went down on one knee and Wolf used me as a stair on which to climb up. I stood and used my arms to push him further up as he steadied one leg on my shoulder while the other searched for a hold on the rock wall. With a final burst and shove, he topped the waterfall. He stood, looked down, and asked, 'Now, how are you going to make it up?'

"'I don't know,' I replied, but began to climb, finding a foothold here, another there. In the darkness, wearing a sixty-pound pack, rubber boots filling with water, I climbed the sheer wall. It was really only a bit higher than I was tall but seemed to tower above me. Suddenly I was on top, lying in the stream, water rushing down my chest. Somehow I had climbed it.

"With great satisfaction and a grand sense of accomplishment, I stood up, proud and tall, which was very unfortunate since I was wearing sixty pounds on my back and totally forgot to compensate for it. As easily as I had stood, I now tumbled backwards, over the waterfall, down the six or so feet. It didn't take long and I didn't have much time to react, but my survival instinct kicked in. I balled up and with that move, and thanks to a rolled sleeping bag in the bottom of my pack, I was cushioned from serious injury even though I landed squarely on my lower back. I lay still, wondering if anything was broken or, indeed, if I was actually dead. Wolf had told me a story once about Peñas Blancas appearing to him like heaven, and now I was having my own celestial experience.

"I saw a dim light over me. Was it an angel? No, it was just Wolf, his pale flashlight beam in front of his dark shadow, peering down from above. He asked, "Are you alright?" and incredibly I was. I picked myself up and we finally decided to call it a night. Wolf came back down and joined me and we managed to sleep for a while beside the stream, waking when our legs would slide down the embankment into the cold water. We would pull ourselves back up, lock our legs in position and begin another round of hopeful rest.

"With morning's light we found our way down to the river where we split up, heading in different directions. I wandered along to Eladio's on my own, remembering the time when I'd asked Wolf what led him to invite me, a wandering, listless young man in search of some meaning and experience, to come and work with him in the forest. He'd said, 'You looked like you could carry my pack.' Wolf always has a way of doing small things that end up being much more profound. Certainly, his simple invitation to work with him had a profound impact on the rest of my life."

Along with physical endurance and strength of mind, it takes a lot of sustenance to keep a person moving down the trail. I was asked once by a friend to question Wolf about what he eats when he is in the forest. I laughed and said, "Wolf survives on candies and coffee." Until his recent diagnosis of diabetes, I had never seen him without a pocket full of something sweet. Of course, the person doing the asking was referring to wild foods found in the jungle that can offer nourishment in the event that someone is lost or injured. Wolf has had incredible luck at avoiding injury while deep in the forest, and would never actually consider himself lost, but I put the question to him.

"The first thing I learned about wild edible foods was that you could eat hibiscus flowers. You don't actually see them much right in the woods, but they're common along roadsides and around large treefalls and old homesteads. Dr. Tosi from the Tropical Science Center was the one who told me that they're edible. They've a little bit of a honeysuckle flavor, a nice sweetness to them. You can also eat wild begonia flowers, which are easily found in our forests.

"I always carry mints to refresh me, though finding any plant in the mint family would be just as refreshing. But if you're caught in the woods with nothing to eat you should be looking for moisture. Since you may not be near a spring or if you can't trust a water source, you can look for moisture on the petals of several flower species. Not only do they trap beads of water and supply you with that nourishment, if you get a little pollen mixed in, there might be some actual food value to it.

"Then there's the fruit of the strangler fig, the *chilamate*. If it isn't real ripe, it's pretty puckery and not very tasty, but if you find some that've fallen down fully ripe, they're pretty good. Wild avocado is another one. At high elevations it's a fairly prominent tree. Wild avocado tends to be bitter, but it has high food value. Of course, there's the heart of palm, the center of the leaf shoots of certain species of palm trees. Now, we don't want people cutting down palms in the forest, but it'd be different if they were all you had to survive. It would be a major job to cut one down if you weren't traveling with a machete. I've read about the roots of some plants, but I've never studied them. And there could be fruits way up in the canopy if you could get to them, such as passion fruit.

"All over the forest are the remains of old homesteads and there you'll find abandoned gardens that provide domestic foods like papaya, mangos, *chayote* and even green bananas. There aren't many edible berries to choose from. Berries don't produce a lot in any one season, so even if you did find them there wouldn't be many to sustain you. *Zapotes* are also around. There was a tree on the edge of Campbell's pasture and the *Ticos* came to collect its fruits, as they'd always been doing. We got to doing the same thing once we learned about them. Occasionally, you got one that was perfectly ripe and it'd be real good. Usually, in the forest, the animals get them as soon as they mature and well before they'd be edible for us.

"There's a nut called *papas* that comes from *Panopsis* trees that are very productive around the edges of clearings. The Costa Ricans taught me to gather them. If you get enough of them you can make dough and fry it. They're a real hard nut to crack and if they've fallen on the ground they've usually been opened and eaten by tree rats or peccaries. But I try to pick them up when I find them.

"The other problem in collecting foods is that some need cooking to be able to eat them, such as green bananas. Eladio has taken palm hearts and cooked them lightly, which gives them a flavor different to eating them raw. If you add cooked palm hearts to cooked rice, it makes a real tasty meal. But you have to know how to start a fire, which is tricky in this wet world.

"The first thing is to have small bits of candle and waterproof matches with you. If there's a palm around, the fiber part of its stem has a little pitch in it and that should fuel a fire. We've learned over the years the one or two species of wood that are good for burning. One is a very red, very hard wood called *sangre de toro,* bull's blood, which is pretty common at the higher elevations. The best tree is called *canfin,* kerosene in Spanish. It has yellow wood and I've seen it used near San Gerardo, though I've only once seen the tree. If you can find some dry dead limbs, they may not be the best depending on the type of tree, but they should do the trick.

"The biggest problem, though, is getting moisture. You can go a long ways without food, but you don't go far without water. I've learned, while hiking up from the highway, that as you dehydrate you get irrational. You make poor decisions, thinking you can get somewhere when it isn't a good idea to even try. You aren't aware of it at the time and it can lead to a fatal situation. I was about six hours without water walking up the mountain once, back in the early days. I didn't think there'd be any problem, but I got off track in the lowlands. I eventually got some water and turned myself around onto the right road, but learned a valuable lesson from it.

"In the tropical lowlands you can sometimes count on getting water from vines. I've done that once, but I've seen it done other times. I saw a good liter of water come out of a vine when I was down in Corcovado. Up here, high on the mountain, we can drink out of the feeder streams. They're fairly common and we can count on them for clean water. However, I'd only drink out of the big river, the Peñas Blancas, if I were desperate. It would most likely lead to diarrhea down the trail.

"We had a chance to test all this several years ago. In 1997 I was deep in Barbilla National Park on the Atlantic side of Costa Rica with a couple of favorite hiking companions, Jim Richards and Marino Serra. We'd planned on going in for the night and coming back out the next day. Well, during the night it rained hard and the streams we'd crossed before had now filled up and the river was impassable. Our guide had a rope but it wasn't really adequate. The current was so strong that there was no way we were going to get across. So we had to find a sheltered place to camp. We were there for three nights because the river never went down. Fortunately, there was clean spring water nearby. The guide went into the woods and came back with an armful of palm fibers from a downed palm. We were able to start a fire and cooked rice for the three days. We had quite a bit of food with us and rationed it.

"Finally, somebody came along the other side, looking for us, knowing we were probably trapped near there. They came back in the morning with ropes, which they managed to throw across the river, and they rescued our packs and then us. The guide cut Vs out of the crotch of a strong limb and we tied the ropes to that and used it to slide across to the other side. In the meantime we'd lived kind of wet for a couple of nights. I got the worst case of fungus on my feet that I'd ever seen the likes of. It took a lot to conquer that.

"We were okay because we had plenty of food to begin with. In all my adventures, I've never been stuck without food. I usually always have some bread and cheese and one extra can of tuna. The Costa Ricans make tamales to take with them. In the early years we usually carried some meat and maybe some potatoes or rice to cook. But the best thing is candy. It doesn't weigh much and it gives you all that energy. If you're already hyper anyway, why, nobody can stop you. Add a few good cups of our delicious homegrown Costa Rican coffee, and you won't want to stop. My old friend José Luis Cambronero claimed my coffee was 'strong enough to walk by itself'. I haven't seen that yet, but it just may come in handy one day.

"The rule is to take more food than you think you need, just in case you need it. And don't pick up anything to eat unless you're sure it isn't poisonous. You definitely wouldn't want to eat the wrong thing. Take only a small sample at first. You may have to go for things that you usually wouldn't think of, such as insects. I learned long ago that if I'm going to take shortcuts, I'd better be prepared for anything."

Wolf's shortcuts are famous. He has never been afraid to set out at whatever hour of the day or night, heading off in uncharted directions, alone or with companions. He has discovered that taking a shortcut is often the most scenic route, and sometimes, though rarely, the quickest.

"Back in 1969, shortly after the mines in Peñas closed, I was planning to go down and do some work at our *finca* by the river. We'd brought the lumber over from the dismantled Camp Four and I wanted to finish putting the siding on our cabin. What didn't work into my plans was a dairy plant board meeting that was scheduled to take place in the same week in the big city of San José. It was important to be there as we were interviewing someone who wanted to be our cheese distributor in the Meseta Central area. So I felt I had to go to that meeting even though it was in conflict with my own work.

"I knew that if I walked all the way into Peñas and then walked back out to Monteverde in time to go the long way around by bus to San José, I wouldn't have time to get my job done. Looking at a map, I realized that San José was directly southeast of my property in Peñas, perhaps 100 kilometers away from my home. Once I was in Peñas I was almost a quarter of the way there! Instead of taking two days to go by way of Monteverde, I figured that one day of hiking out of Peñas and public transportation would get me to San José in time for the meeting.

"So that's what I went for. I did my work on the cabin, spent the night, then got going at dawn. I headed down the old mine trail towards San Miguel. Five hours later I was at the highway near San José de la Tigra, where I remembered that on an earlier occasion I'd caught a bus at noon. I arrived in good time, only to learn that there was only one bus that particular day and it had passed at 5:30 in the morning and there wouldn't be another one.

"So I had no choice but to keep on trekking. I expected I could hitch a ride on a cattle or logging truck, which were pretty common on the roads. As the day went on it got a lot hotter and few vehicles went by. I ended up walking for another five hours on the road, keeping to my straight line, headed to San José. As I was nearing the junction of the main highway at Florencia, I thought I heard a truck coming so I sprinted the last bit to the crossroads. To my good luck, it was a bus, which I caught by the skin of my teeth. I was charged five *colones* to go as far as Ciudad Quesada. We arrived there just as the last bus of the day was leaving for San José. I thought that the Lord was helping me on that one. They charged me another twenty-four *colones* to get to the big city. It arrived an hour before the meeting was scheduled to start.

"I think that was the cheapest trip I ever made to San José. It was definitely the first time I ever walked down Avenida Central in rubber boots! The next day I took the long ride home by way of the highway, which wasn't nearly as much fun. But the experience encouraged me to never fear taking shortcuts. I have great faith that I'll always get to where I'm going and will probably have a better time getting there."

THIRTEEN

All trails lead to home

"It's dawn in the bullpen. Of course, the only bull in this pasture is in its name, as there's not much else by way of bulls around here. Maybe you'll see the odd cow or two. This has been my own path to and from work over the umpteen years that I've walked up to the Reserve. I've had a lot of sightings here in this open clearing, the agoutis feeding on seeds, the skunks and the foxes at night, the deer browsing, the monkeys and *pizotes* traveling through, the biologists looking for animals, and once in a while a couple of two-legged critters looking deep into each other's eyes. I'd say that all the world's woods are connected. Take any trail and sooner or later you'll come out in someone's woods. And all trails lead to home. I've never gone wrong on that one. At this end of the trail, I know I'm getting close to my own home." *Wolf nearing the Guindon farm*

It is a charmed life that I have led. I was born into a loving family, raised with the privilege of having options, and supported in my choices, right or wrong. The older I get, the more I appreciate my good fortune. I remain healthy and strong, but cancer has been hard on my family. Besides my parents and me, my sister also battled cancer, but thankfully, like me, she is a survivor. Maggie and I are grateful for each day that we awake healthy, very aware that any dawn could bring clouds to our horizon. I believe that because of what we have lived through we have become more compassionate souls than we ever knew we could be.

But since that diagnosis sixteen years ago, I am too often reminded that life isn't necessarily fair or kind, rather, it is fragile and can change in the blink of an eye. Sometimes all you can do is hold on to the dragon's tail as it lashes about in the darkness. If the fates allow, you will live to tell the tale. Along with simply being alive, the other true reward of overcoming cancer is being able to encourage others who are facing a life-threatening illness. A positive story of survival is a comforting tonic and I am always happy to share mine.

One of my greatest strokes of luck was taking that hike with Wolf in 1990 and then, over a couple of beers with Art and Maryjka, making the decision to get him a tape recorder. Surviving long enough to follow through with transcribing his stories is another blessing. By way of the little black box in his backpack, I have managed to tag along on his journeys through the rainforest and now have the honor of sharing these stories. Many people find Wolf's speech, often mumbled and indistinct, difficult to understand. Luckily, I have an ear for his dialect, but more than that, I have a profound respect for the man, which has only grown with each trail we have gone down together.

It is a certain kind of person who is happiest in the wilderness, regardless of the reason for being there, whether to study it, record it or face the challenge of it, or simply to be at peace in nature's sanctuary. Most of the earth's population lives in urban environments and many people don't feel the call of the wild or even recognize our collective need for a healthy environment. A woman once told me that, to her, wilderness begins where the sidewalks end. Many people love a city park and that is about as much nature as they want. Others need to go deeper into the forest where the only sound of civilization is the odd jet crossing the sky high above, where being dirty is a treat rather than something to be ashamed of. I have always thought that if you smell like wood smoke from a campfire, it is a sign that you are living well. For those who don't identify with this, it is hard to understand why Wolf and others like him would spend so much time in miserable conditions in the 'middle of nowhere'.

Most conservation areas offer comfortable, well-kept trails for people who want only a small taste of wilderness. In the Cloud Forest Reserve, where the majority of tourists venture no further than the paths of the Triangle, the heaviest impact of human traffic is felt on a very small piece of the forest. The money collected from these visitors and their support for the continuing protection of the area is worth any negative effects their presence has caused. More importantly, the spiritual rejuvenation that comes from time spent amongst the trees is priceless.

For those who want to venture deeper into the jungle, Wolf has cleared the way and others continue to maintain his trails. After over fifty years of wandering through the tropical forest, with the possibility of an accident not nearly as remote as the trails he was cutting, Wolf has sustained few injuries. In his mid-seventies, his body is getting tired, yet mind over matter, he keeps going. There are a few scars that keep account of his mishaps but so far nothing has been serious enough to stop him from returning to his wooded playground.

"My philosophy has always allowed that the longer the stretch in time without a snake bite, crop failure or brush with death, the nearer you are to meeting the said event. But, up until 1990, during twenty years of tropical development and nineteen more of tropical protection, I'd only picked up small cuts for a grand total of fifteen stitches plus several butterfly bandages. I chuckle when I think of the day back in the seventies when I was cleaning *carril* lines with Eladio. I typically had a terribly dull machete and let him sharpen it for me. Right after he'd sharpened my machete, I came up to a log that looked pretty big, twice the width of my leg at least. I was thinking that it was going to take quite a whack, but to my surprise I went right through and the machete hit my knee. I put a handkerchief on the gash and hobbled on down to where Silvia Smith, the nurse, was. She cleaned it up and gave me three stitches. There's a lot of historical value in every meter of these woods and in every scar collected.

"It was in the waning hours of 1990 when I took a serious trip down the accident trail, a path I'd been trying to avoid ever since I sharpened my first twenty-eight-inch machete. On the last day of the year you have to run around and get everything done that you didn't manage to do all year so that you can start the New Year with nothing to do. December 31, 1990, was the day that it would've been better if I'd left my machete at home.

"On this beautiful sunny day I was waiting for some companions near the bridge by the dairy plant in Monteverde. I decided to trim some unwanted growth that was blocking the view of the river. I was finishing the job when, with an easy swing of my faithful machete, I made a three-inch incision on my right leg, just missing my kneecap. My machete had got entangled in some vines and when I pulled it around, it hit me in the knee. For all the thousand good swings you take without cutting yourself, it's the one that cuts that makes history.

"With only a bloody hole in my pant leg to cause alarm, I started off on the accident lane to the clinic, confident that all I needed was a few stitches. Alas, one look into the bottom of the incision sent the nurse calling for the ambulance and I was whisked off to the hospital in Puntarenas. My ever-loving wife Lucky and my son Berto came with me to take care of the paperwork that gets you to the right place. All I had to do was sit there and smile and get wheeled here and wheeled there. The united verdict was to send me up the main trail to San José for patch-up surgery on a tendon and cartilage. They put on a great splint and wheeled me outside and, after a one-hour wait, an ambulance took me to the Hospital México and I went through another scrub and inspection.

"They wanted to sweep me into the operating room ahead of some other victims, but when they asked when the last time I'd eaten was, I struck out. No doctor had mentioned that I should fast, so I'd popped a sandwich at 3 p.m. For this mistake I was punished by being parked out in the hallway until 2 a.m. What a great New Year's Eve event, watching the losers of San José's New Year's Eve parties being rolled by.

"The New Year dawned as I awakened to view my foot sticking out of the end of a cast that reached up to my hip. Out the window was a more attractive view, the Central Valley's volcanic range, with Barva Volcano reminding me that there was another corner of wet, windy ridge top I had yet to climb. At this point I began the month-long camp-out, time spent mostly in San José soaking up the food and tender-loving care and getting completely out of hiking condition. It took a good two months before I could get the old knee over the hill and around the next bend in the trail."

There is a certain amount of good luck involved in not being seriously injured while having adventures deep in the forest. Bad luck and often poor planning is involved when people head off into the wilderness and don't return as expected. Wolf has participated in many search parties for lost hikers. To date, the missing have always been found, perhaps hungry but for the most part safe and sound. Anyone who works in the Reserve knows the anxious feeling of searching for someone who hasn't come home on schedule, wondering what they will find, always praying for the best resolution. In all of Wolf's years working in the forest, there has only been one time when people were called in to look for him.

"I took a trip on one of the last days of December in 1992. I went into the Reserve the back way, through the Santa Elena Reserve. I spent some time in the Rancho Alegre area in the afternoon as I'd heard reports about a mountain lion's den in that part of the woods. I found the tracks and looked around a bit, and then decided to head home a different way than I'd expected to, having mentioned my original plan to Lucky before setting out. I knew that I wouldn't get further than the El Valle cabin before dark, but I figured I could at least make it to there.

"When I started out it was a nice day, and since I wasn't planning on spending the night out I didn't bring any dry clothes, food or my flashlight. At some point in the afternoon the weather turned nasty and by nightfall it was stormy, windy and quite cold. I made it to El Valle by dark and got in with the key I had with me. To my surprise, there weren't any candles. There was gas to cook with, but only one package of Maggi soup left in the supply chest. To stay warm I used the emergency thin plastic poncho from my first-aid kit and it actually worked quite well. I'd never tried that before so it was a real test. It was better than a space blanket that crinkles all night and maybe keeps you warm but is so noisy that it also keeps you awake.

"Anyway, I put it all together and had a good sleep. The storm kept up all night long and the stream came as close to the cabin as I'd ever seen. In the morning I didn't get off as early as I usually do as I had to wait for daylight since I was traveling with no artificial light and it was too dark in the windowless cabin to do anything. With the gas I was able to heat the rest of the soup. I took my time heading back, cutting off the tree limbs that had fallen on the trail through the night in the heavy winds. About halfway back I picked up a seed to examine it and realized that I'd left my glasses in the shelter. I decided to go back to get them even though I knew people would be expecting me home early in the morning. So it was around 11 a.m. by the time I arrived at the Reserve reception.

"It turned out that people were already looking for me in the part of the forest I'd told Lucky I expected to be traveling in. They were sure that I was hurt and not able to make it back on my own. I appreciated the thought because the truth was, with the weather like it was, it could have been real trouble for someone who'd sprained an ankle, fractured an arm, was badly cut or was buried by branches that had come down in the night.

"It was a big deal, the first time anyone had really gone out looking for me. Other times I've been out for maybe three days without anyone knowing where I was, but this time Lucky knew that I didn't have the proper equipment and that I wasn't planning on spending the night, so she alerted people. It was a big day with many people involved in the search. I've spent many hours looking for others who were lost and most often they've shown up in good shape and usually smiling. I know what it means to be out there searching and being concerned for someone who might be in real trouble.

"That's the way it goes, at every crossroads you have an option and sometimes you go a different way than expected. After all these years of going cross-country, sleeping on floors in remote cabins, and often returning home by way of one of my shortcuts, there's no way that anyone is going to know exactly where I am. After that windy night, I saw the handwriting on the wall telling me that I needed to be a lot more conscientious and think about how my actions affected others. As I've gotten older I've realized I'm more apt to get into a serious situation."

After years of wondering about Wolf's well-being, here was the moment when Lucky finally couldn't contain her fear. She describes the same night from her perspective, alone on the farm, watching the storm blow and the cold rain come down.

"I knew that Wolf didn't have a radio and that he'd only gone for a day hike. I knew that he didn't have his flashlight or food or anything from his usual pack full of supplies. Then the night came and the weather changed. It was some of the windiest weather we've had, blowing cold and wet. Trees were coming down and limbs were breaking off and he still didn't come home. I remember him telling a story once of crawling on the ground in the dark, feeling his way along the trail to find his way out of the woods. I know he's very resourceful and can do things like that.

"In the morning I figured that he'd holed up some place overnight. I thought I would give him two or three hours to get back in the daylight. So I waited, knowing he didn't have anything to eat or any coffee and wouldn't waste much time coming home. By mid-morning, when he hadn't shown up, I went and talked to Bruce and Judy, our neighbors who'd seen him after I had, to see if he'd told them of any change of plans. No, they didn't know anything. Finally, I went up to the Reserve and they only had a hazy idea of where he might have gone. When I told them he wasn't back, well, word got out. It's amazing how fast bad news travels. All of a sudden, everybody seemed to know that Wolf was missing and they all came out to look for him. People were still looking for him long after he got back. But, as I've said, Wolf always knows where he is and that he's all right. This was the first time he realized that he really needed to be thinking about others.

"He didn't have his own radio yet. Jan Lowther made a big fuss about that and insisted that the Reserve get him one. I don't necessarily have a lot of faith in those radios, though. Now that he's got one, even here at the house he can't talk to the Reserve, he has to climb up the hill. If he breaks a leg down in a hollow, he'll have to crawl up to a high point to get the radio to work. You might be able to make it squawk and others could find you by the signal, but that only works until the radio goes dead and it stops squawking. Other people have much more faith in those radios than I do."

After that experience Wolf started carrying a radio more for the sake of the folks at home than out of his own concern. Both the Reserve and the League became more conscientious about having someone accompany him on his work details in the forest. For his part, Wolf thought more about not going out alone. There were many people who were thrilled to join him, cleaning trails and listening to his stories over hot cups of coffee.

Wolf continues to make stories in the *bosque nuboso*. In 2003, despite his aching seventy-three-year-old knees, he accepted an invitation to walk up Mount Chirripó, the highest peak in Costa Rica, with his son Ricky and three hiking companions, Jim Richards, Jeff Blair and Tim Sales. Tim recorded a very entertaining and poignant video of the event: the tale of the howling Wolf of the tropical highlands. Tim, Jim and Jeff are part of a select group of perhaps a thousand lucky souls, including Prince Phillip of England, David Suzuki from Canada, and an ex-president of Costa Rica, Rodrigo Carazo Odio, who have followed Wolf on the trail and shared his spirit of adventure and curiosity.

"My doctors said, 'Go on up Chirripó if you want, but if your knees give out, you'll know it.' The doctors wouldn't be worrying about me, so I went and enjoyed it. I also really wanted to go one more time on my Tapir Trail to Arenal. I wasn't able to feel confident that it was the right thing to do and yet I still wanted to schedule it. But there's something that I have to think about if I'm going to keep hiking along these trails, and that's that I don't want to be carried out on a stretcher by Eladio Cruz or Frank Joyce.

"And it would be them doing the carrying. I've often joked to Lucky that if I were to get injured in the forest, it would be Eladio I'd count on to find me, and Frank I'd count on to figure out the logistics of getting me back to civilization. Frank was a young biology student when he came to Monteverde in the seventies and did a lot of volunteering at the Reserve. He was really enthusiastic about going out and patrolling with me as well as learning everything there was to know about the forest. He's one of the volunteers who came back and became an important biologist in Monteverde, continuing on with his education to receive his doctorate in zoology in 1990. He's also done a lot of work with the Conservation League. But to me, he's been a constant strength and a great friend. I've seen him respond to emergencies with intelligence and he'll give it everything he's got. I know that if anyone could get me out of a bad situation, it would be Frank. No doubt I'll always count on both Eladio and Frank in one way or another. My friendship with these two special men and my respect for them has developed over the several hundred wet hours we've spent together in the forest and the several thousand cups of coffee we've shared that have kept us moving.

"I see everything just a little bit differently each time I head out in the forest with different people. I've had a lot of great hiking companions and I've seen a lot of serious work done by volunteers on the Reserve's trails. Whenever I've found a space of time to keep some eager soul busy, I've experienced firsthand the hard work that many people are so willing to contribute. The Reserve has benefited greatly from people who've offered their energy, whether to maintain old trails or clear new ones. If I were more organized and had more time, I could've used this resource more efficiently. As it is, the hours and days spent with these ambitious helpers, whether working or hiking, provided a great social time and were usually very productive. I often remember my companions by names that developed as we got to know each other. So here's to you Shadow, Queen, Blazer, Cinderella, Proper, Tex, Frenchy, Art, Marino, Richard, Jeff, Big Jim, Perennial Luis S. – and, of course, Kay – and the many others whose names my old brain can't quite pull out. The privilege was all mine.

"One of the reasons why I haven't yet got tired of coming down the same old trail is the possibility of another great encounter with new people and maybe an animal or two. Of course, we're all animals, but some of us just have more legs than others. However, now I'm slow and my knees are bothering me, so it isn't as easy as it used to be. Now I can't keep up to the others and my hiking companions are waiting for me. So it's not as much fun in that way. So I would just as soon go on my own, but of course I'm not supposed to do that. Now it's my son Benito who often goes along and carries my backpack and that allows me to keep going down the trail.

"People often ask me if I get afraid out in the woods alone. No! I feel like I'm a part of the *ensalada* out there. I really miss the good hikers and having them to talk to, someone besides this little black box. But it's nice to reminisce about the thousand hours I've walked alone, sometimes on a road, sometimes well out somewhere in the woods, going here and there. And I love hiking in the darkness when the sharp contrast of black silhouettes against the night sky is unlike the complex patterns and multiple shades of green that fill the forest in the day. At night, all the sounds are different. In the stillness of the night, I'm not as conscious of the movement around me, although I may hear it. When I'm in the forest, I realize just how small we are and how big the world is. I just now hear a kinkajou calling and that's more proof that I don't have to feel lonesome."

Besides Wolf, possibly no one has spent as much time in the wilderness around Monteverde as Eladio Cruz. Born in San Luis and exposed as a teenager to the Quaker community up on the ridge, at a young age Eladio wedded his own gentle manner with the idea of conservation. He is a quiet observer and a conscientious absorber of knowledge. Although he is married and has a home in Cerro Plano, he has lived his life in the forest, cutting trails and patrolling, working with biologists and youths. In his cabin in Peñas Blancas, Eladio provides delicious meals to student groups and shares his own stories of the history of the area. His natural instincts and calm spirit have guided thousands through the wilderness. When he talks about his longtime friend, you can sense the depth of their relationship.

"Most people now make their living, if indirectly, from the tourism that followed the establishment of the Reserve. Back when the Reserve started, many people weren't happy with Wilford. When we started to protect the forest, the men who liked to hunt or wanted to cut down trees were not in agreement with him. He had conflicts with some people, though not everybody. There are still some who don't want to understand the idea of conservation, but the majority here live in peace with the protected area. But Wolf and I have always had a great time together in the forest. We go calmly. Neither of us panics if we get off track. Instead, we sit down and drink a cup of coffee.

"I have great respect for Wilford in all ways. He's always had the same spirit. Now his physical strength isn't the same as before, when he had endless energy to walk everywhere, constantly. Many times in recent years when we were on a hike, he'd say, 'You know, Eladio, I'm not the same. I feel that I can't walk anymore and I'm not good for anything.' I'd say to him, '*Bueno*, Wilford, you still do too much.'

"I've always said to him that he shouldn't hike alone. All his life he's gone off into the forest by himself when he couldn't find someone to hike with him. Many times he'd be off swinging his machete on the trails at night. He says that he has problems sleeping, and if he can't sleep then he keeps everyone else awake so he may as well go to work and leave the house quiet. But I've never liked this because it's very dangerous. Hiking at night isn't the same as hiking in the day. But he told me not to worry, that he always went carefully and would return home later to sleep.

"Many of my friends have gone hiking with Wilford and me, and they've developed a great amount of respect and admiration for him. To find someone else who will continue with the same spirit in this hard and solitary job would be difficult. A couple of years ago, I did a hike with Wilford and Lucas Ramírez through Peñas. Lucas is a strong young man from San Luis and is someone I could see following in Wolf's footsteps as a protector of the forest. On this hike, though, he was somewhat nervous about hiking with Wolf, who was so much older. Even then,

Wolf still had a lot of energy and could hike much more than he's able to now.

"On this particular trip we were camping. In the morning, when Lucas and I headed off to clean trails, Wilford remained in the camp to take everything down and pack up so we could start home in the late afternoon. Lucas and I returned for lunch, then got set to go. We wanted to go ahead and keep working on the trail, so we made the mistake of leaving before Wolf. We thought he'd surely catch up to us like he'd always done. However, when it was almost dark, Wolf still hadn't appeared.

"It started to rain, hard like I've almost never seen, an incredible deluge. Then we committed another error. Instead of one of us staying and setting up camp and the other going back for Wilford, we both went back, perhaps afraid of what we might find. When we found him, he was still very close to the previous night's camp. He'd misplaced the cover of his machete and was looking for it and had hardly walked at all. So we found the cover and then carried on with him to the place where we'd left our packs. Now it was completely dark and still raining. This just wasn't a good place to camp as there was no water nearby for cooking, but we had no choice but to make camp there.

"We started to get the camp ready and Wilford said that he was going to look for water as he wanted to have some coffee. Lucas had a small flashlight and I had one, so I gave mine to Wilford. Some time passed and Wolf didn't return. After an hour had passed and he still hadn't come back, Lucas said that he was going to go look for him. He went off with his little flashlight and I stayed put in the tent with no light to do anything. It was pouring rain this whole time and pitch black out. Another half hour passed and neither of them came back. What could I do? Finally, about an hour later, Wilford arrived, but Lucas still hadn't shown up. Wilford said, 'I'm going to go and look for Lucas,' but I told him, 'No, we'll put water on for coffee and then I'll go look for Lucas.' As we were putting water on the little stove, along came Lucas.

"In the night as we were lying down to sleep, Wilford quietly said, 'Well, I've finally made another mistake.'

"I said, *Tranquilo,* Wilford. When we're wandering around in the wilderness, anything can happen. It's normal.'

"He said, 'No, it's my fault. I didn't need to go get water when there was so much running down my back anyway. We could have caught enough off the tent.'

"I replied, 'It isn't your fault.' What had happened was, when Wolf headed off to get water, he'd decided that he wanted to clean up the path down to the stream. It was important to him to open up the side trail that had been used for years to access a good water source but was now completely overgrown. That's what had taken him a long time.

"Wilford always says that he wouldn't mind dying in the wilderness, but I hope that doesn't happen. He once said to me, 'Well, Eladio, one day you're going to have to come and find me in the forest, whether it's because I'm dead or something else has happened to me.'

"I pray that isn't so."

Change comes constantly to Monteverde, to the growing community, the aging inhabitants, the population of endemic species, and the social and natural order that ties them all together. The Guindon clan itself diversifies, expands and contracts, each life as fluid as the water that falls from the sky, nourishes the ground, then transpires to return to the heavens to await the next cloudburst. Despite the years spent working in and worrying about the survival of the surrounding forest, Wolf's heart remains on his farm in the patient care of his wife Lucky.

"We really need to appreciate the times we have together as a family because the years quickly roll by and things change. Now, it's our Sunday-night family gatherings that keep us connected. We don't have to go anywhere to have a good visit with our children and a good time with our grandchildren. That has more and more meaning for us as we get older.

"In the end, things are changing at home. Benito has given up dairying. He's done it since he was young, struggled through all the problems with milking and with the poor setup in the barn. So he's at the top of the totem pole from where I stand. But nobody knows what Benito will do now. He sold the cows and rented the pasture out although when I look I still see a couple cows and a bunch of goats out there. I think he's really in a centrifuge, going around and around about what he's going to do, although he's probably a lot more decided than I am.

"We think it's great for him, but we hate to think that our dairy farm has faded out. It was our original business here and is among the last of the original dairies in Monteverde. We haven't had the family meeting yet where we'll decide how we'll work it out. We make decisions as a family about the future of the property. We're in the process of putting an easement on the forested part of the land to keep it protected. All ten of us, Lucky and I and the eight kids, have a say in things.

"Yes, things are changing. Some of our children's marriages didn't last for the forever that they'd promised. One of my father's sayings was, 'forever is a long time.' When you say, 'I'm going to do something forever,' I'm likely to remind you that forever is, well, forever. You can accept that as your goal and then that's what you strive for, especially in marriage. But a lot of times you use that phrase when you really can't predict the outcome.

"Now I'm trying to get some of this stuff written down that's somewhere in the back of this wrinkled old gray matter. At this age you've got to keep a cap on your head or people suspect that you're wearing out, that the bearings are getting kind of worn and you're loose in the joints. They say, 'Why don't you quit walking the trails and do something like take care of your grandchildren and maybe your grand wife?' People have the idea that you're getting to the time when it's dangerous to head out on the trail. As you grow older you know that you slow down. Even in high speed, giving it all you've got, you begin to appreciate more what you're seeing and what you're doing and that's excuse enough not to hurry.

"It doesn't get any better with age. First your eyes, then your ears, then your functions all get more complicated. I don't like to take pills and it's a struggle to take the ones I do every day. I'm taking medication not only for my bipolar condition, which isn't really a problem anymore, but also for diabetes, which is a problem. At the clinic up here, the doctors have been able to get me on a small dose of medication that keeps things balanced and keeps me clear of really serious diabetes symptoms.

"And then there are my knees. Well, they aren't going to kill me. They're a minor pain with every step I take, but whatever. My doctor warned me that I couldn't go hiking on these trails after the knee replacement, so I wanted to be sure to get on my volcano trail one more time just in case he was right. So I hiked the Tapir Trail in September of 2004, two weeks before having a total knee replacement.

"Anticipating that this could be, heaven forbid, my last trip on the trail, my son Tomás and his wife Gretchen came all the way down from California to experience it with me. I left Monteverde a day before they did and Eladio Cruz, Mauricio Ramírez and a couple of other men joined me on a slow hike to the volcano. It took us three days. One of the hikers came along to carry my pack because my knees objected to its weight. The tropical vegetation had grown up and some of the helpers had to go ahead and clear while we went.

"Tomás, Gretchen and my son Benito left a day later and caught up to us. I was glad to have the opportunity to do the hike with Tomás as he'd never been on my Tapir Trail and we'd always planned on doing that hike together. Benito has now taken groups through several times. He's proven that he inherited the constitution that will keep him rolling down the trail.

"Two weeks after that hike I finally had my left knee replaced. The operation went well. The social security system would have covered the cost of the operation, but it would have meant waiting at least a year, so community members decided to make an appeal to raise money to help me with the cost of going to a private clinic. I'll be eternally grateful for the generosity of those people, which made it possible to have the best doctor and immediate attention.

"I told Luck the other day that I always had the feeling that I was going to die young. During my teen years I had this great belief. It wasn't a fear, just an inevitability that it was going to happen. Then I got through the years in the forest and was doing all those silly things and was sure that sooner or later I would do the wrong thing, perhaps while running the chainsaw. Somehow I always reacted quickly and got away without getting seriously caught. Here in Costa Rica, as well as in other parts of the world, people have gotten physically damaged if not killed while doing protection-type work. In my days as a forest guard I may have been threatened, but there was never any real violence. I always felt that something might happen, but I was lucky and it didn't.

"Here, all of a sudden, I'm aging and starting in on the routine of things that I've seen with old people. If you live a long life, you become old and you don't know what that will be like. I've never thought of death as being a bad thing. We know we're going to die and modern medical science helps us be comfortable to the end.

"But, however it happens, I know I'd like to be buried on our farm. I've always figured on the spot at the edge of the forest up above where a landslide came down against our house. There I'd have a view.

"When I told Lucky, she said, 'Oh, I thought you'd want to be buried in the woods.'

"I said, 'No, I'd like to be buried on our farm near our home.' It might not make a difference in the long run, but I'd still like that."

FOURTEEN

Scenic views

"We're heading right through God's country here. I guess if you come enough times over enough years, well, you're finally going to get the perfect day. It's really clear, no clouds close by, just a few drifting on the horizon. Today's the day you can take a long look to the north, way out over Lake Arenal, to the hills and ridges that stretch from Guanacaste to Nicaragua. To be able to see Lake Nicaragua is the most interesting thing. I've had peeks at it before, but this is the first time I can see the full view. It was worth the trip just for that. Below me, belching nice bits of smoke, is the Volcán Arenal. I think I'll wait around for an eruption. It's been blowing off quite a bit lately. There! Did you hear it?" *Wolf on a ridge top in upper San Gerardo*

The coloring of the Canadian countryside in autumn never fails to excite me. The last fiery warmth of summer bursting into orange, red, rust and gold is like the circus coming to town. For a few weeks the crimson canopy is the greatest show on earth, until finally the spent leaves begin falling to the ground. The temperature drops along with the last tenacious leaves and the first flakes of winter snow. This is the moment that my inner compass orients itself to the south and I start to prepare for my return to Costa Rica. Despite the incredible changes I have witnessed there over seventeen years – more cars, more consumerism, more crime – for me it remains a haven within this turbulent world.

What I see happening in Costa Rica is evident everywhere on the planet. As the country develops, there are immense pressures put on its natural resources. The gap between rich and poor is growing and so is the feeling, among many, that foreigners are dictating their future. Recently, fear seems to have gripped the nation: fear of being assaulted or robbed on the street, fear of not making enough money to make ends meet, fear of the future in a country where people have lost faith in their government and their police.

In 2007 Costa Rica is in the midst of an intense internal debate about whether or not to sign on to the controversial Central America Free Trade Agreement, the southern version of NAFTA, the agreement Canada and Mexico signed years ago with the United States. San José is now covered with graffiti both for and against this controversial pact. The group that supports its ratification because it believes it will protect *Ticos'* jobs calls itself *Trabajo para los Costarricenses,* or TLC. As I move around the city and see spray-painted messages proclaiming NO TLC!!, I can't help but laugh. In Canada, TLC is commonly used for 'tender loving care.' Although I remain unconvinced that any trade agreement with the red, white and blue elephant is in the best interests of the rest of us, I do believe that Costa Rica could use all the TLC it can get.

Fortunately, I still find a society in Costa Rica that is proud of its green and pacifist national character. In Monteverde, I am constantly encouraged by the concern this small community has for their own people and the larger world. Being surrounded by folks who are working towards positive change, whether in a peace march in Ottawa or a Quaker gathering in Monteverde, is one of the best ways I know of to nourish hope for the future. Walking through a forest instead of watching CNN gives me time to contemplate the earth's wonders rather than the global madness. Immersing myself in Wolf's life story keeps me believing in the joy and strength of the human spirit.

In a ceremony honoring personnel from several Costa Rican conservation areas in 1998, Wolf received an award from El Ministerio del Ambiente y Energía and La Sistema Nacional de Areas de Conservacion. He was recognized for his "distinguished work in support of and consolidation of the system of National Areas of Conservation." In 1999 the Monteverde Cloud Forest Reserve and the Tropical Science Center inaugurated a new trail and suspension bridge in Wolf's honor. He had created the kilometer-long trail himself, and the bright red *hamaca* that swings across the ravine in the middle of the Triangle entices wanderers to take another few steps as they explore the hidden delights of the cloud forest.

In November of 2003, in a presentation at the Saint Louis Zoo, Wolf was awarded the Conservation Action Prize from the International

Center for Tropical Ecology in St. Louis, Missouri. He was nominated by Rachel Crandell, a teacher and author who shares her time between Missouri and Monteverde. For years, Rachel and her husband Dwight have worked enthusiastically with the Conservation League for rainforest conservation and education. They began the Monteverde Conservation League US in 2002 and have raised more than $250,000 to support the League's work. She nominated Wolf as "a man of action… full of the stories and the spirit of adventure." This award is presented to "unsung heroes," those people who are particularly active on the front lines of biological conservation, and Wolf was its fourth recipient. His wife Lucky, two of his sons, Tomás and Benito, his grandson LeRoy, and his good friend Frank Joyce were there to celebrate with him.

The award consisted of a monetary prize and a beautiful glass-and-metal sculpture of a raindrop. The irony of the situation was revealed when Wolf and Lucky received the check. Although they had left the United States more than fifty years before because they refused to support the American military complex, the award was heavily taxed by the American government. It is well known that in these stressful times, the U.S. is spending unspeakable amounts of tax money on military operations worldwide. So despite Wolf's strong opposition to war, a part of his lifetime achievement award became a donation to the American war chest. This unfortunate contribution was described to me against the usual backdrop of Guindon laughter. Tears of emotion, be it joy or sadness, well up readily in the eyes of every member of the family, something I've experienced with each Guindon I've met.

I also went to St. Louis to see Wolf receive his award. On the drive back to Canada with my friend Shirley Klement, we found ourselves staying just down the road from Barnesville, Ohio. Curious to see the Olney Friends School where Wolf and Lucky met, we made our way to the school grounds. I could imagine that the place hadn't changed much from the days when young Wilford and Lucille had been courting in the shadows of the grand old brick buildings.

On this crisp Sunday morning in November the parking lot was nearly empty and the grounds were silent. We headed towards the only building where silhouettes were visible through the windows. As we approached the door, it opened and a grey-haired gentleman stepped out. With a friendly smile he asked if we were looking for anyone in particular. I explained that we knew some former students who now lived in Costa Rica and we were interested in seeing this place I had heard so much about. He asked who those people might be. I replied, "Wolf and Lucky Guindon. Would you happen to know them?"

With a peel of familiar laughter, Clifford Guindon extended his hand and replied, "Wolf is my brother." As soon as he said it, I knew it to be true. There was Guindon written all over him. His wife Dottie appeared at the door and introductions were made. They were at the school only briefly, connecting with a cousin who was there for the day visiting her son. It was magical serendipity that brought us together.

Their son Leonard, who teaches at Olney, and their cousin Sue Roth, joined us. We sat for a time and talked. They wanted to know how the award ceremony had gone and were interested in the progress of this book, which they had heard about from Wolf. The discussion came around to the war in Iraq and the government. Cliff, who as a young man had spent time in the Civilian Public Service camps and as a human guinea pig on Staten Island, was still involved in anti-war work. He expressed his strong fear that if the Republicans were re-elected in 2004 (which they were) there would be a new form of military draft imposed. He shook his head as he explained that in multi-denominational gatherings many religious leaders were supportive of the war and the return of conscription.

In 1973 the draft law in the United States expired, but the Selective Service Act was re-authorized in 1980 by President Carter after the Soviet invasion of Afghanistan. Since 1981 there has been no conscription in America, but men of a certain age must register so that there is a list of recruits in case of a national emergency. Many states accomplish this by linking driver's license applications with Selective Service registration. Since the second invasion of Iraq in 2003, National Guardsmen and Army Reservists who signed a contract for a limited time period have had their departure from service delayed by "stop-loss orders" authorized by President George W. Bush. This phenomenon has been termed a "backdoor draft." Instead of young people registering to go to war, older soldiers and reservists are having their service contract extended.

The backdoor draft targets people already serving who are more likely to stay quiet and not protest the extension of their contract. A general military draft is often supported by people who believe it is a way to create a sense of realism about war, to share its burdens more widely and equitably and spread the pain of service. It would also, undoubtedly, lead to a public outcry. The bottom line is, if there is a choice, too many people will forsake the lunacy that is war and stay at home. Also, a draft could reignite the peace movement if the body bags that come home begin to fill with the children of the lawmakers and upper classes. War continues to take its greatest toll on the poor.

Because of Wolf and Lucky's decision to move to Costa Rica, their sons didn't have to make the same choices Wolf and his friends made regarding military conscription. However, their grandchildren, those holding American passports or living in the United States, may be faced with that dilemma, although the period we are now living in doesn't feel quite like the "peacetime" of 1948. In the meantime, the Quakers, along with other peace activists, environmentalists and human rights workers around the world, will continue seeking positive solutions to the problems that fuel war.

What we do know is this: a healthy planet is necessary for a peaceful planet. Our resources sustain us. As clean water, fossil fuels and fertile lands become increasingly scarce, peace and health will also be more elusive. The wars that are now being fought over oil will be nothing compared to those that will be waged over water. Some would argue, quite convincingly, that this is human nature, that we are basically flawed beings with a tendency towards violence. But if *Homo sapiens* consider themselves to be the most intelligent species – citing space travel, medical advances and other technological inventions as proof – shouldn't we be using this intelligence to challenge the aspects of human nature that will otherwise result in our destruction? We must stop accepting greed as justifiable desire and material wealth as comfort, and nations must stop believing that "our way is the only way" if we are to attain a sustainable and harmonious future for this complex world we call home.

Wolf started protecting the rainforest before conservation was fashionable. Once he understood the importance of preserving natural resources, he became a leader, working with others to encourage change. His conviction and inherent optimism kept his legs moving and his machete swinging. Wolf has been committed to the welfare of a relatively small piece of rainforest, but his dedication is a valuable example to others of what one can accomplish when on the right path.

"I'm back out here on the San Luis trail. It's interesting, sitting up here with a bird's-eye view of the valley, seeing the evidence of the value of windbreaks. Where there's been a lot of clearing, the wind has swept away the soil's fertility and eroded a lot of the possibilities of making a living off the land. In other words, it'll go back to just bunchgrass and ironweed and very little good pasture. The Conservation League is working with the farmers to protect their woodlot areas and help them find ways to benefit more directly. So there are more and more windbreaks being planted now. A windbreak is mainly a mixture of fast-growing, weedy types of trees and other species that can stand up to the wind. That's the first step towards reforestation. Once the windbreaks are in, they provide protection for the crops as well as for the slower-growing primary forest species.

"When it was all primary forest, if you climbed up a tree you really didn't see a whole lot except the top of the canopy from one side of the world to the other. That was one of the things we experienced when we were developing our farm. Each time we opened up a new tract, we had a new view with a different angle outwards to the Gulf of Nicoya or down over the San Luis valley. That's what my daughter Helena is now taking advantage of. In her studio she has a place to paint with great views and sunsets. But the importance of clearings isn't just for the tourists to have a good lookout or to raise your children with an idea of what it looks like beyond the cliff edge. When clearing is done selectively, it's also part of the management of the total area. You leave a lot of trees for wind protection and to protect the water source. If you look in any pasture where a tree has been left standing, you can see where the shade has lessened the sun's intensity and kept things green even in the dry periods.

"As I look at the trees and the sky and the sunset, I remember that in most cases every tree I left standing as I cleared land was left deliberately. I'd decide which ones to leave for one reason or another, some of them because they were young and would make good timber another year. Now, after thirty-five or forty years, several of them are quite usable for lumber. Many of the trees that I left because they were good for timber were the ones that furnished the bellbirds and quetzals with a source of food. I didn't know that at the time. Now I wouldn't cut them as we have other options for building materials.

"I believe that no one clears land without having an awareness of the responsibility they have in doing it. This may not come up in the minds of people who clear hundreds of hectares for big farms and big business using machines that do it fast. But in this area, my Costa Rican neighbors and I were aware of it. You may be bringing forested land into production for planting bananas, planting pasture or planting people, but whichever one it is, you're bringing a new purpose to the land. If you clear-cut, you need to be aware of the fact that you're completely changing the use of the land. Of course, even San José is just another big clearing. It must've been beautiful when it was all woods. Now it's full of two-legged animals making tracks everywhere.

"When my neighbors and I were clearing land and cutting down trees, we thought about how many years it took for the big ones to grow. To look up at a tree that's over 100 feet high and to start working away on it, I was very aware that the tree was produced well before me and wouldn't be replaced in my lifetime. It's impressive that with a chainsaw it can take you less than thirty minutes to take down a forest giant.

"The big old oak on our property line was left because it was just one big tree that was going to be one big problem for me on the ground. If I'd taken it down it would've left less space to plant grass because the fallen tree and its limbs would have covered a big area, and oak takes several years to decompose. Also, it was there near our neighbors', the Campbell's, property, so I thought it was a good one to leave. That old oak was still there acting as a sentinel up until a few years ago, and you could see it from a great many miles. I'd look for it from many of the ridges when I was out patrolling and I knew that I just needed to get back close to the base of that tree and I'd be home. That big tree finally came down on its own not so long ago, and we discovered that by that time it was hollow.

"Another famous old oak tree is on the trail to El Valle. On my last hike over to the volcano, it was still standing. I've sat many, many times on a log at the base of that big old oak, its protective fins almost wrapped around me. Like returning to my oracle, I've often asked it for advice.

"So, my old Grandfather Oak, I suppose you were just an acorn about the time that Columbus hit the shore over on the other coast, but you've managed all right. Of course, if we're missing your age, give or take 100 years, I hope you won't mind. Either way you look at it, you've been here a heck of a lot longer than any of us. To have weathered those thousands of storms and still remained so calm, cool and collected, you've given me the strength and assurance to persevere on my own trail. So as one grandfather to another, I thank you."

In the years I have known Costa Rica, I have witnessed changes in communities that have completely obscured their original personality. Small fishing villages, where everyone not only knows each other but is probably related, are hardly recognizable once a resort goes in. When a group of foreigners falls in love with a place and begins bringing in friends, buying land and starting businesses, within a very few years the community will perhaps have prospered, but the lives of the original habitants will have been changed forever. For some, particularly entre-preneurial spirits and the young, changes are welcome, a chance to make some money. For others, transitions can be difficult and not necessarily healthy.

Along with tourism comes development. Having electricity is an improvement in most people's lives. Having a rough dirt road paved not only cuts down on dust and makes for a more pleasant ride, it saves the wear and tear on newly purchased, expensive-to-maintain vehicles. Once electricity and a paved road reach a community, foreigners, land specu-lators and tour operators are sure to follow. In Monteverde, the success of tourism has brought economic prosperity to many. But the commu-nity is now dealing with the impact of the demands of that industry and the development designed to meet those demands. Hotels have expand-ed up the mountainside. Like an out-of-control brush fire, electric lights burn throughout the night, and competition for tourist dollars has divid-ed families and friends.

The conflict that has recently aroused the most passion in the com-munity has been over water. The demand for water has increased great-ly with the increase in tourism and subsequent growth in the local pop-ulation. Water shortages are not unknown in Monteverde, are common in other parts of Costa Rica, and are becoming a tsunami of an issue worldwide as global warming affects weather and precipitation.

In 2004 a small group of private business owners applied for a con-cession to extract water from local streams at twice the rate of consump-tion of the rest of the community. Many people in Monteverde, Cerro Plano and Santa Elena feared the effects this would have on the fragile biodiversity of the streams and worried about what it would mean for the future of water in the area as a whole. When local biologists and landowners demanded an environmental assessment on the impact of the increased water extraction, the government refused to do the study. Despite an intense campaign against the concession by many inhabitants of the area, the business group received permission to start laying pipes and begin drawing water. Then, in 2006, the Minister of the Environment annulled the order and the taps were shut on the concessionaires. Less than a year later the government stated it was revisiting the whole question of granting permission for the concession. The final outcome remains uncertain.

Perhaps the most worrisome aspect of the issue is that if a small group of individuals can assume control of such a precious natural resource in Monteverde, a community comprised of conscientious, educated, concerned individuals with the time and resources to mount an opposition, what kind of precedent is being set for the future of natural resources in other parts of the country?

"Monteverde has a name, and people are going to come no matter what the weather. People continue to come and settle in our Quaker community. There are frequently new people arriving mainly from the U.S. and Canada to settle here and they have a real influence. They often form a completely different social circle. I don't know what you can do to dampen the change in society. I think the Quakers will have less effect and influence as time goes by. All we can do is carry on guided by our own morals and values and hope to have an influence on the next generation.

"I've watched Monteverde change. The landslide of tourism and development came with packaged tours and travel agents looking for a place for their clients. That's when people began to come up here and complain about the road. When the big hotels bring in groups just for two days or the cruise ships bring their passengers up for less than one day, this changes the relationship we have with visitors. Now the tourist agencies are saying that they might just package their tours to different areas instead of Monteverde. Fewer of these packaged tourists could have a good impact on the environment, but on the other hand, if tourism drops off, this community will be in big trouble economically. The government is at fault for not putting enough energy into developing other sectors, such as export agriculture and other sustainable industries.

"Tourism must be proven to be sustainable for people to respect it. At its best, tourism still changes a community. It puts stress on our planning. Even with zoning that decides where to build what, which areas to keep natural and which to develop commercially, the environment changes. The fact that you can put signs up anywhere you want has resulted in our roadsides filling up with advertising. But even tourism can die down. If you lose the attractions – the elephants, the lions, the golden toads or the quetzals – you become vulnerable to the fickleness of the tourist industry.

"What's high on everyone's list is the production of food. In a lot of places in the world people would like three meals a day, but do well to eat one. Here we're in the habit of eating three times a day, and international visitors especially demand a large variety of foods. It's difficult and very expensive to bring it all up the mountain. Raising fresh vegetables, coffee and livestock to feed the tourists and meet our community's needs is a good secondary industry, and hopefully we'll continue to make it an attractive one. With land prices as they are now, this is only going to happen on land already in production and only if people receive a fair price for their produce. With good management of land and methods of irrigation that conserve water rather than waste it, production of food can be sustainable. The headwaters of the streams in this area are very fragile and we're already overextended in our use of this precious resource.

"As I move around on our farm, following the family trail along the property line, I can see the forested ridges of the Continental Divide beyond the San Luis valley. Most all of it is under protection, either by the Tropical Science Center or the Monteverde Conservation League. This view illustrates the new contrast in land values. Up until recently, the land was valued in such a way that you could make it pay for itself by producing crops or having dairy pasture. Now, we're into such escalated prices that all the land being purchased has to be considered as a home site or for its tourism potential. This has been happening for years all over Costa Rica. Once someone is willing to pay the inflated price, this becomes the new standard. Unfortunately, the new land prices make it economically impossible for many people to buy the land or for non-profit conservation organizations to buy it simply to see it protected. We have to rely on the hope that private individuals who have the money to buy the land will also have a social conscience and concern for the forest.

"A lot of the land the League is negotiating to buy to place under protection is quite different from the properties it went after in the early days. We've gotten into properties that are marginal farms with roads and services and these are more expensive. If we're going to pay escalated prices for land, we have to be able to assure the donors that we're getting the best land for their money. Along with this, we must face the fact that money won't be coming in for private reserves the way it did in the past. It's possible the government will make funding available to protect the large area of land in north-central Costa Rica that goes all the way to Nicaragua, which is a seasonal habitat of the great green macaw and the bellbird. So far, it's under the category of Zona Protectora, which gives it the next best protection after being designated a national park.

"I still take great interest in forest protection. There was an organization called CIPACA, an inter-institutional committee for the protection of the ACA, the Arenal Conservation Area, that evolved out of the work Alex Molina and I started back in the 1990s. Along with María Helena Mora, the administrator of the ACA at the time, we worked at building solidarity between the groups that were involved in protecting the region of Arenal-Monteverde. Although CIPACA no longer exists, it started a dialogue between the directors of the various organizations about improving protection in general. Forest guards now participate in joint patrols. Guards at private reserves now carry identification cards recognizing their police authority that are similar to the cards carried by government guards. I'm really glad to see this even though I'm no longer involved.

"It's important that energy and resources are spent on coordinating patrols, transportation and facilities for the guards. All this is finally coming into being and I think it's great. As proof of the integration of our protection systems, on National Parks' Day, August 24, 2006, Frank Joyce, Eladio Cruz, Gerardo Céspedes, Bob Law and I, along with several National Park forest guards, received Honorary Parks Guard certificates.

"I always benefit when the Reserve changes directors, as it did recently for the tenth time. It gives me a chance to share my experience and opinions with a new colleague. Along with the new director at the Reserve, there's a new administrator of the Tropical Science Center and a new director at the Conservation League. All three of these people are open and wanting to work together. That's real attractive to me and makes me want to stay involved. It's good to hobnob with people who have that kind of willingness and availability. I challenge all the organizations and their directors to accept their responsibility and build on this opportunity to work together in a positive fashion.

"Nowadays, I just talk to visitors and try to stay out of the way. A few years ago Lucky and I started giving talks together to visiting groups about Quakerism and the history of our community. It's something we can promote and at the same time make some income from. It's probably not what we most enjoy doing, but to do a certain amount is okay and what we've done so far we've enjoyed.

"I'm basically a trail person and I really should've promoted trail development more. I look at trail use as an arm of protection as well as a source of information about the area. The trail from Monteverde through to Poco Sol remains undeveloped. Thanks to the two mules, the League and the Reserve, each one pulling for its own interests instead of creating a system of cooperation, this trail has never reached its full potential or been used as I envisioned it could be. But with the new administration, there are always new possibilities."

Now seventy-seven, still recovering from the operation on his right knee while delaying the decision to get his left knee replaced, Wolf continues to plan his next trip down a tapir trail. He has taken a position once again on the board of the Conservation League and he makes his way a few times a week to the Cloud Forest Reserve. Wolf's time spent in the forest is diminishing, but his desire to see it protected is as strong as ever. His spirit guides every visitor who ventures down the trails he cut, through the forest he nurtured. His hope is that there will be an endless supply of dedicated individuals who will continue to support conservation in whatever way they can, by writing letters to their government, raising funds or donating money, working collectively on issues and creating paths for others to follow. Our hope is that telling his story will encourage others to take action. Whether it is for the health and well-being of a local forest or the larger community, we need to walk together towards a sustainable future for this precious planet.

"I'm grateful to have played a part in establishing this preserve in Monteverde. It's attracted an incredible number of biologists who have contributed greatly to our understanding of what's here in this forest and how valuable it is. It was a real treat to meet my son, Dr. Carlos Guindon, on the trail explaining the importance of this environment to students who are really interested and who have the chance to hear it from a person who's both experienced and educated.

"It takes a whole team. We don't, any one of us, have a corner on it all. The input is going to have to come from many people, not only in this speck of woods but in wild areas around the globe. With better management, we'll hopefully recover some of what we lost as we went from having a mostly forested earth to one that's pretty well chopped up with only a bit of forest left.

"What we need to dedicate ourselves to is getting the most productivity out of the best land, protecting our streams and water supply, and protecting the habitats of multiple species of flora and fauna. We're only beginning to truly appreciate that land at all elevations and forests of all types must be protected to give any assurance of survival to a majority of the species. Man needs to accept that he's just one species amongst many. We must find a way to manage our natural resources that respects our desire for clean air, pure water and uncontaminated soil. We can't go on wasting and polluting these precious elements, especially since our need for them grows along with the world's population.

"We have more scientific knowledge and understanding now than when I started out down this path. In my lifetime, I've seen the beginning of environmental awareness and a strong level of concern and commitment to positive change that has grown from almost nothing. Terms such as ecology, recycling and sustainability all came about while I was wandering about in this tropical tangle. This gives me faith that there will be intelligent and conscientious leaders who will know how to proceed to keep the planet spinning. But it's going to be more demanding every year and each future generation will have to show the same commitment. Fortunately, I can already see that some of my children and grandchildren are working to be part of the solution. I'll be satisfied if they continue walking down this path. And I'm thankful that through my talks with Kay and the creation of this book, I've had this special opportunity to tell about my role in conservation and to share my love for the tropical forest."

FIFTEEN

Across the wrinkled ridges

In the first week of April, 2007, during *Semana Santa,* I once again followed Wolf into the forest. Along with a small but enthusiastic group of hikers, we walked his magnificent Tapir Trail from the entrance of the Cloud Forest Reserve to its conclusion in the pastures at the base of the Arenal Volcano. Over the four days of hiking I finally saw for myself the obstacle course he had cut through this incredibly soggy and muddy, yet phenomenally vibrant forest. For most of its twenty-eight or so kilometers the trail snakes along the spine of several steep ridges, passing through patches of permanently swampy terrain, continuing doggedly towards the light at the end of its deep green tunnel. It often disappeared under enormous piles of branches created when trees succumb to the intense wind, but thanks to Wolf's son Benito and a couple of companions who had traveled the trail a few days earlier, the path could always be found on the other side of the treefalls that they had chopped up and cleared away. It was impossible not to marvel at the work done by the visionary who imagined the trail in the first place, and it was joyful to finally be walking it with him.

We spent our first night in the *refugio* at El Valle, a deluxe hotel in comparison to the two nights of camping that followed. A drizzle had begun falling gently in the early evening but we were comfortable inside the cabin. However, by the end of the second day we were no more than human sponges slogging through the steady rain, absorbing moisture through every pore with absolutely no hope of drying out. In our pack we each carried what we referred to as "our pot of gold," a small plastic bag of dry, clean clothes we could change into at night. The trick was putting on our sleepwear without getting it wet, then managing to crawl into our tents without bringing in the ubiquitous black mud. In the morning we would put on our cold, damp, dirty clothes once again, none of us wishing to carry any more than necessary in our packs. We walked across the wrinkled ridges amidst the sound of rolling thunder, an occasional grunt from the volcano, a cacophony of insect noises, frog songs and birdcalls, the varying tones of the rain as it changed its rhythm, and the ever-present melody of Wolf's voice.

Besides Wolf and myself, there was another Canadian, J.R., a Monteverde resident who had joined Wolf on the Tapir Trail before. He kept track of our progress and urged us onward after each rest stop, concerned that we arrive before nightfall to set up camp. He knew that we needed to reach the campsites because they were located close to the streams that would provide our drinking water. My young friend from San Carlos, Andrey, came along as a "sherpita," offering his strong six-teen-year-old back to help carry the heaviest packs. This was the first time he had experienced the emerald intensity of a primary cloud forest. There were three lively *Ticas,* Mercedes, Rose Marie and Elena, who were aware that they had the honor of sharing in an extraordinary adventure and they celebrated their good fortune with a steady chorus of appreciation. We also had the very pleasant company of a young Japanese woman, Takako, who had recently started a business bringing people from her country to experience eco-tourism in Costa Rica. On our first night she and I discussed the nature of eco-tourism and shared our observations over the years, both positive and negative, as visitors to Costa Rica. At the end of the hike we agreed that this trek – this immersion in the forest with all its delights and discomforts – was eco-tourism at its finest.

The last two members of our party were employees of the Reserve. At Easter time the Reserve traditionally increases the presence of guards throughout the area in anticipation of the hunters and palm-tree cutters who are more likely to appear in the forest during this season. Men who normally work in maintenance are absorbed into the protection program and spend the days of *Semana Santa* patrolling the Reserve and beyond its borders. We were lucky to be joined by Nano, a strong but humble gentleman who was hiking the Tapir Trail for the first time. We were also very fortunate to have Luis Angel Obando with us. Luis, who is the brother-in-law of Eladio Cruz, was one of the shy young *Ticos* working in the Reserve when I first went through Peñas in 1990. He started on the maintenance crew in 1988 when he was 21, eventually became Head of Maintenance, and in 2002 moved into the position of Head of Protection. I was thrilled to spend time in the forest with Luis. His calm strength and constant joking kept us laughing and moving forward without complaint. Men such as Luis and Nano, not to mention Wolf, Eladio and others like them, are a wonder to behold, running like deer down the trail, jumping like rabbits over fallen tree trunks, carrying as much weight in their packs as a horse. I always feel at ease in the presence of people who are so capable and comfortable in the wilderness and each time I am with these men of the forest, my respect for them and the work they do increases.

The members of our group came on the hike for a variety of reasons, understanding that the physical demands would only last for a few days. The forest guards, on the other hand, head into the jungle on a regular basis, year round, in the torrential downpours of winter and the hot humidity of summer, constantly accompanied by horseflies and on the lookout for snakes. At any moment they can be called upon to deal with a dangerous situation, be it an aggressive hunter or a missing hiker. Despite the miserable conditions and possible dangers, the guards manage to maintain a steady chorus of laughter and gossip as they cook their meals in the dark, oblivious to their wet clothing and tired bodies, their families and comfortable beds left far behind.

When Luis spoke to me about his job as Head of Protection, his pride was obvious. After years of working in maintenance, clearing and cleaning the trails to keep the tourists happy, he had discovered that with protection work he was looking after the welfare of the flora and fauna. It was ultimately more satisfying. Luis appreciates that in the Monteverde area people are basically nonviolent and accepting of the Reserve, and so he feels no need to carry a gun, though he understands why guards patrolling in areas where there are still conflicting attitudes towards conservation may want to be armed.

Luis believes that the answer to the ongoing problem of hunting is to hire the hunters as forest guards. This would provide them with a livelihood as well as a new purpose to be in the wild. They would learn the benefits of preservation while sharing their own valuable knowledge of the forest. Luis grew up in San Luis and was a hunter all his life, right up until the day he started working at the Reserve. He never went hunting again. He credits Wolf and Ricardo Rodríguez, a former director and Head of Protection at the Reserve, for teaching him how to deal in a non-confrontational manner with violators. "You first ask them to put down their guns or machetes," Luis says. "It lessens the tension. Then you can talk reasonably and work towards a peaceful solution together."

No doubt he also employs humor to diffuse serious situations, just as Wolf did through his years of patrolling.

With about an hour of daylight left on our third day, we made it to camp. The last part of the trail had been pretty much straight down the steep ridgeback, constantly sliding through mud with the rain never letting up. Despite being very wet, dirty and tired, the mood was one of general euphoria when we arrived at the simple blue tarp that marked the campsite. We had made it to our last pit stop before walking out to civilization the next day.

Realizing that there wouldn't be enough room for all of our tents under the tarp, the men worked on in the rain, putting up other shelters as the women set up the gas stoves and started making coffee and preparing food. Wolf and J.R. went off in search of trees from which they could hang their hammocks under sheets of plastic. Nano and Luis cleared the wet vegetation from a relatively flat piece of ground and laid down large heliconia leaves that would serve as the groundsheet for their tent.

After hanging his hammock, Wolf came to the edge of the tarp where we were cooking our dinner and stiffly lowered himself onto a damp log. His thin poncho was stretched around his hunched shoulders and his hands cradled a warm cup of coffee. As we all huddled near the stoves for warmth, breathing in the wonderful smell of *tamal mudo* sizzling in the frying pan, Wolf quietly said, "This is a super group to be out with on my last hike on this trail."

The candlelight softly lit up the shadows around the tired man. The rest of us exchanged looks. "Ay, Wolf, I don't want to think that could be true," Mercedes replied.

He talked on without looking at any of us. "Well, you know, I think I've lost the spirit for this. I'm pretty sore. I'm not sure that I'll be able to come out and do this again."

No one said anything. Everyone was feeling enough of their own discomfort to thoroughly understand Wolf's sentiment, though none of us wanted to believe his words.

We settled down to eat in whatever spot we could find. After a few minutes Luis came and crouched close beside me, just outside the protection of the tarp, unperturbed by the drizzle. He looked like he wanted to say something as he pushed the rice around his plate with his fork. Finally, he said, "I can't believe we're out doing this hike."

"Why do you say that?" I asked, watching the raindrops slide down his face and off his nose.

"I was just thinking about when you left that first year. How long ago was that?"

"Seventeen years," I replied.

"Well, I remember that the last time we saw you that year, you were so thin and weak. We knew there was something wrong," he continued. "Then Susana Schik told us you had cancer. She said you might die." In those days Susana taught natural history classes to the employees of the Reserve. She and I were friends and exchanged letters after I left Monteverde. "We thought it was a miracle when you came back, *gordita y saludable*. So to see you now, doing this hard walk, strong as you are, well, I'm amazed."

It was true. At 48 years of age I was surviving this mountainous endurance test better than ever, my worse complaint the slivers in my hands from grabbing the wrong trees as I slid through the mud. "*Bueno,* Luis," I said. "To be able to be here, walking with you and Wolf and everyone else, it's a great gift. May we all have the chance to do it again someday."

"*Si,* Kay," he said. "*Ojala que si.*"

The night passed accompanied by a chorus of raindrops, the howling of the wind and the occasional roll of thunder. We were kept awake by the deep voices of Luis, Nano and Andrey as they talked and laughed in their tent through half the night, the result of much too much coffee. At last there was silence – for about a second – before the screeches, warbles and singsong chatter of the early morning birds started up. Slowly, light seeped through the seams of the tent. The rain had slowed to the occasional tremolo of droplets. I lay in my warm sleeping bag, stretching out my legs, thinking about the three more hours of walking we had to do, wondering if the going would truly get easier, all downhill as Luis and Wolf were insisting. I had come to realize that they often stretched the truth, telling hikers what they want to hear just to keep them moving happily down the trail.

"*VAMANOS!* Let's go!" came the familiar voice from somewhere off in the forest. "Where's the coffee?"

I quickly crawled out of my sleeping bag, unzipped the door, pulled my disgusting socks and shoes on for the last time, and went to put the water on the gas stove to heat. As the fluty song of a black-faced solitaire pierced the mist and merged with Wolf's voice, I smiled. I knew that for as long as he was able, Wolf would continue walking, chopping and talking his way through this incredible forest that he loves. A month later, after I had gone home to Canada, Wolf hiked the trail once again, this time accompanied by Benito, Melody and six of his grandchildren. How wonderful is that?

Kay's Acknowledgements

Over the many years that I have been preparing this book, I have been encouraged and assisted by more people than I can possibly name, but I will never forget the kindness and support that surrounded this project from the beginning. It is a testament to the respect and affection people have for Wolf Guindon.

I must first thank Maryjka Mychajlowycz and Art Pedersen for helping to develop the idea of collecting Wolf's stories, and Nalini Nadkarni and Teri Matelson for lending us the first, of several, tape recorders. For providing technical assistance over the years while I painfully learned about computers, my appreciation goes to my techno-gurus Bob Law, Mike Yarrow, Marlene Leitón Campbell, Pablo Brenes, Sam Hicks, Cheryl Tyson, Jamie Grant, John Bak and David Willis.

I am very grateful to my good friends who at various times provided me with a home as well as cheered me on while I worked on this project: Joe Muething and Kathy Martin, Jack and Mireille Lapointe, Zulay Martínez and Keith Maves, Horacio Montero and Vilma Martínez, and Patricia Maynard. For their enthusiasm which kept me energized when the tasks seemed overwhelming, thank you to Jim Crisp, Mary Stuckey Newswanger, Dennis Lee, Paul McKay, Freda and Mike Cole and especially Jim Oake.

Andy Sninsky and Inge Holecek, publishers of Good Times in Central America, and Gord Pullar at CFMU radio in Hamilton have been publicizing *Walking with Wolf* long before its completion - my heartfelt gratitude for your efforts. For their help in making sure I kept the facts straight, I also want to thank Patricia and Michael Fogden, Wendy Rockwell, Karen Masters, Bill Haber, Willow Zuchowski and Turid Forsyth. Brett Cole, Wagner Lopez, Jim Richards and Carolyn Avery contributed their wonderful photographs, and I sincerely appreciate their generosity.

Mil gracias a Yúber Rodríguez por haber dibujado los mapas; Luis Angel Obando por compartir sus palabras; y un gran abrazo a Mercedes Díaz Herrera por su enorme ayuda con las comunicaciones entre Wolf y yo.

I must acknowledge the directors and staff over the years at the Monteverde Cloud Forest Reserve, the Monteverde Conservation League and the Monteverde Institute for giving me access to their records and facilities. A special thanks to Carlos Munoz at the League for allowing us to use excerpts from Wolf's writings that were originally published in Tapir Tracks, the League's newsletter. To Adrian Forsyth, Gary Diller, Fermín Arguedes, Bill Buskirk, Eladio Cruz and Richard Butgereit, who added so much character to the narrative with their personal stories, I'm grateful for the time you took to share these memories.

To everyone who read the manuscript at some point and gave invaluable input – Christine Carleton, Joanne Snow, Shirley Klement, Al and Jean Bair, Lynda Lehman, Dean Huyck and Lisa Wirtanen – my profound thanks. Also, I'm deeply indebted to Mark Wainwright, who edited an early draft and saved me from stepping into controversy (and also fed me innumerable delicious meals). Later our editor, Jane Pavanel, embraced the manuscript, and with tenderness, reverence and intelligence helped Wolf and me tell our stories more clearly. Jane, you are tremendous.

Through cyber-serendipity, I was reunited with my friend Laurie Hollis-Walker, who became my mentor in the design process and helped me transform the manuscript into this book. I also had the great fortune of meeting Ken Kroesser, who worked with me to design the cover. Both of you are imaginative, talented and enthusiastic, and because of your participation I was able to truly enjoy the scariest part of the publishing process. Thanks also to Bruce MacLean who completed the indexing as well as the final preparations to get the book to the printer.

I want to acknowledge Dr. Ralph Meyer and Trish Haines for helping me stay alive. Because of the care they provided, I was able to remain positive during the cancer-fighting process and considered my yearly checkups to be little more than visiting with friends. My sister, Maggie Shanklin, not only said "you can do it" a thousand times, but designed the Wandering Words Press logo and the snippet of vine that appears throughout, adding her personal touch to this family project. Although my parents didn't live to see the results, it was their hard work and careful living that provided me with the funds to complete *Walking with Wolf*. Their love taught me to believe that I could do anything, including finishing this commitment. I know that they would be amazed and proud. I spend my life full of gratitude for the privilege of having such a fantastic family.

This book took shape and grew along with my love and respect for Wolf. The bonus of the exercise has been getting to know Lucky and the rest of their family. I made many apologies over the years for the length of time it was taking to get these stories to print, but now believe this was according to some grand design – for it allowed me to linger amongst the Guindons, as well as the tall twisted trees, for a wonderfully long time. That has been the greatest blessing. I thank each member of this remarkable family, as well as everyone in the community of Monteverde, for allowing me the opportunity.

Wolf's Acknowledgments

This book is the result of the dedication and determination of Kay Chornook. In 1990, she presented me with a tape recorder to record the stories I had been telling along the trail and over cups of coffee. She then returned to Canada and transcribed the tapes, using the sixth sense she developed for interpreting my way of describing events. I continued to fill those tapes until about 2002, but Kay kept including material from conversations until 2007. Now we have a written history of these experiences that otherwise would have been lost in the wind.

Once we thought we might have the material for a publication, the traumatic events in Kay's own life proved to be only temporary delays to the tremendous project ahead. The introduction she added to each chapter and her interviews with family and friends brought more personal tales into the mix and elevated our efforts from an account of an individual's life to the story of a whole community.

I join with Kay in dedicating this to her mother, Vi Chornook. I became acquainted with Vi when she took an interest in my dream of establishing a long trail from Monteverde to Nicaragua. She furnished me with the *Bruce Trail Comprehensive Plan*, a document that detailed how that 850-kilometer hiking path in southern Ontario was designed and managed. She had a real interest in the creation of this book and I regret that we never met.

Another key person who contributed to our project is my super wife Lucky, who was left with all the responsibilities of our family and home. Her love and support always accompanied me while I worked full time in the Cloud Forest Reserve and no matter how far from home I was patrolling. Lucky and all our children assumed a role by taking on extra responsibilities. So Alberto, Tomás, Helena, Carlos, Benito, Ricardo, Antonio and Melody, I thank each one of you.

We all give thanks to George and Harriet Powell, who planted the conservation seed and by their visionary efforts overcame all obstacles to make the Reserve take root and grow. This was no small task in 1971, when forest development was the popular movement. I am also grateful to the Tropical Science Center, which voted me in as a member of their association. They had confidence in me to represent them in many positions, from administration and land purchase to protection and public relations.

I am greatly indebted to the people who shared their expertise with me both on and off the trail, such as Dr. Leslie Holdridge, Dr. Joe Tosi, Gary Hartshorn, Gary Stiles, Alvaro Ugalde and Mario Bosa, to name just a few. These learned people helped so much in broadening my knowledge of tropical ecology. I also want to extend my thanks and appreciation to the founders and others who sustained the Monteverde Conservation League and to the biologists and community members who by joining together gained local and international support: Bill Haber, Richard Laval, Bob Law, Willow Zuchowski, Alan Pounds, Patricia Fodgen, Michael Fogden, John Campbell, Cynthia Echeverría, Jim Crisp, Jim Wolfe, Bob Lawton, Eladio Cruz, Frank Joyce, Adrian Forsyth and Giovanni Bello. It was their concern and support that inspired me as I was swinging down the many trails described in this book.

Of course, one of my greatest gifts is being a member of the Monteverde community. It is my home. As a group of concerned families we set an example of conservation and careful use of our natural resources. We put aside that tract of 554 hectares to safeguard our water supply, and it was while protecting this area that I first realized my fondness for exploring the woods.

I must acknowledge my fascination for this small but dynamic forest, which I have had the pleasure of sharing with so many people – its ambience of ever-changing degrees of sunlight, diffused by cloud cover and the blowing mist... the fact that there is always something new to observe and enjoy... that when you run out of sunlight, which happens at least once a day, a whole new world of sound and life emerges... the sharp silhouettes and varied patterns of its shadows... even the plant life with its own routines, some blooms coming alive at night while others are closing. Add to all of this the moon with its constantly changing phases, bringing its own rhythm that drives the pulse of the forest at night. So I give thanks to God's creation and for the blessing of having played a role in its protection.

Wilford F. Guindon Hall

Glossary

al suelo!	timber!
ayote	kind of squash
azufre	sulfur
bodega	storage shed
bosque nuboso	cloud forest
boyero	oxcart driver
breñero	jaguarundi
bueno	well/good
cabro de monte	red brocket deer
cajeta	caramel fudge
canfin	a kind of tree, meaning kerosene
carril	boundary
carta de venta	bill of sale
cascajo	coarse gravel/sandstone
casona	large building (reception building at Reserve)
catarata	waterfall
caucel	oncilla (or margay)
cazadores	hunters
cedro	cedar
cedro amargo	bitter cedar, a large tree important in recovery of natural areas
centimos	one hundred centimos = one colon
chamol	root crop
chayote	vegetable pear
chicharrones	pork cracklings
chilamate	strangler fig
colindantes	adjacent property owners
colones	Costa Rican monetary units (in 1950 $1US = ¢8 colones; in 2006 $1US = ¢510 colones)
congo	mantled howler monkey
Cordillera	Continental Divide
cuecha	a plug of chewing tobacco
danta	tapir
denuncia	formal denouncement or accusation of an illegal act
Dios paga.	may God pay you
Dos Aces	Two Aces
dueño de la montaña	mythical semi-human creature

283

El Alemán	The German
El Lobo	The Wolf
El sendero de mil miradores	The trail of a thousand lookouts
El Valle	The valley
ensalada	salad
fábrica	factory (Cheese factory in Monteverde)
finca	farm
gallo	rooster
gancho	hook
gemelos	twins
gordita y saludable	chubby and healthy
guayabera	a man's light tropical shirt
hamaca	hammock or suspension bridge
higueron	strangler fig tree
laguna	small lake
La Liga	The League
Las Calaveras	The Skulls
lata	a tin can
lechería	dairy plant
leona	lioness
león	mountain lion or puma
lomo	loin of meat or ridge between valleys
manigordo	ocelot
manzana	land measurement: 7,000 square meters
mejoras	improvements
mono carablanca	white-faced monkey
mono colorado	Central American spider monkey
mono	monkey
mortadela	kind of processed meat
mucho sol	lots of sun
naranjilla	fruit from tomato family used for juice
nueva canción	new song: a movement in Latin music combining traditional folk and rock rhythms with relevant often political lyrics
ojala que si	I hope so
palmito	heart of palm
paloma	dove
papas	potato or kind of nut
pava de agua	water turkey (also sunbittern)
peine de mico	monkey comb tree

284

pensión	small inn
piquete	rough partially cleared trail
pizote	coati
playón	small sandy beach
Poco Sol	little sun
Portal	entrance
pueblo	small community
pulpería	general store
pura vida	common Costa Rican expression literally translates as "pure life" and means "great"
quebradas	streams
rancho	humble hut with dirt floor
refugio	shelter
rio	river
sangre de toro	bull's blood tree
sapos dorados	golden toads
Semana Santa	Easter week
si	yes
tamal mudo	a simple tamale made with corn and possibly beans but no meat
temporal	several days of rainy weather
tepezcuintle	paca
terciopelo	fer-de-lance
Ticos/Ticas	Costa Ricans
tigre	jaguar
tigrillo	margay (or oncilla)
Trabajo por los Costarricenses	Work for Costa Ricans
trapiche	sugar mill
tranquilo	peaceful or "take it easy"
una más	one more
vamanos	let's go
venado	white-tailed deer
Ventana	the "window" on the Continental Divide overlooking the valley
vivero	tree nursery
volcán	volcano
volcancillos	naturally occuring steaming sulfur mud pots
zapote	fleshy tropical fruit
zona protectora	protected zone

Bibliography

Asociación de Amigos de Monteverde. 2001. *Monteverde Jubilee Family Album*. Monteverde, Puntarenas, Costa Rica.

Baker, Christopher P. 1999. *Costa Rican Handbook, Third Edition*. California: Moon Publications, Inc.

Lober, Douglas J. 1992. *Using Forest Guards to Protect a Biological Reserve in Costa Rica: One Step towards Linking Parks to People*. Journal of Environmental Planning and Management, Volume 35, No. 1, pages 17-41. Routledge.

Nadkarni, Nalini and Nathaniel T. Wheelwright. 2000. *Monteverde: Ecology and Conservation of a Tropical Cloud Forest*. New York: Oxford University Press.

Mendenhall, Mildred. 1995. *Monteverde*. Canadian Quaker Pamphlet. Series 42. British Columbia: Argenta Friends Press.

Monteverde Conservation League. 1986-1994. *Tapir Tracks*. Monteverde.

Phillips, Kathryn. 1995. *Tracking the Vanishing Frogs: An Ecological Mystery*. New York: Penguin Press.

Stiles, F. Gary and Alexander F. Skutch. 1989. *A Guide to the Birds of Costa Rica*. Comstock: Cornell University Press.

Tropical Science Center website. Available at www.cct.or.cr

Wainwright, Mark. 2002. *The Natural History of Costa Rican Mammals*. Miami: Zona Tropical Publications.

Index

M